KNOWLEDGE AND NATIONHOOD

Also available from Cassell:

P. Ainley: *Class and Skill*
P. Ainley: *Vocational Education and Training*
P. Alheit: *Taking the Knocks*
D. Atkinson (ed.): *Cities of Pride*
D. Atkinson: *Radical Urban Solutions*
M. Barber and R. Dann (eds) *Raising Educational Standards in the Inner Cities*
L. Cantor, I. Roberts and B. Pratley: *A Guide to Further Education in England and Wales*
L. Glover: *GNVQ into Practice*
P. Hodkinson and M. Issitt (eds): *The Challenge of Competence*
T. Hyland: *Competence, Education and NVQs*
D. Thomas (ed.): *Flexible Learning Strategies in Higher and Further Education*

Knowledge and Nationhood

Education, Politics and Work

*James Avis, Martin Bloomer, Geoff Esland, Denis Gleeson
and Phil Hodkinson*

CASSELL

Cassell
Wellington House
125 Strand
London WC2R 0BB

127 West 24th Street
New York
NY 10011

First published 1996

British Library Cataloguing-in-Publication Data
A catalogue record for this book is available from the British Library.

ISBN 0-304-33580-0 (hardback)
      0-304-33581-9 (paperback)

Typeset by Action Typesetting Ltd, Gloucester
Printed and bound in Great Britain by Redwood Books, Trowbridge, Wiltshire

Contents

Contents

Foreword

Education is the central plank of our civilization. It is the essential transmission mechanism that allows the individual to become a thinking and empowered citizen. Congratulations to five men who in their passionate belief in this proposition seek to rescue education from those who insist that its duty is rather to propel Britain up the international economic league table. While it is true that education contributes to economic growth, paradoxically it can only deliver on this promise if it stays true to its mission to educate – and if the wider system is designed with this aim in mind. *Knowledge and Nationhood* makes this case effectively and compellingly, and is a welcome antidote to the domination of the debate by propagandists for the New Right.

Will Hutton
Editor, *The Observer*

Acknowledgements

We should like to acknowledge the support of the Economic and Social Research Council (award number R 000-23-3582), The Leverhulme Trust (grant F.144X), and the Central England Training and Enterprise Council. Their funding was essential for various projects which have informed this book. We are also grateful to the Universities of Keele, Manchester Metropolitan, Oxford Brookes, Exeter and The Open University for providing us with accommodation, time and resources for the completion of this collaborative initiative. In particular, we would like to thank the young people and teachers who contributed to the various empirical sections of the book and also a number of colleagues, John Ahier, Margaret Bird, Bruce Butt, Richard Edwards, Mike Flude, Ali Harwood, Heather Hodkinson, Lesley Kydd, Debbie Morgan, Mike Murphy, Andrew Sparkes and Geoff Sparks, who engaged with us in the generation of ideas, offered critical comments on aspects of our work and gave practical assistance, but to whom no blame is attached. Last, but not least, our thanks are due to Naomi Roth of Cassell for the interest she has shown throughout our writing of the book, and to Gladys Pye for her superlative secretarial support services.

Preface

A word of explanation about this book is in order for several reasons. Societies, world-wide, are now in a moment of transformation as educational, social and economic policies built on ideas of the New Right, and market policies based on rampant individualism, are crumbling. The New Right is in disarray and crisis. Moreover, the changed circumstances which face Western nations, notably those resulting from the globalization of economic change, together with transformations in Eastern Europe, have spawned new thinking by both Right and Left in terms of the economy, education and state relations. We offer *Knowledge and Nationhood* as a contribution to what we consider to be an urgently needed open debate about the relationship between globalization, education and national development. While our main concern is with education, our arguments also have a wider purpose, addressing related economic, social and political questions. Our book provides a critique of policy issues associated with post-compulsory education and training – treating the British, and most frequently the English experience, as a case in point.

As a group of writers and researchers, we worked together from 1993 to 1996 on this and other projects. Individually, we have been researching and writing about post-compulsory education and training for a number of years, though often in conjunction with one another. For much of our professional careers we have experienced the onslaught of the New Right upon education and in these difficult circumstances, along with colleagues, teachers and students, have remained committed to critical educational ideals and values. With others we have observed the central tenets of progressivism – student centredness, active learning, problem-solving – being subverted and appropriated by the New Right, resulting in an ongoing but unequal struggle over different versions of these tenets.

Our view of education is organized around a number of agreed concepts. These are couched within an understanding of education as having a critical and central relation to wider society: to personal growth and development, to social cohesion and to economic stability. It is not an understanding which asserts only economic efficiency and the market. Our view is that education is a social and collective process involving an intimate relation between knowledge and the promotion of individual and collective studentship in the development of each person's full potential. Educators and policy-makers must offer learners the means to generate and reflect upon knowledge, to critically assess its usefulness and to interrogate knowledge in the light of, and for the purposes of deepening, their understanding of themselves and their society. Allied to this is the generation of skills that bear an intimate relation to knowledge and its production. A critical educational practice does not seize upon once-and-for-all answers and solutions but remains open to perpetual critique and interrogation. Within this book we have attempted to sustain such a practice. Central to our analysis is the importance of a political economy perspective which entails the location of education within a national and global economic context, though not exclusively so. One of the major developments of the present time is the declining authority of the nation-state and its capacity to contain or challenge the destabilizing effects of globalization. We pose questions about the relation between post-compulsory education and what is sometimes called a post-Fordist economy and the function of this relation within a changing society.

Knowledge and Nationhood is a collective endeavour. The introduction and final chapter were jointly written, with leads being taken by Geoff Esland and Denis Gleeson respectively. All the other chapters were individually written but collectively worked on and developed through a process of debate, good humour and sometimes attrition. Differences may well be apparent within our work but these represent part of our collective refusal to close an ongoing debate – allowing an opening for further discussion and critique.

James Avis
Martin Bloomer
Geoff Esland
Denis Gleeson
Phil Hodkinson
September 1995

Introduction

This book is, as much as anything, about the rise and fall of a political strategy: a case study of the use of the state by a dominant political party to attempt to promote and achieve economic modernization. It is also about the part played in that strategy by an education and training system – principally those sectors of it carrying responsibility for the provision of post-compulsory education and training.

The case study is the United Kingdom[1] – a choice which derives partly from the fact that its education system is one in which we have professionally worked and researched over a number of years; but the UK also provides a major example of a single-minded, *modernist* political strategy, dedicated to the reversal of Britain's economic decline and loss of status as a world power. A defining characteristic of this political strategy has been the uncompromising belief of its originators in the correctness of its principles – a view sustained for the greater part of two decades by four Conservative governments. The conviction that no alternative strategy was available led to the determined and populist cultivation of nationhood and a corresponding statecraft to ensure that it would remain unchallenged by internal dissent. Despite the fact that during the 1980s the British electoral system repeatedly produced popular majorities opposing its policies, the Conservative Party felt able to impose its radical agendas in order to bring about what it saw as the only viable solution to the problem of Britain's long-term economic decline.

The programme on which the British New Right embarked in 1979 marked a major ideological and political departure from anything attempted by Western governments since the end of World War II. It was not long, however, before other national governments followed the example of the radical Right in Britain and introduced similar policies of economic modernization. The United States, with whom Britain had long shared a strategic and ideological affinity, became, under the presidency of Ronald Reagan, the most celebrated supporter of New Right principles and the source of further free market reforms later adopted in the UK. But during the 1980s, Australia, New Zealand and Canada, among others, also embarked on similar programmes of radical economic reform. In common with Britain and many of the Western European states, these countries regarded education and training as a central element of their modernization strategies, and set in place a range of labour-market reforms based on new forms of vocational education and training (Finegold, 1992).

Although there are a number of factors specific to Britain's modernist strategy, it shares with other national economies the necessity of responding to problems arising from the 'globalization' of capitalism and, in particular, the remorseless rise in unemployment and social instability which has been consequent upon it. With few alternative options to put before their electorates, almost all of the Western nation-states have settled on the reform of education and training as the panacea for economic renewal and prosperity – a policy which increasingly appears to be either an act of faith or a cynical gesture, depending on one's political persuasion. The following extract from a British government White Paper is typical of many official statements in which rhetoric substitutes for objective assessment, as the state purports to harness the nation's intellectual capital to its future competitive strength:

> To compete internationally the UK needs a highly motivated and well qualified workforce. We need young people who are well prepared for work, employers who see the importance of developing the skills of their employees, and people in the labour force who take their development seriously. The Government's role is to help create the necessary conditions for this to happen.
>
> (White Paper, 1995, p. 78)

Statements such as this are commonplace. 'National competitiveness' is seen to rest on the need for individuals to improve their skills and to prepare themselves to be 'flexible' in meeting the 'challenges' of the modern global economy. But such statements are also disingenuous, showing little recognition either that skills are often eclipsed in importance by other factors affecting employment (such as investment) or, more fundamentally, that the international economy has outgrown the political, economic and intellectual resources of the nation-state. To paraphrase Reich (1991), emphasizing the importance of education and training to national competitiveness has come to constitute a kind of vestigial mantra – the refuge of a nation-state stranded in a time warp.

What makes the extract quoted above particularly misleading is that it sits in contrast to the more realistic assessment of an earlier White Paper in which we are told that

> Many of the drivers of change are beyond the control of governments. In the increasingly global market there is no hiding place, no comfortable backwater. Change will not stop and others will not rest. They will strive to pass us by. We must continually improve our performance.
>
> (White Paper, 1994, p. 8)

The problem with continually trying to accentuate the skills and motivation of the workforce as the key solution to the social and economic impact of the global market is that there is so much evidence which counts against such an exercise. As we survey the current scene in Britain we see a great deal in its employment policy which both *demotivates* and undermines the workforce. Not only is there growing insecurity for those in employment, but in a deregulated labour market, many are working longer hours for low pay. A survey published in the *Employment Gazette* (June 1995) showed the average working week for British workers to be 43.9 hours, one of the highest in Europe. Likewise, workers' rates of remuneration and rights of protection against the arbitrary powers of employers have progressively been eroded (Hutton, 1995a), just at the time when huge increases in the levels of top executive pay have become the norm.

Similarly, with regard to education and training, there are many who see in the current structure of vocational qualifications little that will help either to raise the skill levels of the workforce or to increase the numbers of skilled jobs in the economy. A recent critic of the system of national vocational qualifications in Britain has claimed that the competence-based approach to education and training 'is fundamentally flawed, disastrously misguided and entirely inappropriate to our current and future education and training needs' (Hyland, 1994, p. ix). In similar vein, Smithers (1993) has claimed that the current system of vocational education and training threatens 'a disaster of epic proportions'. As we argue in Chapter 2, one of the charges which can be levelled at the prevailing paradigm of education and training is that its inherently behaviouristic ideology fosters a superficial instrumentalism in learning which promotes a 'dumbing down' of the population. Likewise, the current denigration of theoretical knowledge and obsession with standardized forms of assessment closes down an individual's capacity for intellectual innovation (Pring, 1995). A form of cultural degradation is being visited on the nation as the dead hand of business managerialism drains its educational institutions of intellectual vitality. Despite the widespread publicity given to the judgement of Finegold and Soskice (1988) that Britain's economy is founded on a 'low skills equilibrium', there is little in current policies which is likely to change this judgement. The problem with Britain's economy continues to be one of weak demand for skills rather than weakness in supply.

As well as being modernist, the economic strategy implemented by the UK government has also been aggressively *nationalist* in its commitment to a British supremacist view of global competition. At the same time, British governments have maintained a steadfastly *unionist* view of their political heritage, resisting any attempts by Scotland and Wales to secure greater economic and political independence – despite the fact that by the mid-1990s, Conservative political representation in these two national communities had been virtually eliminated.

Although, in a number of significant ways, education and training provision are organized differently in the various national communities of the UK, the prevailing jurisdiction of the Westminster parliament means that Scotland, Wales and Northern Ireland remain subject to most of the national political and economic agendas which are our prime concern in this book. While respecting the institutional differences between the various nations making up the United Kingdom, all parts of the UK are included within our analysis in so far as they form part of the totality of the ideological and economic construction of nationhood undertaken by the British state. However, we would suggest that this is an enterprise which has become increasingly Anglocentric.

We set out in this book to examine the current conditions surrounding post-compulsory education and training in Britain after a decade and a half of reform since the first Thatcher government came to power in May 1979. As with all areas of domestic policy, that date marked a fundamental turning point in the ways in which education and training in Britain were perceived by its newly elected government.

Our prime purpose here is to examine the political and economic contexts of the policy changes that have been introduced and to view education and training within the broader framework of Conservative social reform. Although we shall be considering some of the implementational aspects of change – in curriculum, organization and governance – we do so only in so far as they illuminate the guiding principles of reform undertaken by successive Conservative governments. Central to this objective are the main agendas and discourses which have provided the driving force behind their introduction – the principles and rationales underlying the enormous upheaval brought about during four Conservative administrations.

Within this framework, our prime concern is that so dominant and deeply rooted have those agendas been in the political project of the New Right that it has been difficult, if not impossible, either to question them or to put forward alternatives. Least of all have those most affected by the changes – practitioners and their students – been allowed opportunities to debate or challenge them. This situation has in our view brought about an undesirable democratic deficit in the formulation and operation of policy – a state of affairs common to all areas of education. More important still is the fact that the intellectual foundations of the reforms in post-compulsory education and training are themselves manifesting serious signs of strain as the damaging social consequences of free-market ideology become increasingly evident. Within three years of the Conservatives being returned to power in 1992, it was becoming obvious that the 'flexible labour market' – that totem of New Right orthodoxy – was inflicting serious damage on middle-class aspirations and sense of personal security. Fears about unemployment co-existed with worries about 'negative equity' among a substantial proportion of house-owners and a stagnating housing market; and for those approaching retirement, whether voluntary or otherwise, there were growing fears of infirmity and old age, as neither state provision nor private pensions were seen as capable of providing anything more than basic support.

One of the key issues which we seek to address in this book is the association between the shaping of public knowledge and the cultivation of nationhood which has been such a fundamental feature of the New Right agenda for education. So central has this process been that it has become the legitimating base for most of the reforms of the past two decades. In spite of its populist power, our view is that the New Right's concept of nationhood can no longer sustain credibility, but, as the tentative proposals for educational reform put forward by the Opposition parties indicate, the problem is that there is as yet no clear intellectual consensus for an alternative future policy.

That this should be the case is due in no small measure to the massive investment by the New Right in establishing an institutional apparatus for education which has been the managerial equivalent of a black hole – the kind from which neither light nor radiation is emitted. Within the past two decades, the British state has created a degree of centralization within the education system which is without precedent. By exploiting to the limit the opportunities allowed by the custom-based British constitution, the New Right has established a structure of power and control which enables the ruling party to define almost everything that passes for education in this country. It has done so for three main reasons. These are, first, the profound and undiminished mistrust of professional workers employed in education which has informed many of the New Right's education policies. With only occasional but brief respite, the ruling party has consistently derided or ignored the professional values of educational practitioners and installed managerial systems to ensure that the will of the executive carries to almost every institution in the country – or at least to those remaining within the state system. The ostensible reason for the high level of supervision and control is that only on this basis can the state act as guarantor of 'standards' in education, with the implication that left to themselves, without all the apparatus of inspection, audit and 'quality control', educational institutions would be unwilling or unable to prevent a fall in such standards. However, as the writings of New Right academics have indicated (Scruton *et al.*, 1985;

Lawlor, 1990), the real purpose of establishing so much control has been the desire to contain and neutralize the so-called 'left-wing' values of what is often disparagingly referred to as 'the educational establishment'.

A second reason for the unprecedented centralization has been the determination of the state to drive down the costs of education by retaining tight control over the content of the educational process itself. By refusing to recognize the claims of educational professionals for more generous levels of investment for the advancement of teaching and learning, the state, continuing to treat educational expenditure as a cost, has, where possible, intervened in both curriculum and the teaching–learning process in order to rationalize the knowledge bases of the curriculum (some more than others) and their associated teaching costs. All sectors of education have experienced rationalization of this kind, although the forms it has taken vary from one to another. Schools have experienced a massive intervention in their curriculum and forms of assessment; they have also seen their budgets cut and, particularly in recent years, there have been substantial numbers of redundancies among teachers. Within the post-compulsory sector there has been substantial rationalization of teaching costs through the imposition of new teaching contracts, as well as major intervention in the knowledge base of training. As far as the universities are concerned, for much of the New Right's period of ascendancy they have had to absorb year-on-year 'efficiency savings' of 2 per cent while accepting large increases in student numbers.

A third reason for the high level of centralization has been the determination of government to bring about a much closer relationship between educational provision and what are claimed to be national economic requirements. During the 1980s, this applied particularly to educational policy as it affected schools, but from the 1988 Education Reform Act onwards it has been built much more explicitly into policies for further and higher education. As part of their justification for tighter control over public expenditure, governments have felt it appropriate to apply a more rigorous cost-benefit analysis to educational budgets. By means of targeted funding, only those projects which conform to departmental policy can expect to receive financial support. The crucial point about this form of regulation is that few outside the relevant state departments have been involved in the formulation of policy itself. Certainly, there has been little consultation either with educational professionals or with parents and students for whom ostensibly the reform process was designed.

A major success of the New Right in Britain has been the way in which it has established a dominant discourse that is rarely publicly challenged. This discourse has been marked by the development of a shared framework of taken-for-granted ideas, moulded into a new settlement (Avis, 1993a; Centre for Contemporary Cultural Studies, Education Group, 1981), and is quite visible in post-compulsory education and training policy, in numerous analyses of the economy and elsewhere. The notion of settlement, which we make frequent use of throughout this book, extends beyond that of consensus in providing for the possibility of inconsistencies and contradictions. Settlements are based upon superficial consensus and, though prone to rupture and disintegration, are marked by their capacity to hold diverse interests together within an unstable equilibrium which has to be continually reworked and remade.

Most recent and current developments in post-compulsory education and training have taken place on the basis of a settlement to which educationists, politicians of all major parties, industrialists and trades unions have contributed. While the contributors represent quite divergent interests, they appear to subscribe to common assumptions and analyses of a number of crucial issues, notably those concerning relationships between education and the economy. The Conservative government, the Labour Party, the Confederation of British Industry and the Trades Union Congress have all made pronouncements on those relationships in somewhat similar fashion, suggesting that they each subscribe to New Right analyses or, as seems more likely, that they have not subjected their own assumptions to any great critical scrutiny (John Major in DES/DE, 1991; Labour Party, 1991; CBI, 1993; TUC, 1989).

To its supporters, the New Right project, which set the framework for the current settlement, has been a necessary political challenge to historical complacency and a cause for which the opportunistic exploitation of the British constitution was wholly justified. To its critics, the era of the New Right has brought economic failure and an increase in social breakdown, poverty and inequality. In our view, it has also brought to the world of education an impoverished culture and the depletion of intellectual resources – a form of enfeeblement which sits peculiarly alongside the slogans calling for 'empowerment', 'investment in people', 'lifelong learning' and the necessity for high levels of education for the 'knowledge-based society'.

In 1992, this modernist strategy suffered a major setback with the withdrawal of Britain from the European Exchange Rate Mechanism (ERM) after the so-called 'Black Wednesday' on 16 September. This event signalled a loss of confidence in the financial markets that Britain had sufficient industrial capacity to enable it to continue trading with the pound at its then current value. The resulting devaluation brought about some improvement in Britain's trading position, but the low levels of domestic demand and consumer confidence in Britain (brought about by the need for increased taxes in order to reduce the budget deficit) have meant that the quantum leap in investment required to rebuild industrial capacity has not been forthcoming. As Hutton (1995a) has argued, from the recession of 1990–92 the British economy has become locked into a vicious spiral in which a combination of a weak domestic market, low levels of industrial capacity and investment and high costs of borrowing – all within a low inflationary corset – acts as a massive constraint on economic growth, and therefore on the creation of jobs. The relevance of education and training to this kind of scenario looks increasingly problematic.

The future of Britain's economy is also impeded by its ambivalent stance towards the challenges of globalization. As we prepare this book for publication, the Conservative Party, while still in office, is in serious internal disarray over its core beliefs. The blend of nationalism, free-market liberalism and social authoritarianism which has played such a major part in the New Right intellectual armoury has begun to break up over further moves towards a federal European Union. The contradictory pull of national sovereignty on the one hand and the desire for an effective presence in the global market on the other is fuelling an acrimonious split in the party. As Marquand (1995) put it, 'free-market Tories are ... impaled on a contradiction. They are for the sovereign market, and they are also for the sovereign state. They cannot have both at once.' From the spring of 1995 most political commentators were of the opinion that as the failures of its free-market adventurism were becoming increasingly evident, the long hegemony of the New Right was coming to an end.

But in spite of the decline in the New Right's intellectual dominance, there is as yet little evidence that either of the two Opposition parties, New Labour or the Liberal

Democrats, has made any significant progress towards fashioning a set of alternative agendas for an education and training policy. Indeed, all the available evidence suggests that they may well be prepared to continue the existing policy of maintaining a centralized, managerially regulated system of market-driven institutions. Similarly, with regard to the curriculum, although there has been some exploration of an alternative post-16 system of provision, featuring a 'British Baccalaureat' (Finegold *et al.*, 1990), there has been little political debate as to the adequacy of the current system of competence-based, output-funded, vocational qualifications.

The central theme of the book is that the hitherto presumed connection between Britain's education and training policy and its nation-state-based strategy to modernize the economy, improve its global economic performance and generate high-skill jobs, has broken down. As this has happened, Britain has become increasingly trapped in a regressive and ultimately self-defeating nationalism, while perpetuating a narrow, backward-looking, cost-driven, mechanistic system of education and training. The claims that current policies can lead to a high-skill economy and an expanding number of job opportunities look increasingly hollow. This book is intended as a contribution to a debate which we feel to be increasingly necessary. The effects of the centralized domination of radical right policies must not be allowed to continue unchallenged while in our view they threaten to inflict substantial damage on the future opportunities of the British population. Although the thrust of current policies is towards greater intensification of competition, whether between nation-states, organizations or individuals, there will, we believe, have to be a greater readiness to explore the possibilities of a more co-operative ethic in the furtherance of a concept of the public interest.

The canvas of the book is necessarily broad. It draws on a number of theoretical perspectives, most notably that of political economy, in which political and economic policy is seen in relation to its social and cultural implications. Along with Hutton (1995a) and Ormerod (1994) we take the view that anything less than the interdisciplinarity which such a perspective allows runs the risk of failing to acknowledge the complex social consequences of political and economic policy. Such a perspective enables the exploration of a much wider web of interconnections than would be available from within a more specifically political, economic or sociological frame of reference. We therefore seek to move freely between the various 'levels' of analysis embracing political and economic structuration to policies and their implementation through to discourses and agendas, knowledge bases and paradigms, and the rationality of practice. Our theoretical focus draws on current literature in the sociologies of work and the economy, education and social policy. It is also informed by developments in industrial geography and political and educational philosophy. Throughout, it has been our intention to bring together policy and practice within the overall analytical framework.

In Chapter 1, Geoff Esland examines the New Right's construction of nationhood and the ways in which it is currently being undermined by the processes of globalization. He argues that a central feature of Britain's modernist strategy has been the New Right's subjugation of the education and training system to the narrow managerialist agendas of the state, while proclaiming its centrality to economic renewal. The chapter reviews the ways in which the New Right has been able to build up and sustain its discursive and managerial controls over the work of educational professionals to the point where they have become separated from their own intellectual traditions and banished from public debate on the operation of policies for which they have become merely the technical exponents.

Chapter 2 continues the political economic analysis by examining one of the central elements of the New Right's agendas – the requirement for education policy to play a major role in Britain's economic renewal. Drawing on analysis suggesting that the New Right's macro-economic policies have seriously weakened Britain's industrial base and locked the economy as a whole into a downward spiral, Esland suggests that without a major commitment to investment, requiring fundamental reforms of the City's financial institutions, the contribution of education and training to a high-skill, high-technology economy is unlikely to happen – for the reason that the appropriate jobs will not exist. He goes on to argue that, far from producing the 'high-quality' system of post-compulsory education and training called for in White Papers, current policies are simply reproducing a narrow instrumentalism founded on short-term notions of skill requirements.

The theme of Chapter 3 is the 'myth of the post-Fordist society'. Central to the prevailing agenda underpinning post-compulsory education lies a particular construction of the economy which stipulates the need for skilled labour. The concern to develop 'a highly motivated and well-qualified workforce' is placed within an understanding of global economic relations which sets a premium on the 'value-addedness' and the development of a high-skills, high-trust society. It is supposed that such a society could break out from the low-skills equilibrium which is a characteristic of the British economy. James Avis argues that there are many mythical features within this scenario. The development of a high-trust society cannot rest upon the development of labour power alone and has to be matched by interventions into the economy and wider society. Such interventions would need to be informed by commitments to social justice and the development of democratic participation. The continuation of existing global trends and the secular decline of manufacturing means that interventions into education alone would be seriously compromised and certainly would not be able to deliver the more optimistic scenario depicted by proponents of the 'learning society'.

In Chapter 4, Denis Gleeson considers ways in which policy–practice issues in post-compulsory education find their expression at the interface of global and nationalistic responses to change. He argues that the apparent consensus over post-school education, embodied in national ambitions for a 'learning society' or 'skills revolution', is a sham. Despite the apparently progressive rhetoric associated with new market concepts: 'flatter, leaner' systems, credit culture and 'enterprise' in education, such concepts have, in reality, become associated with cost-cutting and deprofessionalization. In schools, colleges and higher education, the market and managerialist revolution is associated with, on the one hand, fewer teachers handling more students with fewer resources and, on the other hand, professionals working to nationally prescribed curricula and conditions of work. Gleeson's argument is that it is a mistake to believe that the new post-school education agenda can be held together by a credit and contract culture, allowing employers, students and institutions to *trade* in the market place. In so doing, he questions the fashionable assumption that deregulated forms of employment represent inevitable, post-modern features of progress towards the twenty-first century. Increasingly, terms such as flexibility, diversity and choice have, he argues, become euphemisms for inequality, control and deprofessionalization. The rediscovery of post-industrial and post-Fordist perspectives, now defined in terms of neo-Fordism and old

Taylorism, represent little more than a distraction or gloss on inequalities generated by market and business reforms. Gleeson argues that attention must now be given to education *in* and *of* the community, in ways which transcend New Right ideology and the pedestrian dogma of managerialism and vocationalism which supports it.

In Chapter 5, James Avis explores a number of themes and questions dealing with quality, managerialism and the development of alternative practices within post-compulsory education and training. He draws out the link between the surveillance and the control of labour and their articulation with post-Fordism. The rhetoric of empowerment is used as a mechanism of control. Many of these issues are taken up in the new managerialism that reflects neo- and post-Fordist tendencies. These tendencies can be seen in the appropriation of the work of management gurus in the discourses surrounding post-compulsory education, behind whose emancipatory rhetoric lies a concern with cost-effectiveness and efficiency. A technicist rationality is present that precludes a real engagement with social justice and the development of democratic participation. Current curricular developments are lodged within this managerialism and so are far from liberating.

In Chapter 6, Phil Hodkinson focuses on the impact of current policies towards vocational education and training on individual young people. Basing his work on data from a recent research study funded by the Economic and Social Research Council, he shows that current market approaches are derived from a version of technicism that bears little resemblance to the cultural complexities of the training process. He puts forward an alternative theory of careership and pragmatic rationality which better fits the research data, while raising fundamental questions about current market policies for education and training. For many young people, the results of such policies will be very different from the official rhetoric of empowerment and upskilling. At best, key questions, for example about growing inequality and persistent high unemployment, remain hidden and unaddressed.

In Chapter 7, Martin Bloomer focuses upon students' experiences of learning, drawing from a research project funded by the Leverhulme Trust, 'Teaching and Learning in 16–19 Education'. The concept of studentship is introduced to describe ways in which young people 'act upon' prescribed curricula in their constructions of personal knowledge and learning careers. The chapter argues that New Right concepts of curriculum are an inadequate response to the needs of learners in post-16 education. Specifically, the potential of studentship is stifled by the technical rationalism which underpins the plans of the New Right and, for that matter, New Labour, despite their frequent use of rhetoric such as 'empowerment', 'entitlement', and 'student-centredness'. And yet it is the harnessing of studentship which offers the greatest potential for the creation of the holistic, practical and critical curriculum so essential for the achievement of personal effectiveness, social cohesion and economic stability.

In the final chapter we consider the implications of the growing disjunction between education and training policy conceived as an instrument of Britain's economic modernization and the actual progress of globalization itself. Increasingly the education system appears to be moving further away from serious engagement with the employment implications of the global economy, as the jobs that remain become scarce, temporary and insecure.

Throughout the book, we stress the importance of moving forward from the sterile and stultifying managerialism in which the education and training system is currently locked, and in which there is too little tolerance of professional debate. The limitations of nation-state capitalism as a basis for education policy are becoming increasingly obvious, and there is a serious danger that there is too little to build on in terms of alternative values and priorities. The centrality attached to efficiency, cost-cutting, intellectual containment and managerial control is now becoming exposed as a totally inadequate platform for future innovation. We argue that the combination of market and managerialist policies fragments practitioners and institutions and denies the possibility of seeking common purpose. Claims about the importance of a learning society and life-long learning will remain simply slogans unless there is a serious recognition that learning consists of much more than crude and limited output measures.

NOTE

1 The political and historical distinctions between Britain, the United Kingdom, Scotland, Wales and England bedevil many British educational writers. In the main, we use the terms 'Britain' and 'UK' synonymously, for the distinctions between them are largely irrelevant to our argument. However, readers should be aware that much of the detail of educational policy and practice which we discuss is drawn from experience in England and Wales. Northern Ireland and, especially, Scotland are significantly different in some important respects.

Chapter 1

Knowledge and Nationhood: The New Right, Education and the Global Market

Geoff Esland

We live in an increasingly knowledge-based economy. The education and skills of all our people are crucial to our prosperity and national success ... The White Paper sets out the steps we are taking, in partnership with industry, to realise our ambition that Britain should have the best qualified workforce in Europe.

(John Major, Introduction to White Paper, *Competitiveness: Forging Ahead,* 1995, p. 3)

The global market-place which the new-style Tories celebrate is cold and hard; in a profound sense, it is also subversive. It uproots communities, disrupts families, mocks faiths and erodes the ties of place and history. It has created a demotic global culture, contemptuous of tradition, hostile to established hierarchies and relativist in morality. Above all, it has made a nonsense of national sovereignty, at any rate in the economic sphere.

(Marquand, 1995)

The importance of 'globalization' to British political and economic life has become an increasingly familiar feature of popular understanding and discourse. Its implications for employment are frequently rehearsed in official government statements and through the media, where the public is often reminded that Britain's ability to compete in the global market depends on increasing proportions of its population acquiring higher level skills. As the *Competitiveness* White Papers (1994, 1995) make clear, at the level of rhetoric at least, 'globalization' has now become a central defining frame for education and training policy in the UK. Yet many of the economic and educational policies enacted by Conservative governments since 1979 have done little to substantiate the rhetoric. If anything, they have rendered the relationship between globalization and education and training progressively more opaque, problematic and confused, and have increased the probability that the UK will be unable to participate in the globalization process from anything other than a position of weakness. Without major changes of policy it is likely that the damaging social consequences already apparent from Britain's failure to generate new investment and employment will continue to worsen.

This chapter will argue that the preservation of a narrow form of national culture has been inscribed on an education system designed to prevent its practitioners from challenging the state's authority in defining the purpose, content and process of education. The institutionalized antagonism engendered by such policies represents the antithesis of the democratic and co-operative culture required to address the complexities and demands of globalization. Innovation and intellectual creativity are now so tightly circumscribed by an over-regulated, over-managed, neo-Taylorist system that they are unlikely to find substantive expression in any but a few areas of the education service. Far from being an energized resource for Britain's global future, the education system has now become disabled by the narrow, authoritarian agendas to which it has been subjected, to the extent that an effective educational response to globalization is unlikely to be possible without major changes.

THE CHALLENGE OF GLOBALIZATION AND THE GEO-POLITICAL CONTEXT

The declining political authority of the nation-state has become one of the major issues facing the world capitalist system as it approaches the millennium. The combination of an expanding global information technology with the growth of world markets in finance, services and manufactured goods has led to the re-formation of economic deci-sion-making, which, as it becomes increasingly concentrated in transnational conglomerates, is simultaneously devolved to networked locations throughout the world. As these trends develop further there will, as Reich (1991, p. 3) puts it, 'be no *national* products or technologies, no national economies, at least as we have come to under-stand that concept. All that will remain rooted within national borders are the people who comprise a nation.'

This process has been advancing for two decades at least. By the mid-1970s, the expanding operations of multinational companies during the early post-war years had already brought about substantial transfers of capital, production capacity and techno-logy from Western states to the newly industrializing economies – particularly in the Far East; but it was the advent of micro-electronics and information technology, accom-panied by the massive explosion of Japanese exports during the 1970s, which brought the 'globalization' phenomenon to public consciousness.

In some senses, as Redwood (1993) observes in his book *The Global Marketplace*, the impulsion towards globalization is not a new one. The expanding European economies of the sixteenth and seventeenth centuries, for example, were founded on international trade links – particularly with the countries of the Far East – in which the British and Dutch East India Companies, supported by joint-stock capital, took a leading role in the export of manufactured goods in return for imported raw materials. The trading patterns established during this period continued well into the nineteenth century as Britain was able to exploit its lead in establishing the first industrial revolu-tion. The wealth generated by Britain's economy then proved to be crucial in supporting its growing imperialist ambitions as it set about imposing its hegemony on 'underdevel-oped' countries throughout the world. As the Empire continued to grow during the nineteenth century, the resulting expansion of British interests led to a nascent form of globalization in which trading relationships were buttressed by the military, financial, administrative and transportation systems designed to secure Britain's position as a dominant presence in international markets.

What is new and distinctive about the contemporary global economy, of course, is the impact of the revolutions in information and telecommunications technologies. It is they that have made possible the global reorganization of economic activity by removing the constraint of national boundaries in the movement of information and capital. When harnessed to the resources of the transnational company, these technologies have the power to create huge economies of scale and transfers of capacity in virtually all aspects of the industrial process: product design, production, marketing and financial management. Data-processing, distribution networking and the control of production flows and stock movement are particularly amenable to geographical transfer and can be carried out at locations far removed from where the demand originates. At the same time, the development of 'world markets' for goods and services and the concept of the 'world product' have led to the emergence of an international market for labour – at least for that minority whom Reich (1991) calls 'symbolic workers', employed in various high-skill forms of 'knowledge production'.

The harnessing of new information and telecommunications technologies to the economic process – the system known as post-Fordism – is, then, a defining feature of globalization, but in many of its other characteristics the international economy continues to follow the evolutionary track of what has long been described as the system of 'monopoly capitalism' (Baran and Sweezy, 1966; Braverman, 1974). The key features of this process derive from the trend towards greater concentrations of corporate ownership and wealth and the drive towards transnational production and marketing. The absorption of rival companies and their products through takeover and merger, and the adoption of management structures capable of integrating complex international networks are also central features of the process. All are recognizable elements of an economic landscape familiar in political economic analysis.

By contrast, the discourse of *'globalization'* gives rise to a rather different set of resonances. Reflecting its location within post-modernist and post-structuralist analysis, where much of its development has taken place, the globalization discourse maintains a fairly weak intellectual connection with the political economy of monopoly capitalism, thereby contributing different and more socially emollient nuances to the politics of the global market. The post-modern notion of the 'global village', celebrating diversity, is somehow a less threatening and more culturally accessible concept than a world seen to be dominated by expanding multinationals.

This leads to a second aspect of the discourse of globalization which concerns its popularization as a 'folk-concept'. In this form it draws from a different well of legitimation. Readily concretized through the iconography of the Internet, extra-terrestrial broadcasting and the satellite, the computer, modem and fax machine, globalization is perceived as part of a dynamic consumer culture offering individuals new forms of communication, flexibility and choice. These technological signifiers of the global market therefore help to substantiate the 'reality' of globalization, moderating some of its harsher features while increasing the sense of its inevitability.

A third feature of the globalization discourse lies in the fact that the emphasis on technological innovation renders invisible the interplay of political and economic forces which are mobilizing and defining the globalization process in specific ways. The imagery and discourse of globalization celebrate its existence as a cultural form, but are often less sensitive to the political and economic agendas underlying it. Although the education system in Britain is expected to 'prepare' young people for the global market, it does so from a position of non-participation in the political shaping of the process and, by the same token, it has little or no public purchase on the implications of globalization for the British citizens it educates. Globalization may well involve every individual in terms of its effects, but the only agendas on offer in the UK have been those of the Conservative political establishment.

The 'challenge' of globalization is simply stated. As the process continues, there will be a continuing tendency for markets for goods and services to expand in volume and become enlarged geographically. As the available technologies extend the 'reach' of producers in terms of both manufacture and distribution, and as economies of scale intensify the monopolization process, ownership and control will be exercised by fewer but larger companies. Where once, for example, there were numerous small independent car manufacturers or producers of 'white' electrical goods, there are now far fewer, each with an appreciably larger market. Takeovers, mergers and competitive success have provided the means of eliminating weaker performers and consolidating a company's hold on the market.

This trend is already a recognizable feature of Britain's national economy over the past thirty years or so. Each wave of mergers and takeovers – particularly during the 1960s and 1980s – has led to the consolidation of surviving producers and suppliers of consumer goods and services, a phenomenon apparent in the reduced diversity of high street retail outlets. The standard appearance of urban shopping centres is testimony to the dominance of the large retail companies. First supermarkets and more recently hypermarkets are now responsible for an increasing proportion of retail sales at the expense of the small supplier. Mail-order purchasing and 'electronic shopping' are likely to continue the decline of the local retailer. Local markets will remain for goods and services supplied and consumed locally – specialist engineering suppliers, firms of solicitors and accountants, restaurants and hairdressing salons, for example – but as a proportion of economic activity, their contribution to gross domestic product is likely to be progressively reduced, or at least subsumed under the turnover of the companies they supply.

Under globalization, this process will continue and expand over greater geographical areas, encompassing particularly those markets previously closed to Western industrial expansion. The inherent tendency of world capitalism towards greater monopolization will lead to the major conglomerates controlling ever-larger areas of the consumer market. The American software company, Microsoft, for example, now supplies its operating system for personal computers, *Windows*, right across the world. Likewise, global companies such as Sony and Philips are dominant in the consumer electronics market while also being a major presence in the recording industry. Although the illusion of diversity can be maintained by the retention of trading names of subsidiary companies and by the customization of products made possible through 'flexible specialization', ultimate financial and policy control remains with the parent or holding company. The forty varieties of the car model, each of which has an identical chassis and body shell, while offering different stylistic options and fittings, is a current example of what will become a familiar phenomenon. National boundaries, already barely visible in the transfer of global capital, will become less relevant under further intensive globalization. In August 1995, for example, a recently privatized British regional electricity company, South Western Electricity, was taken over by the American Southern Company, wishing to diversify out of its home market, amid suggestions that this sale was likely to be followed by similar bids from other US companies. Thus, what only a few years earlier had been a publicly owned UK utility had now become absorbed into the globalization process.

It is the competitive logic underpinning capitalist expansion which feeds the monopolization process. The productivity gains available through consolidation and rationalization create 'efficiencies' in the form of more intensive uses of labour and technology which in theory can be translated into reduced – or at least constant – prices. Rival companies are then obliged to follow suit. Thus increased capitalization and job losses often go together – a process which is intensified by the prevailing commitment of the advanced economies to keeping inflation at very low levels. It is the combination of the tight disciplines imposed by the global financial markets and the competitive pressures leading to rationalization and labour shedding which has given rise to the growing fear of unemployment and job insecurity as the natural concomitants of the globalization process.

In parallel with the tendency towards monopolization is the countervailing pressure on large companies to subdivide and sub-contract parts of their business, again in order to promote efficiencies. Much contemporary management theory exhorts companies to concentrate on their core business and to out-source the rest. Carrying in-house operations as an overhead is seen as an unnecessary cost burden. One of the more extreme examples of current cost-reducing strategies is the practice of so-called 'hot-desking' whereby employees are deprived of their right to a designated office and desk, having instead to work from a collective office, from home or where their clients are based. Although sub-contracting and out-sourcing have become common practice, the structure of control often remains unaffected by virtue of the fact that it can be locked into the contract. It is this that provides the underpinning regulatory structure to the interdependent networks of suppliers and agencies. Although the appearance is one of fragmentation, the reality is that managerial control can in many cases be strengthened while employment becomes less secure.

The challenge to the nation-state of the increasing concentration of economic power is to create the conditions in which its economic producers and companies secure as strong a presence among the global performers as possible. This can be achieved either through overseas capital investment, where income may be repatriated in the form of profits, dividends or interest payments, or through indigenous research and development where new enterprise is created through product or service innovation combined with capital investment to bring new products to the market. Although the former strategy is the one most prevalent in the UK, there is a strong body of opinion which would see the latter as being a more fruitful means of generating employment for those whom Reich describes as 'remaining rooted within national boundaries' (1991, p. 3). A third strategy – that of inward investment, the aim of which is to persuade foreign-owned companies to base some of their production capacity within the UK – has also been strongly favoured by British Conservative governments since 1979. The past decade has seen substantial increases in the numbers of foreign-owned companies based in Britain. They include newly established Japanese-owned consumer electronic and motor vehicle companies, but also many former British firms taken over by others of European and US origin.

Although the theory is simply stated, the process itself is hugely complicated by the interplay of diverse national agendas as each nation-state addresses the implications of globalization. Financial and industrial cultures, resources and infrastructure will vary one from another, as will the presence or otherwise of favourable conditions for economic stability and growth. These variations give rise to the further interplay of decisions relating to the deployment of capital investment, technology and labour as they are differentially directed to locations according to their potential for conferring competitive advantage.

Although international investment has long been a feature of the international economy, the 'promise' of globalization rests on the opportunities it offers for securing dominant positions in supplying global markets, particularly those of previously inaccessible economies such as those of China and the East European states. The fundamental problem is that individual nation-states – and trading blocs for that matter – are competing on unequal terms. The 'level playing field' desired by business communities does not exist. Different capitalist economies adopt different strategies towards investment and employment and operate through very different financial institutions. They have also developed contrasting concepts of capitalist culture which materially affect both economic performance and the working conditions of their populations (Albert, 1993). Will Hutton (1995a), one of the more trenchant critics of the British system, compellingly argues that Britain's performance in the global market is, and will continue to be, seriously undermined by its adversarial political system and the dominance of free-market ideology in its economic culture. The implications of his analysis for education and training provision in Britain are serious and will underlie much of our discussion in this and subsequent chapters.

The position adopted by national governments towards the global market is often an ambivalent one. It is sometimes depicted as a kind of economic tidal wave – unstoppable, carrying with it the detritus of industrial failure and human dispossession while threatening to overwhelm those who stand in its path. The message put out is that globalization is an inevitable process transcending political control, and that there is little alternative but to accept its unremitting progress. But governments also invoke a different image of the global market – one which likens it to a huge zero-sum game where individual nation-states engage in economic combat for access to new markets, each trying to secure competitive advantage over the others.

Each image has some validity, due to the fact that the discourse of globalization and the world political system – at least in Britain's conception of it – mutually reinforce an antagonistic or 'competitive' concept of international economic relations, albeit within the framework of the General Agreement on Tariffs and Trade (GATT). But each of the images of globalization disguises the political energy and commitment which are promoting the global market as a desirable and necessary form of economic relations between advanced industrial economies. Each seeks to present it as an inevitable consequence of technological development while playing down the political opportunism involved in seeking new markets to exploit. Neither image, of course, need go unchallenged. A much less determinist and ruthless social and economic system could be devised, founded on a commitment to democratic co-operation rather than competition. Indeed, from an environmental viewpoint, such a system might be regarded as long overdue. As Gray has expressed it,

> The danger of the rhetoric of globalisation is that it reduces the scope of democratic political life to marginal adjustments in the management of market institutions. It thereby closes the political process to questions about the contribution made by market institutions to the satisfaction of human needs.

(Gray, 1994a)

If there is a neo-imperialistic ethic at the heart of the globalization process it is because the world political order still retains vestiges of nationalist ideologies basically little changed from those which gave rise to the 'scramble for Africa' at the end of the nineteenth century (Cain and Hopkins, 1993). But now it is the control of information and telecommunications networks which constitutes the currency of power and wealth.

The response of the main capitalist economies to the globalization process has been simultaneously to promote the global deregulation of trade and investment on the one hand while in many cases pursuing protectionist cultural and political agendas on the other. The paradox at the heart of this objective has been the insistence on pursuing global ambitions while attempting to maintain national identity and sentiment.

Recent British governments have tended to represent the global market in unequivocally determinist terms. In tune with Britain's imperialist traditions, the global market is perceived as a killing field for British financial institutions and multinational companies, each seeking opportunities to exploit the investment potential of developing economies, as Western capital and technology fuel their expansion. It is a game played by the powerful for the powerful, in which the consequences for the rising numbers of unemployed are likely to become ever more baleful. Free-market capitalism, it is claimed, allows the state little alternative but to give business its head through deregulation and the maintenance of low social overheads. If in consequence, the argument goes, the nation reaps a declining manufacturing base and falling numbers of skilled jobs, inward investment by foreign-owned companies can be relied upon to make up the shortfall (White Paper, 1995).

EUROPE, GLOBALIZATION AND THE BRITISH NATION-STATE

In spite of their enthusiastic endorsement of free-market capitalism, successive British Conservative governments have been torn by increasing tensions between their commitment to the globalization process and the nation-state centredness of Britain's political, economic and cultural institutions with their historic sentiments of national sovereignty and identity. This has taken place during a period when Britain's empire is drawing to a close and its standing as a world power has been in decline. The ending of the so-called cold war which came about with the collapse of the Soviet Union and the East European communist states has led to a world realignment in which Britain has found its 'special relationship' with the United States substantially diminished. Lacking the strategic necessity for a military presence in Britain, the United States has gradually withdrawn from its British and European commitments. At the same time, Britain has been obliged by the Single European Act of 1987 to take on a new, politically co-operative role with its European partners, one which is likely to require Britain to cede increasing control over its economic policy to the institutions of the European Union.

Although the management of macro-economic policy and the budgetary accounting that goes with it are still the responsibility of the nation-state, an increasing number of elements of the 'real' economy involving industrial production, finance and trade regulation are taking place within broader economic frameworks – or trading blocs – of which the European Union is but one. This enlarged economic formation is seen by its European supporters as the only viable means of national economic survival in the face of powerful competition from the US and the Far East. Even in its implementation of macro-economic policy the nation-state is heavily circumscribed by the power of the international financial markets to exert influence over a nation's exchange and interest rates as they continually assess its economic performance. As was made apparent by the events of so-called 'Black Wednesday' on 16 September 1992, when Britain's currency was forced out of the European Exchange Rate Mechanism, even the economic institutions of the European Union were unable to prevent the financial markets from overriding the British government's wish to maintain the then current value of the pound.

As many see it, the opening up of a single European market ultimately carries with it the necessity, and indeed the desirability, of a single European currency and the acceptance of some degree of supra-national economic decision-making – logical consequences of the argument advanced for the Common Market in the first place, that a Europe consisting of several small, competing domestic economies is both inefficient in the short term and ultimately unsustainable (Cecchini Report, 1988; Rajan, 1990). Although Britain still retains ambitions to exploit the global market as a single player, its circumstances ordain that it will increasingly have to do so from within the European Union. As the likelihood and significance of a more federal Europe have become apparent during the 1990s, vociferous sections of the British Conservative Party have struggled to reconcile their political attachment to the sovereignty of the nation-state with the dynamics of world capitalist development. Thus, in neo-Marxian terms, 'globalization' has brought with it a classic historic conjuncture exposing profound contradictions between economic necessity and the political and ideological superstructures of the state and civil society.

This conjuncture claimed its first major victim with the resignation of the British Prime Minister, Margaret Thatcher, on 22 November 1990. Although it did not bring about the end of her party's hegemony, her resignation was a significant turning point in the New Right's political and intellectual ascendancy in Britain. Although other factors were involved, the events of her resignation were precipitated by her increasingly vociferous repudiation of the implications of the Single European Act which she had signed in 1986. Her growing rejection of its terms was based on her observation that her own minimalist concept of the European Economic Community (which became the European Union in 1992) as an *economic* alliance of nation-states was not shared by most of the other European leaders. Her brand of Conservative philosophy saw in the economic alliance of European nation-states opportunities for British business to take advantage of the trading and efficiency gains available through access to a larger free market which could offer both greater deregulation as border controls were eliminated and resulting economies of scale as companies merged; and, provided that British business could match the investment and training records of its European counterparts, there would be untold possibilities for economic growth.

Her philosophy allowed no recognition of the social consequences of what for her was essentially an economistic policy. Individuals affected by these changes would have to look to their own or their families' resources as they faced up to new employment demands which might include possible unemployment and the necessity of migration. As was widely understood from other elements of Conservative policy, in which people were constantly exhorted to 'stand on their own feet', individual initiative and enterprise were seen as the only viable means of coping with the negative fall-out from greater European harmonization. But this view was not shared by most of Britain's European partners, who recognized that substantial numbers of Europe's population could be displaced and economically damaged by the large-scale rationalization implied in the European project. Although there was optimism among Europe's leaders that growth and expansion would result from greater harmonization, they also recognized that some would be adversely affected by the shake-out of surplus and inefficient capacity (Rajan, 1990) – especially in those countries on the periphery of Europe. For them, some form of social policy offering a degree of protection from the operation of free-market forces was essential.

The resulting contest between two conflicting forms of capitalism – Britain's individualistic system on the one hand, and the more communitarian 'Rhineland' capitalism of Europe (Albert, 1993) on the other – was to persist after Margaret Thatcher's resignation. The European agenda for a Europe-wide social policy, however much it may have been watered down during the negotiations of the 1990s, has still proved to be unacceptable to many British Conservative politicians.

Five years after Margaret Thatcher's resignation, the issue of a 'federal' Europe again precipitated the resignation of a British political leader – that of John Major who, while in office as Prime Minister, resigned as leader of the Conservative Party. When, on 15 June 1995, after three years of internal strife within his party, he offered himself for re-election, he was responding to his party's failure to withstand the pressures building up beneath the fault lines within it. The increasingly vociferous 'Europhobes', becoming fearful at what they saw to be the potential threat to British sovereignty resulting from closer ties with Europe, were pressing for the restitution of the Thatcherite goals of nationalism, free-market liberalism, low taxes and a minimalist welfare state. The internationalist Tories, on the other hand, had found themselves increasingly frustrated by the surge in xenophobia and the determination of the Thatcherite wing of the party to regain its former dominance. As Marquand (1995) put it at the time, 'Free-market Tories are ... impaled on a contradiction. They are for the sovereign market, and they are also for the sovereign state. They cannot have both at once.'

Although in the event Major was re-elected, the fault lines responsible for the political upheaval remain in place as the economic momentum for a more federal Europe continues. At the time of writing, Britain seems to have opted for the worst of both worlds: a lack of commitment to further Europeanization with no clear idea as to how the limited economic structures and resources of the nation-state can be made to function as part of the globalization process – except through some form of competitive nationalism.

Between 1993 and 1995 it was becoming increasingly apparent that the pursuit of nationalist, free-market global capitalism was seriously threatening the economic and social interests of the British middle classes. During one period, newspapers were falling over one another in their concern to feature some new aspect of the 'plight of middle England'. Not only were the middle classes continuing to suffer the damaging consequences of the 1990–92 recession which had left them with a huge mountain of debt and negative equity in the housing market, but through direct experience they were also becoming increasingly conscious that 'becoming internationally competitive' translated into rising unemployment, exploitation and job insecurity for those in employment, and growing poverty, increasing crime, and social polarization for the country as a whole. The '30–30–40' society depicted by Hutton – in which 30 per cent of the adult population are either unemployed or economically inactive, 30 per cent are in marginalized and insecure forms of work and only 40 per cent are in full-time employment – describes a situation in which 'more than half the people in Britain who are eligible to work are living either on poverty incomes or in conditions of permanent stress and insecurity' (Hutton, 1995a, p. 109). By the mid-1990s the conviction politics of the New Right were seen by many to have been responsible for the economic failure and social fragmentation documented by the Joseph Rowntree Foundation (1995). In such a context, the resignations of Margaret Thatcher and John Major were merely the outward signs of the political contradictions which have led to the gradual unravelling of the Conservative hegemony; and the issue at the centre of it all has been the nature of the British nation-state.

EDUCATION AND THE GLOBAL MARKET

The relevance of these political and economic changes to the British education system may not be immediately obvious but, as we shall suggest in the chapters which follow, there is a profound and critical relationship. For the past two decades British education policy has been drawn increasingly into the national game-plan for Britain's participation in the global economy. Education's traditional liberal humanistic values have been derided and abandoned by the New Right and replaced by a totalizing and unreflexive business-oriented ideology expressed through a discourse based on markets, targets, audits, 'quality performance' and human resource management. Opportunities to influence future policy priorities have been extended increasingly to employers, both as individuals on boards of governors and collectively on numerous quangos – at the same time as they have been withdrawn from educational professionals. As job opportunities for young people have declined, priority has been attached to preparing them for low-cost, 'flexible' labour markets capable of attracting inward investment and of undercutting the higher labour costs of those countries which British governments insist on calling their 'competitors'. In short, the acquiescence of educational institutions in what are seen to be the demands of global capitalism is regarded by political and business leaders as axiomatic. During the past two decades, educational practitioners and institutions have been coerced into accepting a variety of organizational changes designed to minimize and control their professional discretion and to sustain a centrally defined curriculum that bears the strong imprint of Conservative ideology. Safeguards, in the form of managerial controls, targeted funding and performance assessment, have been installed to ensure that conformity to this regime by institutions and practitioners is secured.

Above almost all other national institutions, the British education system has been regarded by the state as a prime agency in its attempt to reconcile the ideological tensions between economic modernization for the global economy on the one hand and the preservation of the culture and values of the nation-state on the other. As a consequence, it has been made the scapegoat for failing in a task which was misconceived in the first place – whether this be defined as 'meeting the needs of the economy' or providing the legitimation for competitive nation-state capitalism. As with the political establishment's failing attempts to hold these contradictory forces together, the prospectus on which the current educational agendas are based is rapidly losing credibility and will eventually be impossible to maintain without a major reassessment of the role which education should play in the formation of the values and obligations attached to

British participation in a global society. It is our view that the political, economic and moral appropriateness of the New Right's educational agendas has been insufficiently challenged and debated – a situation which arises not from a lack of commitment to such a task but because the assertion of political closure over debate has itself been a part of those same agendas, and, where there have been challenges, alternative arguments have often simply been ignored or dismissed.

As with its broader political strategy, the New Right has tried in its education and training policies to face in two directions at once: towards economic modernization on the one hand and the preservation of Britain's national culture on the other. In essence, these objectives are irreconcilable; or, at least, they are reconcilable only if Britain persists in regarding the global economy in competitive nationalist terms. But, on its own admission in the 1995 *Competitiveness* White Paper, the British Conservative government also wishes to present the UK as an *internationalist* participant in the global economy:

> In proportion to GDP, the UK is more actively engaged than other major industrial countries as an overseas investor and as a host for inward direct investment. This reflects *the UK's traditionally international outlook*, cultural accessibility, foreign exchange liberalisation in 1979 (earlier than in most other European countries), and its attractions as a location.
>
> (White Paper, 1995, p. 26, emphasis added)

The confusion and contradiction which surround the education and training policies of the past decade and a half are founded on the fact that in trying to meet their different political objectives, successive Conservative governments have singularly failed to address either the implications of globalization for more internationally-oriented approaches to education and training or, secondly, the inconsistencies that arise between their economic policies and those prescribed for the education and training system in Britain.

The second point will be explored more fully in Chapter 2, but with regard to the first point it has to be said that there has been almost total silence. Instead of a concern to examine the consequences for education of both citizenship and employment issues inherent in globalization, there has been a determination to press on with a 'national curriculum' for schools and a system of competence-based vocational qualifications for post-compulsory education totally different from – and, some would argue, inferior to – any other system in Europe (Green, 1995). In spite of the importance attached to the advance of globalization, Britain's education and training provision has remained resolutely nationalistic and backward-looking (S. J. Ball, 1994).

Britain's response to globalization has lacked any real underlying coherence. On the one hand, the New Right has unleashed a system of unfettered free markets in capital and labour, while being unclear as to whether the enterprise is founded on the nation-state or the European Union; and on the other, it has created a highly centralized system of education and training designed to serve its national political philosophy – albeit one riven by serious contradictions. By definition, deregulated companies and financial institutions are free to follow their own agendas wherever they may lead and with whatever consequences for unemployment, while an overmanaged education system is tied to a narrow conception of national self-interest which bears a diminishing relationship to what is happening in the global economy. Simply to call on educational institutions and practitioners to raise qualification levels and to prepare young people for 'change' (in whatever forms that may take), while denying them the intellectual and financial resources to do so would seem to be a serious misjudgement of the problem.

Education and training policies have become bound by the defensive and protectionist nationalism which underlies many of the initiatives taken by the New Right since 1979. Because education and training are part of both the economic and the cultural fabric of the nation-state, their institutions embody these contradictions more than most. On the one hand, education and training are seen as fundamental to Britain's successful accommodation to the new global economy, but on the other, they are seen as the preservers of national identity and cultural stability.

These contradictory tendencies are, to a degree, present in all public education systems. The task for the state is often one of balancing the critical and sometimes destabilizing potential of education with the necessity to reproduce in each generation internalized acceptance of society's rules and historical culture. These contradictory forces become particularly acute when national identity is under threat. This is especially the case when the self-seeking opportunism of capitalism begins to break down the economic structures which have hitherto contained it. During such periods, established interrelationships between economic structures and those which regulate the political institutions of the state are also likely to experience profound tension and instability. So, too, do cultural agencies such as schools, colleges and universities as they perceive the context of their core function undergoing dramatic change.

Although it was apparent at the time, it has become even clearer in the intervening years that such a conjuncture occurred during the first half of the 1970s. Many of the elements of what later came to be called the process of 'globalization' were already in place and rapidly burgeoning. However, what was less understood was that the nation-state itself was under threat as the main political unit of economic interest and identity. Movements of capital and labour as well as decisions about investment and the location of production were taking place without reference to the political institutions of Western states, thereby forcing their political leaders into a variety of reactive adjustments. For much of the previous century and a half, the world order had formed around the nation-state as an economic, political and cultural entity. Imperialism, two world wars and a variety of smaller confrontations had all drawn their energy from struggles to define nationality and national interest. Alongside the political consolidation of national identity developed cultural institutions such as those of education, the media and the legal system, the core functions of which include those which give expression to the formation of national identity, culture and belief.

Recent contributions to the debates on the nature and direction of the globalization process have shown particular concern for the transformations of national identity and culture which are entailed in the changes it is bringing about (Featherstone, 1990; King, 1991). As the capacity of nation-states to stem and influence the movements of capital around the world becomes further diminished and their political and economic institutions increasingly trapped within an anachronistic framework, the temptation for politicians to assume greater control of the cultural agencies within their jurisdiction becomes harder to resist. Aware that their electorates see daily their compromises with other nation-states over the basic terms of economic policy – interest rates, exchange rates, taxation, public expenditure, industrial and agricultural production and trading rights – politicians are inevitably forced on to the defensive, faced as they are with public recognition of diminishing autonomy. With this comes potential loss of authority as national jurisdiction becomes more tenuous and provisional. Cultural institutions, on the other hand, continue to remain largely (although not entirely) within the bounds of national jurisdiction, and it is significant that in Britain in particular these have become increasingly brought under the centralizing authority of the nation-state. Universities, schools and colleges, the broadcasting media, and even the established church have experienced a succession of government incursions into their values and practices, their financing and management and their commitment to open debate.

While it would be unwise to claim that there is a necessarily systemic relationship between the leakage of nation-state political and economic influence to the new global networks and the growth of state power over cultural institutions, there is nevertheless a high probability of this occurring. A particularly clear example is the concern over the pornography reputed to be transmitted via the Internet and extra-terrestrial television – an issue which has been perceived by politicians as a clear case of British standards of decency being undermined by more permissive nation-states. In such cases, arguments over cultural differences stand as proxy for the greater loss of economic influence. As the institutions of the national polity are seen to be losing ground, there remains a strong temptation for political leaders to unleash the defensive forces of national culture and identity and to foster a competitive nationalism *vis-à-vis* other nation-states. As Stuart Hall puts it,

> when the era of nation-states in globalisation begins to decline, one can see a regression to a very defensive and highly dangerous form of national identity which is driven by a very aggressive form of racism.
>
> (Hall, 1991, p. 26)

The paradox of a government simultaneously wishing to experience the economic opportunities of a deregulated global economy while retaining control over its powers of decision-making in fundamental areas of social policy is seen in a particularly acute form in the UK of the 1980s and 1990s. A central feature of the New Right regime has been its determination to exert increasing control over cultural institutions and at the same time to prescribe for them a set of values approved by itself. Where direct intervention does not take place, there are alternative controls which include exercising jurisdiction over their funding and markets and their organizational and management systems. As Gray (1994b) has argued, a central feature of the New Right – at least in its more recent manifestations – has been the restructuring of the state apparatus in order to secure the dominance of its own position. In the course of doing so it has severely restricted the democratic opportunities within British culture.

The educational policies of Conservative governments have in the main been founded on a partial and restricted concept of economic change and a regressive form of nationalism. Allied to other elements of the New Right agenda – notably the determination to ignore professional contribution to debates in education and the introduction of a marketized and managerial culture in education – these features of the post-1979 settlement have produced both instability within educational institutions, and an education and training system which no longer has a clear relationship with employment and economic change.

It is now apparent that the British state's ideological and policy positions with regard to globalization are in serious disarray. The internationalist neo-liberals in the Conservative Party, attaching a higher priority to the exploitation of world markets than they do to the preservation of national symbols, have had to confront increasing opposition from the neo-conservative wing fighting to hold on to what it regards as a paramount 'national sovereignty'. As Richard Johnson (1991a) and Stephen Ball (1994) have argued, similar tensions have been present within Conservative educational policy, where neo-liberal 'economic modernizers' lost ground during the late 1980s to neo-conservative 'cultural restorationists' who saw in the Education Reform Act opportunities to press for a more nationalist, subject-based National Curriculum.

On current evidence, the continuing pursuit of free-market global ambitions is likely to exact an even higher price from the nation's social fabric in the form of persistent poverty and unemployment. In view of the social risks involved, it should be the purpose of any mature democracy to foster a constant and wide-ranging debate capable of addressing the fundamental issues associated with increasing globalization. Such a debate would of necessity have to confront the social and economic costs of globalization as well as the trumpeted material benefits. It would also need to explore the ethics of an ideology of competition between nation-states and to consider policy areas better served by a more co-operative stance. As Redwood (1993) acknowledges, there are now numerous areas of international policy ranging from the environment to the health and safety features of quality control and the exploitation of cheap labour which call for a strengthening of co-operation between nation-states. Educational institutions and practitioners should be centrally and professionally involved in debating those issues – as should their students – and be encouraged to examine the complexities of the new global order rather than be obliged to accept the sloganized managerial agendas which the British state decrees they should follow.

Many of the current post-16 education and training policies have been promoted on the premise that economic modernization requires a narrow vocationalism: competence-based learning targeted at the acquisition of specific work-related skills. Overlaying this form of vocationalism is a managerial system drawing on the principles of technical rationality which shows scant regard for humanistic concerns (Hodkinson and Issitt, 1995; see also Chapters 5 and 6). It is a system which renders both human labour and its skills as commodities to be utilized or discarded as circumstances – and profits – determine. There is at the heart of technical rationality an ethical indifference towards the non-economic value of employment and the social costs of an oppressive employment environment. In the utilization of human skill for economic production, it is often cost-driven calculations which determine the nature and duration of work. If the key determinant of training and employment is 'fitness for purpose' at minimal cost, it becomes possible to define employment strictly in terms of economic utility. In spite of liberative-sounding management-speak emphasizing 'empowerment', 'motivation' and 'team work', the 1990s have seen a veritable explosion in 'delayering' and 'downsizing' as workers deemed to be surplus to requirements have been stripped out of corporate payrolls. At the same time, the intensification of working hours for those in work has become an increasingly conspicuous feature of British employment practice. The deepening deregulation of labour markets makes the involvement of educational practitioners extremely problematic, in that it forces them to become agents of the same technical rationality in their professional practice – a process in which they and their students also become 'technicized' as units of cost and labour.

As we argue in Chapter 2, because of the failure to bring macro- and micro-economic policy into line during the 1980s, the goal of matching training to available employment could never be achieved. This has resulted in a lack of demand for those occupational skills that have been created and a high level of disillusionment among the educated and trained who are either unemployed or employed in low-grade work (Brown and Scase, 1994). It is the political unwillingness to recognize and address the *systemic* nature of Britain's economic underperformance that has given rise to an economy seriously under-capitalized and a labour force with diminishing opportunities for meaningful work.

The state's determination to suppress professional debate in British education has been and will continue to be highly damaging both to Britain's economic and political future as well as to the personal and social well-being of its population. As the evidence mounts up during the 1990s of rising levels of poverty and social breakdown, the collapse of secure employment and growing fiscal strain in relation to pensions and welfare, it will become increasingly necessary to break the stranglehold on broad democratic involvement in debate about alternative political and economic futures. Already, the rising levels of activism in single-issue politics are an indication of both a disillusionment with the conventional political process and a frustration that stakeholders other than politicians, and major shareholders and employer organizations are excluded from most forms of decision-making (Mulgan, 1994). The authoritarian and utilitarian thrust of much of the New Right's educational policy is likely to lead to increasing diminution both of personal effectiveness and of social and national cohesion. It has brought low morale to the teaching profession at all levels of education and given rise to a narrow, regressive, superficial instrumentalism which has impoverished national culture and debased the notion of what Pring has called a 'community of educated people' (Pring, 1995; Smail, 1993; S. J. Ball, 1994).

DISCOURSE MANAGEMENT AND THE NEW RIGHT'S RECONSTRUCTION OF NATIONHOOD

The reconstruction of the British nation-state and the political manipulation of public knowledge about its character and future development are intimately related aspects of the task which the New Right set itself in 1979 and which has largely continued into the 1990s. Although aspects of policy have been adjusted and the presentational tone has become less strident, the underlying commitment to the free-market transformation of Britain's economy and public institutions has continued unabated within a substantial section of the Conservative government – in spite of mounting evidence during the 1990s of overwhelming popular rejection of such policies.

A central feature of the New Right's determination to achieve a permanent cultural revolution in Britain has been its extraordinary attentiveness to the knowledge, language and conditions defining public discourse and debate – what some might call 'propaganda' – knowing that the control of these is fundamental to the formation and maintenance of a 'social reality' which is both public and private. Central to this objective has been the infusion into all areas of public life of the language and ideology of what Smail (1993) has called the 'Business Revolution'. The deployment of concepts such as 'freedom', 'choice', 'efficiency', 'effectiveness', 'accountability', 'value for money', 'quality', 'ownership' and 'empowerment' – all with carefully designed populist inflections – has been a fundamental feature of New Right statecraft and, by seeking to dominate both message and medium, the New Right has had considerable success in erecting a discursive platform which has been able both to define the legitimate terms of debate and to exclude and marginalize those who do not share its values and assumptions.

Of all the areas of social policy subjected to the New Right's 'cultural revolution', the reform of education has arguably been the most central to its moral and political project. As with certain other policy areas, the education system has seen long-standing organizational practices overturned and been forced to operate as a quasi-market for the delivery of its services; and, like those in other parts of the public sector, educational institutions have been compelled to incorporate elements of the 'new public management' designed to eliminate 'waste' and 'inefficiency' and to induce a greater responsiveness to the new 'customer culture'. However, where education differs from other areas of social policy is in its significance as the prime cultural agency in the formation of identity and the reproduction of social values and moral principles – especially those of nationality and citizenship. It is this function of the education system in particular which has led to almost every part of it being subjected to major political intervention with the aim of neutralizing – if not eradicating – values deemed inimical to the moral, political and economic project of the New Right.

In the decade and a half since 1979 all sectors of education have seen their curricula and methods of teaching and assessment transformed – the only real exception being the preservation of A-levels. In post-16 education and training, the knowledge base of the curriculum has been comprehensively redrawn through the substitution of a competence-based system of learning and assessment drawing its sustenance from employer-determined skills. Having come to power in 1979 determined to root out the cultural sources of what it saw as the 'British disease', the New Right has sought to create an education system in its own image, which embodies its narrow managerialist prescriptions for national renewal and nationhood.

One of the essential features of the New Right project in confronting the 'British disease' has been its determination to 're-moralize' the nation – to root out those causes of 'decadence' which according to Margaret Thatcher and her supporters had contributed so much to Britain's economic and moral decline, and to put in their place a moral economy founded on the 'vigorous virtues' of 'uprightness, self-sufficiency, energy, independent mindedness, adventurousness, loyalty and robustness' (Letwin, 1992, p. 35). This crusade, according to Letwin, embraced in one great unity of purpose the individual, the family and the nation. At the heart of Britain's malaise was believed to be a culture too imbued with 'dependency', drawing on the 'softer virtues' of 'caring, sympathy, humility and gentleness'. Transposed on to the national stage this cultural imbalance had produced a country lacking in dynamism and independence:

> For the Thatcherite, British society should be organized in such a way that individuals who do practise the vigorous virtues have room to flourish; and it should be a country which, as a result, is rich, powerful, culturally dynamic and universally respected by the other nations of the globe.
>
> (Letwin, 1992, p. 37)

It was sentiments such as these that led Hall to observe that

> Thatcherite populism is a particularly rich mix. It combines the resonant themes of organic Toryism – nation, family, duty, authority, standards, traditionalism – with the aggressive themes of a revived neo-liberalism – self-interest, competitive individualism, anti-statism.
>
> (Hall, 1983, p. 29)

Such was the certainty with which the New Right analysis was upheld and proclaimed that it felt entirely justified in 'taking on' those institutions which were seen to be 'part of the problem' – among them the various professional establishments.

> In each case, what was being 'taken on' was an establishment which was thought to constitute a 'cosy cartel', a source of complacency, a centre of defeatism, an obstacle to vigour, an instigator of dependency, a cause of poverty or powerlessness.
>
> (Letwin, 1992, p. 41)

The fundamentalist zeal with which this crusade was undertaken gave rise to a political style in which contempt and derision were visited upon any organization or individual who dared to put forward policies derived from a different value position. Hugo Young in his study of the Thatcherite decade, *One of Us*, refers to the Prime Minister's 'image of severity and adamant righteousness' (1989, p. 73) and comments that 'her style was built on domination. None of her colleagues had ever experienced a more assertive, even overbearing, leader. Certitude was her stock-in-trade, the commodity with which she planned to exorcise the vapid compromises of post-war politics' (p. 137). Young refers also to 'the expression of a conviction that brooked no interference from reason' (p. 152).

Alternative sources of intellectual influence such as the BBC, the universities or the church were either attacked if they appeared to constitute a threat or, more usually, were ignored or treated with dismissiveness:

> Like the so-called intelligentsia, the so-called moral leaders in their palaces and pulpits were deposited outside the walls: a discardable class whom government found it could easily do without. With the political will behind it, it could afford to ignore these excrescent bodies, save only to flatten them with outrage whenever they dared speak for different ideas.
>
> (H. Young, 1989, p. 425)

The orchestration of what Stephen Ball (1990a) has called a 'discourse of derision' has been a major feature of the New Right's attack on the professional values of the education community. Originating in the *Black Papers* and press attacks on 'progressive teachers' and comprehensive education in the early 1970s, it has been a more or less constant refrain in all subsequent New Right educational reform. As recently as 1993, for example, the Prime Minister, John Major, told the Centre for Policy Studies,

> This ancient prejudice was then reinforced by the Left, with its mania for equality. Equality not of *opportunity*, but of *outcome*. This was a mania that condemned children to fall short of their potential; they treated them as if they were identical – or must be made so. A mania that undermined common sense values in schools, rejected proven teaching methods, debased standards – or disposed of them altogether. A canker in our education system which spread from the Sixties on, and deprived great cohorts of our children of the opportunities they deserved. I, for one, cannot find it easy to forgive the Left for that.
>
> (Pring, 1995, p. 141, quoting from an unpublished paper by Sir Peter Newsam)

Pring rightly condemns this kind of statement as 'an absurd caricature, a total distortion of what actually took place', but such fundamentalist views of educational history have been far from uncommon, as a number of New Right political memoirs published during the early 1990s indicate (Batteson and Ball, 1995). The classic form of attack, in which ministers announce the existence of a crisis in education and at the same time denounce teachers for incompetence, ignoring the interests of young people, preaching 'Marxist' or other 'subversive' doctrines, or for otherwise 'failing the nation', has been used on numerous occasions during the past two decades to provide the legitimating context for New Right 'solutions'. The 1988 Education Reform Act was a particularly clear example of this kind of strategy, where the spectre of 'the incompetent teacher' was invoked to legitimize the formal requirement for teacher appraisal; but similar strategies also featured in the passage of the Further and Higher Education Act of 1992 and the establishment of the Teacher Training Agency in 1994, where teacher training institutions were condemned by the New Right for their propagation of 'left-wing' views (Lawlor, 1990).

In common with most fundamentalist bodies, New Right supporters have found it impossible to tolerate any form of critical questioning of traditional British culture and have been particularly resistant to the notion that learning should involve the learner in a genuine exploratory dialogue over issues and ideas. Notions of pluralism and diversity are cast aside while only the knowledge sanctified by New Right approval is thought fit for inclusion in the curriculum. Government reforms are virtually non-negotiable and there has been minimal commitment to evaluating their effects. Where there has been genuine professional concern about the kind of educational provision on offer – as is currently the case with the system of vocational qualifications in post-compulsory education – educational practitioners are rarely consulted. The message constantly replayed during the past two decades has been that educational professionals cannot be trusted, and therefore have to be made more accountable and to be more closely monitored and controlled.

The naturalization of New Right derision and the scathing denunciation of cultural progressivism and intellectual values in educational institutions might well be dismissed (as it has been by a number of Conservatives) as the product of a demented and philistine cadre of backwoodspeople – as so much visceral prejudice and rhetoric. But, in Foucault's terms, such discursive practices come to constitute 'a regime of truth' which, when harnessed to broader political and managerial agendas, has enormous power to constrain the expression of alternative values:

> Discourses are about what can be said, and thought, but also about who can speak, when, where and with what authority.... Thus, certain possibilities for thought are constructed. We do not speak a discourse, it speaks us. We *are* the subjectivities, the voices, the knowledge, the power relations that a discourse constructs and allows.... In these terms we are spoken by policies, we take up the positions constructed for us within policies.
>
> (S. J. Ball, 1994, pp. 21–2)

As evidence from research carried out by Stephen Ball (1994, pp. 50–3) and Halpin *et al.* (1993) testifies, discursive restrictions can apply even within schools and colleges, where the imperatives of financial survival, public relations and image management have so taken priority over other forms of professional activity that concerns about the curriculum or student learning are driven from the agenda. What was once the core of educational practice is now becoming peripheral to the all-consuming demands of the market.

The practical significance of the constraints created by the political control of educational discourse is well illustrated by a comment made by the former Chief Inspector for Schools, Eric Bolton:

> One of the side-effects of conviction politics is the labelling of any critical voices as self-interested whingeing: 'They would say that, wouldn't they?' It has been an effective tactic,

ensuring that informed and reasonable critical voices have been shut out from debates even before they get started.

(Bolton, 1994)

A striking feature of the New Right's approach to 'discourse management' has been its reliance on denunciation through the public campaign and the medium of the press, rather than the considered exchange of views through the academic journals. To a degree this emanates from its unwillingness to recognize the validity of the social science disciplines, particularly when applied to the study of education. Both theory and research are derided and overridden by the 'common sense' of experience, so that from the early 1970s onwards the New Right has made little use of the academic outlets for the presentation of its arguments, preferring instead to concentrate its contributions in the publications of the right-wing 'think-tanks'. But even here its literary canon is surprisingly sparse, as those who have attempted to engage with its ideas have discovered (S. J. Ball, 1990a, 1994). While such an approach to discourse management might well provide evidence of the profound anti-intellectualism which afflicts the radical Right's philosophy, it also underlines its unerring instinct for the mobilization of political power in negating the traditions of research which underpin educational professionalism.

Potent though they have been in generating antagonism between the New Right and the educational community, derision and discourse management alone could not have provided sufficient leverage for Conservative governments so totally to dominate the educational agenda without the financial and managerial controls which have been progressively added to the armoury of the state. It is to these that we now turn.

GOVERNMENT BY 'DOMINOCRACY'

It was a former Conservative Lord Chancellor, Lord Hailsham, who coined the phrase 'an elective dictatorship'. He had in mind a possible future left-wing Labour government which would be able to exploit the opportunities available to it through the various loopholes he perceived in the unwritten British constitution. In the event, his fear was groundless, but he was more prophetic than he knew in that it was a government of his own party which qualified for the description. The visceral politics of the New Right, combining hostile rhetoric towards its 'enemies' with a determination to exploit the power allowed to it by the British constitution, have produced a one-party state in Britain unparalleled in peace-time this century.

One of the most significant and unremitting features of the Thatcherite and post-Thatcherite programmes has been their determination to exercise domination over all areas of public life which come under the jurisdiction of the state. Since 1979, many of these have been privatized, others disposed of, closed down or substantially reduced, while a few have been grudgingly retained. Those that have remained – essentially those in education, health, law enforcement, and a few remaining areas of the civil service – have been subjected to huge managerial transformations which in many cases have left their professional employees with the sense of having been de-skilled (S. J. Ball, 1994). Through the discourses surrounding 'consumer choice' and 'value for money', the state has determined the reform agendas (often using management consultants) while showing an almost total disregard for professional expertise and the research traditions within the public sector institutions themselves. What for New Right supporters has counted as 'firm government', for its opponents has been the exercise of autocracy and dogma (Young, 1989; Gilmour, 1992).

Both in scale and in extent, the New Right's deployment of political power has been immense and without precedent. It has also been a complex and highly sophisticated enterprise which has both exploited the openings allowed by the lack of a formal British constitution, and, as we suggested above, has relied heavily on the assiduous construction of discourses capable of both regulating the terms of policy and intimidating those deemed to lie outside their legitimate frame. But perhaps the most central aspect of the state's expanding control has been the widespread imposition of the 'new managerialism', disseminated and monitored by ministerially-appointed quangos. When, as has happened in all sectors of education, regulations relating to quality assurance and financial audit are combined with output-related funding and techniques of human resource management, the state and its agencies are in possession of immense and far-reaching powers to regulate the operations and personnel functions of an organization such as a school or college.

There remains one final dimension in this catalogue of power methodologies which should be mentioned and that is the preparedness of the New Right to incorporate a postmodernist stance into its political strategy – particularly in its readiness to promote anti-intellectualism and selective relativism as active elements of policy (R. Johnson, 1991a; S. J. Ball, 1994). The debunking of 'expert' knowledge (unless it originates in the City) and its displacement in the national pantheon by a mishmash of folk myth, 'common sense' and the inflated prescriptions of business management give rise to the bizarre paradox of relativism and absolutism existing side by side.

Taken together, these powers constitute eloquent testimony of the New Right's mistrust of educational institutions and professionals. We shall briefly examine each of them in turn.

FEEDING THE LEVIATHAN

Both Hutton and Wright have made much of the fact that the maximizing of executive power and minimizing of the limited constraints placed upon it by the British constitution has been a conscious political strategy for the New Right. According to Hutton,

> There has not been such a determined effort since the advent of universal suffrage to use the machinery of the British state to prosecute a particular party programme as that undertaken by the modern Conservative Party. Every nook and cranny of the constitution has been exploited to consolidate the party's hold on power; as far as possible implementation of its policies has been delegated to those inside and outside government who actively support it.

> She (Margaret Thatcher) pushed the system to its limits, using the traditional legitimacy offered by 'parliamentary sovereignty' for her very untraditional ends.
>
> (Hutton, 1995a, pp. 32 and 29–30)

In his Fabian pamphlet, *Beyond the Patronage State*, Wright refers to this systematic exploitation of executive power as a form of 'dominocracy', in which

> Parliament has become the pathetic creature of the executive. In the name of ministerial responsibility, real accountability is dissolved. The constitution is what is made up as

governments go along. This endangers liberties, erodes legitimacy, encourages bad legislation and threatens the integrity of all intermediate institutions. A modern Bagehot might describe the efficient secret of British politics as the ability of ministers to do what they can get away with in exchange for being shouted at once a fortnight in the House of Commons.

(Wright, 1995, p. 1)

Of particular concern to Wright is the enormous expansion of what he calls the 'patronage state', which has brought with it a massive increase in the number of quangos and the exercise of the power of control over the public appointment process leading to a *nomenklatura* of political sympathizers (Gray, 1994b). The effect of such an expanding state apparatus is to extend the reach of government itself through the devolution of power combined with an appointments policy which ensures ideological compatibility between government and its agencies. By the same token, the distance created between government and agency also enables ministers to disclaim responsibilities which were formerly theirs.

According to Wright, in 1989 a Cabinet Office *Review of Public Appointments* noted that there were 51,000 public appointments, with ministers making 10,000 new appointments or re-appointments each year. It went on to comment that 'new appointments are often the most effective means at Ministers' disposal for changing the direction of arms' length public bodies'. 'In other words,' as Wright puts it, 'patronage was to be seen as a crucial engine of policy, with appointees no longer charged with the task merely of running public bodies but with a mission to redirect them in line with the prevailing ideology' (1995, p. 10). He goes on to note

the extent to which the party in power has seen itself as engaged upon an ideological mission to change the character of the state and so needing its army of shock troops to engage with the enemy on every front. Patronage was seen as a powerful weapon, providing the means whereby non-believers could be despatched and those of true faith installed, giving a new character to public institutions and new directions to state activities. ... The partisans who were deployed from the private to the public sectors were frequently uninhibited by public service traditions or conventional public interest baggage. ... If there often seemed to be a clash of cultures ... it is because there was. Their mission was not to serve a traditional concept of the public interest but to subvert it ... the new patronage class is a product of a political project to replace elective with appointive government over wide tracts of executive territory in order to advance the ideological purposes of the party in power without having to recognise rival legitimacies or the pluralities of mediating institutions.

(Wright, 1995, pp. 10–11)

The establishment of quangos – many of which have been granted executive authority – has been of paramount importance in securing the implementation of the New Right's education and training policies. Indeed, between them they control virtually every aspect of government policy in this field, creating a chain of managerial regulation extending from the state to local institution to individual practitioner.

Within the area of compulsory education, the 1988 Education Reform Act established the National Curriculum Council (NCC) and the School Examinations and Assessment Council (SEAC), both since superseded by the School Curriculum and Assessment Authority (SCAA). Alongside the installation of these executive quangos the Conservative government in 1992 took away responsibility for inspections from Her Majesty's Inspectorate and conferred it on the privatized Office for Standards in Education (OFSTED). More recently it set up the Funding Agency for Schools as the executive agency for controlling the budgets of opted-out schools, which, according to its Chairman, is seen as the eventual replacement for local education authorities (reported in *The Guardian,* 11 September 1995).

Within the post-compulsory sector, ultimate accountability is to the Audit Commission. Control of governance, funding and quality assessment is the responsibility of the Further Education Funding Council (FEFC) while the 81 Training and Enterprise Councils (TECs) in England and Wales (there were originally 82 TECs but the South Thames TEC went into receivership in 1995) and the 22 Local Enterprise Companies in Scotland are responsible for supporting local training and for promoting the efforts of schools and colleges to meet the government's training targets. Those targets are themselves the remit of the National Advisory Council for Education and Training Targets (NACETT), while the National Council for Vocational Qualifications (NCVQ) is responsible for managing the system of vocational qualifications in England and Wales (SCVQ in Scotland). In higher education the three Higher Education Funding Councils for England, Scotland and Wales (HEFC) are responsible for the allocation of funding and assessing the quality of institutional performance in teaching and research; and with regard to the national management of teacher education the relevant authority is the Teacher Training Agency established in 1994.

Most of these bodies carry executive responsibility for the implementation of education and training policy within the UK. Their members are largely appointed by government ministers, and they have authority to act as executive agencies independently of any local democratic process. They may or may not choose to consult with educational practitioners, and, as Wright and others have pointed out, a number of surveys confirm a high proportion of quango members as being either Conservative activists or sympathizers (Cohen, 1994). A typical example of this process at work, according to Hutton, is the membership of the Funding Agency for Schools. Referring to the position in 1994, he points out that:

> The Chairman of the Funding Agency for Schools is Sir Christopher Benson, head of Sun Alliance, Costain and director of MEPC – all important contributors to the Conservative Party. Other members include Sir Robert Balchin, chairman of the Conservatives in the South-East and Edward Lister, Conservative Leader of Wandsworth Council.
>
> (Hutton, 1995a, pp. 327–8)

The establishment of executive agencies as part of the operation of government has been a central feature of Conservative political management since 1979, and came out of the Efficiency Strategy under Sir Derek (later Lord) Raynor set up by Margaret Thatcher in 1981 (Metcalfe and Richards, 1990). The basis of the strategy was the necessity, as the government saw it, of changing the culture of the civil service from one of public administration founded on the 'meeting of need' to an ethos of public management based on the control of costs (*ibid.*). The importance of cost reduction in the public services and minimizing the role of the state were part of the initial rationale for such a policy, but during the 1980s it developed into a powerful feature of the New Right's political strategy right across the public sector.

If the executive agencies responsible for education and training constitute the *managerial apparatus* for their regulation and control, the introduction of various forms of managerialism *within* institutions has been at least as important in securing the compliance of the educational community to the will of the state. It is this aspect of the New Right's political strategy to which we now turn.

THE NEW MANAGERIALISM IN EDUCATION AND TRAINING

One of the striking paradoxes underlying the New Right's education and training reforms lies in the contrast between the progressive rhetoric of the post-Fordist vision, with its emphasis on co-operation, teamwork and the need for 'lifelong learning', and the profoundly *Fordist* culture of British employment relations established by the Conservative reforms (Brown and Lauder, 1992b; see also Chapter 3). This phenomenon has been singularly apparent in Britain's public sector institutions – and notably the education system – where employees have had to endure significant elements of neo-Taylorism as the defining feature of the new managerial culture (Pollitt, 1993; Fergusson, 1994; S. J. Ball, 1994). As a consequence, teachers and lecturing staff have experienced significant degrees of deprofessionalization involving various forms of work intensification combined with diminishing responsibility for the content of their work. Specialist curriculum knowledge-bases have been redrawn by government-nominated 'experts', and for many practitioners it is no longer possible to incorporate into their teaching the new developments taking place within their field of expertise. In the classic separation of the conception of work from its execution, the role of the teacher is now to implement the policy set down by the state and not to challenge or engage critically with it – even if this means accepting procedures which are perceived to be unjust or 'anti-educational'. For many lecturers in the post-compulsory sector, formerly held curricular responsibilities have been transformed into the assessment of competence, often without explicit curriculum content. Assessment of students at various levels in the education system has been simplified and reduced to the administration of standardized tests designed to be independent of the teacher's judgement. Initial teacher education has been largely emptied of its theoretical content in the desire to restrict teachers to the learning of 'practical' skills, and serious attempts have been made to reduce the influence of universities in the professional preparation of teachers (Fergusson, 1994).

Under the market reforms introduced since 1988, educational practitioners in all sectors have seen the price mechanism invade every aspect of education so that, as one of Ball's respondents puts it, 'each child has a price tag on it, and the sixth formers have the highest price tag – so, in pure financial terms, one is obviously trying to raise the most money one can' (S. J. Ball, 1994, p. 52). Co-operation and collaboration between institutions are virtually impossible, and the importance of trust between government and profession is seen by the state as irrelevant. Teachers and lecturers themselves are tied to the operations of such a system by means of performance assessment through formal appraisal (S. J. Ball, 1990b). The major instruments ensuring that this culture and its practices prevail within the education system are the precepts of 'managerialism', which now form the prescribed basis of working relationships and practice in almost every institution.

A number of commentators, including ourselves, take the view that in characterizing the organizational reforms introduced into schools, colleges and universities since the mid-eighties, the concept of 'managerialism' conveys more readily their ideological and political significance in the establishment of Conservative hegemony than does the more conventional term 'management'. Supporters of the notion of 'management', both as a generic socio-technology and as a set of specific instruments for the implementation of organizational reforms, often present it as a neutral body of principle and practice designed to establish appropriate disciplines for the maintenance of organizational functionality. As Pollitt puts it,

> 'better management' sounds sober, neutral, as unopposable as virtue itself ...
>
> [It] is usually presented as if it were a politically neutral 'good', a set of more-or-less scientific techniques which, when properly applied, will produce large benefits without distorting normal constitutional and political relationships.
>
> (Pollitt, 1993, pp. 49 and 57–8)

Such a view renders invisible the social and political basis of management, both in its implementation and in relation to its objectives and outcomes. 'Management' does not exist in an ideological vacuum as an all-purpose, value-free technology, as some of its exponents would have it: it is invariably the servant of broader political and social agendas which it often fails to disclose or question in the procedures of its everyday practice. And of few cases has this been more true than the managerialism within the 'reformed' education system.

In his critique of the managerialism which now pervades British higher education, Martin Trow (1994) draws a distinction between its 'soft' and 'hard' versions and suggests that during the 1980s, following the publication of the Jarratt Report (Committee of Vice Chancellors and Principals, 1985), it was the former which largely prevailed in British higher education. By contrast, following the 1991 White Paper, *Higher Education: A New Framework* (DES, 1991), the Further and Higher Education Act of 1992 installed a hard managerialism which for Trow 'is a substitute for a relationship of trust between government and universities, trust in the ability of the institutions of higher education to broadly govern themselves' (Trow, 1994, p. 14). Attributing responsibility for the new policy to 'those in government and business rather than in the universities themselves', he goes on to suggest that:

> Business models are central to the hard conception of managerialism; when applied to higher education, as the current government does, the commitment is to transform universities into organisations similar enough to ordinary commercial firms so that they can be assessed and managed in roughly similar ways.
>
> (*ibid.*, p. 14)

The determination of the New Right to infuse every sector of the public services with a business-oriented, cost-driven managerialism can be seen as one of its most persistently pursued goals. Indeed, throughout the whole of the Conservative Party's period in office it has remained a constant feature of its agenda and, as a generic form, has powered the organizational transformations of each of the major public services. As Metcalfe and Richards put it,

> the political impetus behind reform has been sustained long beyond the time when many, inside and outside Whitehall and Westminster, had expected it to fade. ... [T]he central place accorded to the concept of management ... has set a new direction and instigated changes in the culture of Whitehall which will be difficult if not impossible to reverse.
>
> (Metcalfe and Richards, 1990, p. vii)

The centrality of 'management' to the Conservative project was first articulated in 1980 by Michael Heseltine, then Conservative Secretary of State for the Environment:

> Efficient management is a key to the (national) revival ... And the management ethos must run right through our national life – private and public companies, civil service, nationalized industries, local government, the National Health Service.
>
> (quoted in Pollitt, 1993, p. vi)

Fifteen years on, Heseltine's commitment to the reform of public-sector management and his belief in its importance for 'national competitiveness' was undiminished and to be found being proclaimed in the 1995 *Competitiveness* White Paper – produced by the Department of Trade and Industry where he was Secretary of State – in which the subject was accorded 44 paragraphs. One of the significant points to come out of the White Paper review is that total employment in the public sector in 1994 was 5.3 million, compared with 7.4 million in 1979 – much of the difference being accounted for by the transfer of function and personnel to the private sector.

The centrality of management reform to the New Right agenda became established during the early 1980s where it grew out of the Efficiency Strategy. At first its key relevance was seen to be in relation to the government's commitment to cutting the costs of public welfare and to 'rolling back the state', but it quickly developed into a more elaborate reforming policy founded on the goals of 'economy, efficiency and effectiveness' which were to form the basis of policy in all areas for which the state was financially responsible. During the 1990s, as part of the Conservative reforms of the National Health Service and education and training, the focus of New Right managerialism has become enlarged to incorporate the functioning of quasi-markets, 'quality service' and the charter initiative (see Chapter 5).

The managerialist revolution introduced into education and training embodies both in theory and practice many of the political principles dear to the New Right. It contains another 'rich mix' of Thatcherite precepts, combining the objectives of privatization, 'efficiency', 'value for money', accountability, marketization and consumerism, while significantly incorporating surveillance and central-control-at-a-distance. Although the 'three Es', economy, efficiency and effectiveness, are often cited together, the main driving force has undoubtedly been the striving for economy and efficiency rather than effectiveness, where the pressure on reducing inputs has been paramount. If efficiency is defined as the optimal ratio between inputs and outputs, the prevailing emphasis has been on driving down the costs of inputs – especially of what are now called 'human resources'. As Pollitt (1993) puts it, '"efficiency gains" so often become a matter of trying to get the same service from a smaller resource base rather than investing a few extra resources in order to procure a disproportionate increase in outputs' (p. 139).

It may be thought that by focusing at a systemic level on policy agendas and regulations, an analysis of this kind runs the risk of promulgating an over-determined view of educational practice. It is often said, with justification, that it is impossible for the state to police all the areas under its jurisdiction and that teachers in their own classrooms or lecture halls still retain relative freedom to determine their teaching methods and even, to some degree, curriculum content. This is, of course, true up to a point, and there will be significant variations in the discretionary options available to teachers across the different sectors. But it is much less true of the 1990s than it was for most of the previous decade when the Education Reform Act began the process of redefining and more tightly specifying the role of the teacher/lecturer. Individual practitioners will continue to use the spaces available to them to create some discretionary variation, but such are the systems of delegated authority and accountability established by the state that even day-to-day practice is now visible and available for inspection or assessment.

As Ball has pointed out, a central feature of the managerialist revolution has been the system of *self-management* prescribed for schools and colleges in the market reforms introduced from the 1988 Reform Act. The statutory requirements for accountability, budgetary control and human resource management – central to which is the appraisal process – oblige the headteacher, principal or, in some institutions, the chief executive to act as proxy for the Secretary of State in seeing that they are met. Ball has likened the role of headteacher/principal to that of 'state vavasour' – a chief vassal owing allegiance to a great lord and having other vassals under him (S. J. Ball, 1994, p. 58). Such a system enables the state to maintain the appearance of devolving responsibility while virtually tying the hands of those to whom it is devolved – an illusion of statecraft which one commentator has called 'steering at a distance' (Kickert, 1991). An important aspect of this process is that the organization itself 'takes over' the responsibility devolved to it – and for which it remains accountable. This is well conveyed by Raab, who suggests that:

> Government's hope must be that the implantation of the systems and ethos of management will take root sufficiently to legitimise new mechanisms and routines and to make them appear to be self-imposed, or collaboratively adopted, from top to toe. In this headteachers are pivotal, and a massive reaffirmation of their role as managers is being undertaken. Lay members of school boards and governing bodies are likewise being inducted and trained to a conception of their function within a management paradigm of school governance.
>
> (Raab, 1991, p. 16)

While some who fulfil managerial roles have undoubtedly seen the reforms as beneficial for their institutions in terms of the increased autonomy they are able to exercise, for others it has been a poisoned chalice which has led to hardening divisions between categories of staff. According to Ball, the managerialist policy in the education system is leading to 'the emergence of a professionalised cadre of specially trained teacher managers', a phenomenon which he sees as creating 'polarisation between the values of professional responsibility and those of efficient management' (S. J. Ball, 1994, pp. 57–8). The introduction of performance related pay, leading to substantial pay differentials between senior management and other employees, further exacerbates those divisions.

A similar two-edged process is also at work with regard to financial management. Although there may be some gains to be made from having the power to allocate resources within the institution, the formula-driven nature of its budget of necessity confirms ultimate control as resting with government on the one hand and the capacity of the local student 'market' on the other. If a school or college finds itself in competition with others in a declining market, major pressures both on professional and teacher–learner relationships are highly probable.

It is in the nature of managerialism – particularly in a quasi-market economy – that managerial operations become separated from, and invariably take precedence over, those performed by professional employees. The centrality to the institution of financial control, public relations, marketing and income generation inevitably reorient its priorities and further exacerbate the cultural divide between managers and professionals. In large organizations particularly, 'strategic planning' becomes the dominant concern of the 'senior management team' while the former mainstream tasks of teaching become subordinated to the structures emerging from its decisions. As often as not, the price mechanism will dominate. Decisions as to whether a course will run are likely to depend on the numbers of students it will attract and therefore how much income will be brought in. 'Popular' courses will survive while those serving more 'marginal' interests will suffer and may well disappear. Thus educational institutions are made to share the classic features of what Hutton calls 'degenerate capitalism': short-termism, price-mediated relationships, the commodification of curricular knowledge and training packages as consumable products, and internal hierarchization of function where status and priority rest with the goals of managerialism.

AN IMPOVERISHED CONCEPT OF MANAGEMENT

Of all the elements of the New Right's political strategy to contain and de-limit the professional discretion of educational practitioners, and to maintain its own limited concept of national education, the imposition of a hard managerialist regime on educational institutions has arguably been the most significant. The state's enforcement of a narrow concept of efficiency has further helped to strengthen the grip of the executive over the operations and discretion of educational institutions, while also generating *inefficiencies* as overworked staff try to cope with the additional workloads and bureaucratic demands imposed upon them. In larger organizations, the operation of managerialism itself leads to further costs as the process of internal transactions creates additional demands on resources.

One of the most significant features of the restrictive regime created by this form of managerialism is the notion of the *organization* as the paramount unit of operation. The recent growth of Human Resource Management as a managerial philosophy in many educational institutions takes the process further. In almost every respect, intra-organizational activity is the ultimate point of reference – whether it be expressed in the form of mission and vision statements, the discourse of public relations and market strategy, the search for income generation, the school/college development plan, or in the commitment to the institution expected of staff. Almost the entire managerial and operational energy of the institution's employees is focused around the organization itself.

On the surface, such a preoccupation with the managerial demands on the new market-driven institution may appear to be perfectly defensible and rational. The problem that arises from it is that the culture of the school or college runs a high risk of becoming transformed from one dedicated to wider educational concerns to one driven by extrinsic business objectives. Through the instruments of managerialism, the traditional professional commitment to learning as the development of understanding is converted into the marketing and development of products. By such means, the original and the innovative, the speculative and exploratory, the challenging and the critical become too difficult to incorporate into the curriculum – even supposing that the legislation permits it. By the same token, issues which might benefit from co-operative action between educational institutions in the interests of improving the overall provision in a geographical area come up against the barriers of competitive market relationships. In a global economy characterized by the constant 'change' so often referred to by politicians, such cultural closure seems extraordinary and indefensible.

The deficiencies of New Right managerialism have been well-documented by its critics. Pollitt (1993) comments on its negative impact on staff morale and motivation, noting that the main political objective has been one of control rather than the nurturing of commitment. Fergusson (1994) is critical of the dominance of extrinsic measures of performance derived from business culture and the corresponding disregard for the intrinsic values which have been the bedrock of professional culture in education.

Metcalfe and Richards (1990) refer to the Conservative governments' management reforms as reflecting 'an impoverished concept of management', noting that it is hierarchical, intra-organizational in its emphasis and designed to operate as an executive function which presupposes 'the clear definition of objectives, policies and, if possible, corresponding performance measures'. They go on to observe that as a consequence,

> These elements in combination impose severe restrictions on the scope of management. They limit the role of public managers to programmed implementation of predetermined policies. They disregard the problems of adapting policies and organisations to environmental change. If this is all that management means, giving more weight to it is likely to cause confusion and frustration rather than lead to long-term improvements in performance.
>
> (Metcalfe and Richards, 1990, p. 17)

The heavy reliance on managerialism as the main defining philosophy for inter-professional and institution–learner relationships can clearly be challenged for its negative impact on the learning experiences of students and teachers. Its predisposition to instrumentalism, its capacity to restrict and narrow down curricular knowledge which should be opened up for extended dialogue, and its tendency to supplant educational concerns with those relating to the institution as a business all raise important value and moral issues, some of which we explore in later chapters. At the same time, there is an issue relating to the hidden costs of managerialism. A finance-driven model of efficiency undoubtedly *creates* inefficiencies elsewhere in the system and brings about a decrease in effectiveness as resource-starved institutions are obliged to give priority to crisis management strategies which themselves generate costs. The widely-publicized effects of the 1995 budget cuts on a number of schools and local education authorities in which experienced teachers had to be made redundant and class sizes increased are a clear example of this process. Similarly, increased stress levels borne by practitioners carrying expanding workloads while fighting the effects of disillusionment and demoralization are also part of the wider calculus of cost and effectiveness.

For the nation as a whole there are costs arising from the neglect of public institutions and the narrowing of educational experience. The managerial reforms have led to a system so rigidly encased in an apparatus of state control that it is unlikely that any significant innovation in educational practice can occur without the approval of the state or its executive agencies. This has, of course, been the intention underlying many of the New Right reforms. But, leaving aside for the moment the ethics – and political consequences – of placing limits on the intellectual horizons of both professionals and students, there is likely to be a high price to pay for an education system which is drained of much of its potential for creativity and innovation in the face of the scale of existing and future global problems. If, as has happened in most sectors of education, practitioners continue to function as technicians of state-defined curriculum policy, an enormous responsibility rests with the state to ensure that the system remains capable of addressing the demands both of the present and even more of the future. The current situation gives rise to the ultimate irony of a political party which has steadfastly anathematized the model of the 'command economy' adopted by former communist states being itself responsible for setting up a command education system. Why the latter should be thought to be any more successful than the former in its responsiveness to innovation and change is difficult to comprehend.

CONCLUSION

Our concern in this chapter has been to examine the political and ideological strategies of the New Right in their construction and implementation of policies for education and training. The garnering of the latent powers available to it within the British constitution has allowed the New Right to use its electoral mandate and parliamentary majority to define the conditions of service for public sector workers in uncompromisingly Taylorist terms. Having been defined as a critical source of anti-market values and degenerate liberal humanism, educational professionals have been subjected to a total onslaught on their intellectual identities as well as their conditions of practice. The dedicated authoritarianism and anti-pluralism of the reforms have been central to a thoroughgoing attempt to ensure that educational culture should itself be imbued with the values of free-market capitalism, in which commodification, marketization and competitive individualism reign supreme.

The vision set out by Pring (1995) for a 'community of educated people' is far from being realized. The dominance of the New Right's agendas during the past two decades has ensured that educational culture has been resolutely anti-democratic, anti-pluralist and resistant to expression of critical reflection on educational policy directives. Although educational research has continued to be published and professional development can still provide occasional opportunities for the social and political analysis of education, this happens in a context which is increasingly constrained by the human resources management regime which defines teacher training in terms of organizational functionality. The intellectual challenges and uncertainties which are fundamental to any area of enquiry are gradually being put out of bounds for educational professionals. Separated from its parent disciplines in philosophy and the social sciences, 'educational knowledge' is defined increasingly in terms of technicist solutions to practical or managerial problems. With few exceptions, the New Right in government has denied any right to public-sector professionals to contribute to policy agendas. On the contrary, they have been required to implement whatever has been enacted and to perform the degrading task of complying with the terms of their own de-skilling and deprofessionalization.

The underlying rationale for the New Right's education reforms has throughout been the Thatcherite determination to install an uncompromising version of free-market capitalism in which an economically restored, newly enterprising and revitalized Britain would reconstitute itself as a vigorous adversary in the intensifying global struggle for markets. As we shall argue in the following chapter, in the event this ambition has not been realized, nor, on the terms on which the Conservatives set out in 1979, could it be. The contradictions between the nationalist and internationalist thrust of its economic policies are part of the story, but even more undermining have been the consequences of its unswerving commitment to deregulated, free-market capitalism.

Chapter 2

Education, Training and Nation-State Capitalism: Britain's Failing Strategy

Geoff Esland

Chief among the non-economic factors degrading British industrial performance are those rooted in our education system. The disdain for industry and commerce which has long been a feature of our educational establishment within public schools and universities is now partnered and supported by an outright hostility towards business, stemming from the modern left-wing public-sector education establishment.

(Tebbit, 1991, p. 99)

Despite the claims of her propagandists at the time and her apologists later, [Mrs Thatcher's] actual achievement was modest, even destructive – for in economic and political terms she did no more than entrench the vicious circles in which the country is trapped.

(Hutton, 1995a, p. 30)

Left to itself – possibly encouraged to be so by extreme free marketeers – capitalism embraces a Darwinian power struggle within society.

(Keegan, 1992, p. 190)

INTRODUCTION

In the previous chapter we looked in some detail at the political strategies of the New Right in relation to education and training policy, noting their reliance on both a narrow, protectionist view of nationhood and a Taylorist form of managerialism designed to maintain a tight regulatory control over the culture, content and practice of education. We also suggested that although the economic demands of globalization feature frequently in government declarations of its priorities for education and training, the internal divisions within the Conservative Party have ensured that the determined defence of Britain's cultural sovereignty has prevented any serious engagement with their implications for a more international concept of citizenship. Although there has been some degree of recognition – albeit reluctant – of the need for the supra-national management of economic policy, there has been a consistent refusal to yield on the defence of national culture and practice within education and training.

The blend of nationalism and authoritarianism which currently characterizes British education, and its coexistence with neo-liberal economic policies, raises important issues as to the relationship between the two spheres of policy. If globalization represents the economic track along which Britain feels obliged, but also chooses, to travel, the question arises as to the nature of the relationship between the economic and social demands of the global economy and the kind of education and training policies currently being pursued in the United Kingdom. How realistic, for example, are government exhortations to the educational community to raise qualification and skill levels in an economy that remains incurably resistant to investment in and utilization of high-level skills? Then again, how sufficient to the task of raising standards of education and training is the current competence-based system of post-compulsory education? Underlying these questions is the yet more fundamental issue of the moral and political agendas which have fashioned the New Right's educational reforms in which the expulsion from the system of liberal humanist values has been accorded the highest priority. Related to this is the problem of 'unrealistic expectations' and the fear of producing an 'over-educated' society in an economy with persistently high levels of youth unemployment. It may, therefore, be more pertinent to understand the Conservative education and training policies in terms of their role in institutionalizing and legitimating the moral economy of the free market than as a serious attempt to realize what John Major has described as 'our ambition that Britain should have the best qualified workforce in Europe'.

It is undoubtedly the case that the political and ideological agendas of the New Right have been fundamental to the shaping of education and training policies, in which almost every essential detail of the system has been required to embody the precepts of consumerism and the market. As part of this process, the globalization discourse promulgated by the New Right has incorporated an instrumental view of education founded on skill and qualification acquisition in which the outcomes of education and training are perceived as tradable commodities in the job market. Such an approach is consistent with the individualistic nature of British capitalism, under which the learner or employee is expected to become 'competitive' by acquiring the skills appropriate for employment. As a result of this emphasis of policy, there has been little, if any, recognition of the importance to society of an education system capable of fostering in young people a broader critical understanding necessary for dealing with the ethical and value issues arising from the pursuit of a global market. As we argued in the previous chapter, the political prerogative claimed by the Conservative Party under Britain's unwritten constitution has included the right to determine the value system to which all public institutions are expected to subscribe. In consequence, the education system has been virtually purged of whatever capacity it had for ethical debate and intellectual pluralism and has been formally obliged to confirm in its organization and practice those values favoured by the New Right – notwithstanding the fact that many educational practitioners would not themselves endorse them.

One of the most widely criticized features of Conservative policies has been their encouragement of a moral economy in which the values of competitive individualism have been promoted over all others, giving rise to what many believe to be an amoral culture marked by growing inequality, social polarization and the promotion of individual consumption over social citizenship (Hutton, 1995a; Commission on Wealth Creation and Social Cohesion, 1995). Boardroom excess, workplace insecurity for employees and the sense of declining standards in public life documented by the Nolan Committee (House of Commons, 1995) are the symbols of an unfettered capitalism which the education and training system is, by default and association, obliged to endorse. So determined has the New Right been in trying to suppress value positions different from its own that in many sectors of education access to alternative concepts of social and economic morality has all but disappeared.

In considering these and related issues, our task in this chapter is to spell out and explore some of the economic implications of globalization for British citizens and to consider how effective the economic policies pursued by the New Right over the past sixteen years have been in meeting the challenge of the global market. If the central objective for Mrs Thatcher – and by implication, her successor – was the revitalization of British capitalism, for which the reform of the education and training system was an essential prerequisite, we need to consider how those policies have interacted together in order to meet that objective.

In attempting to address this issue, we conclude not only that there is very little evidence of the sustained regeneration of British capitalism, but also that the overriding concentration on supply-side reforms in attempting to meet such an objective was seriously misconceived from the outset. Other features of economic policy – notably the attachment to *laissez-faire* policies in relation to the UK's financial system – have had an immeasurably greater impact on the country's economic performance. In consequence, the education and training reforms carried out in the name of economic renewal have led to a narrowing education system which has been deprived of its capacity to engage seriously with the social, economic and *intellectual* demands of globalization, and which itself reflects and reinforces the 'low-skills equilibrium' on which much of Britain's economic uncompetitiveness is founded (Finegold and Soskice, 1988). At the same time, it has been obliged to perform the ideological task of habituating young people to low pay, job insecurity and unemployment. As *The Guardian*'s Economics Editor, Larry Elliott, expressed it following an interview in September 1995 with Gillian Shephard, then Secretary of State for Education and Employment,

> At the root of her thinking is the notion that the world of work is changing irrevocably. In the next century, workers will have to face up to the reality of 'short-term contracts, some uncertainty and even a period in unemployment', *and that is why the provision of training and good quality education are vital.*
>
> (Elliott, 1995, emphasis added)

The implication of such statements is that under the impact of globalization the role of the nation-state has been reduced to 'little more than invest[ing] in infrastructure, training, and education in order to make their countries more attractive to investors' (Schmidt, 1995, p. 80). As Schmidt suggests, liberalization, deregulation and privatization are contributing to a reduction in the ability of the nation-state to deal with its social problems while increasing the power of business interests. Under its pursuit of the neo-liberal global market, the state is effectively 'handing over' control of employment and the labour market to the large corporations.

As the social implications of globalization become more apparent, there is a growing concern about the democratic deficit within the UK and the long-term consequences of an adversarial business culture. We would agree with those commentators who believe that the political, economic and social adaptation necessitated by the national commitment to further globalization requires a more consensual and co-operative culture in which innovation and investment coexist with employment relationships founded on high levels of trust. According to the RSA (1995) publication, *Tomorrow's Company,* the adversarial, class-riven, finance-dominated culture of British business, in which minimal regard is shown for its wider responsibilities to employees and community, seriously impedes its ability to compete with the kinds of 'world companies' which are proving to be successful performers in the global market. In the face of the growing problem of social exclusion arising from current economic policies, the RSA report concludes that the only viable option for UK business is to develop a culture of *inclusion* – a goal which will be impossible to achieve without a major change of public values.

CAPITALISM AND EDUCATION IN BRITAIN

The relationship between a nation's economy and the kinds of values and systems it promotes in its education and training provision has long been a central issue within the sociology of education and work. With the publication of their book *Schooling in Capitalist America*, Bowles and Gintis (1976) launched a long-running debate concerning the inherent tendency for capitalist states to bring their educational practice into line with the prevailing labour requirements of their economies. Central to this process is the role of educational institutions in regulating access to the socially favoured positions in the labour market – usually via higher education, but also, most notably in Britain, through the privileged networks of the public school system. As a consequence, the criteria of social differentiation engendered through educational selection – both tacit and overt – were said to be the main instruments of legitimation for inequalities pertaining to society as a whole.

One of the arguments put forward by Bowles and Gintis was that political pressures on educational institutions to provide ideological authentication and support for the state's economic objectives are likely to intensify and become more overt during periods of major structural change within the economy. Although the provision of education entails the pursuit of a broader set of values predicated on the development of the 'self as citizen', powers are available to the state to enable it to change the balance of priorities in favour of those aspects of education believed to promote improved economic performance – hence the emphasis on 'basic skills' and attitudes of deference and self-discipline as central aspects of the work ethic.

Taking these arguments further, Dale has suggested that capitalist states face three core problems:

- support of the capital accumulation process;
- guaranteeing a context for its continued expansion;
- the legitimation of the capitalist mode of production, including the state's own part in it.

(Dale, 1989, p. 28)

Although these may appear to be complementary processes, Dale is careful to point out that they give rise to a number of contradictions and discontinuities in education and training policy as the state tries to reconcile the conflicting pressures which they create. One of the most significant of these concerns is the contrasting implications which arise from giving priority to the process of accumulation as distinct from its context:

The basic question of whether the *process* or the *context* of accumulation is to receive priority treatment, reverberates through education policy. The process argument calls for an élitist system of education, devoted to the early recognition and fostering of 'ability' and its processing through a largely 'instrumental' curriculum. Such a policy clearly has enormous implications for several of the 'basic myths' which comprise the legitimating function of the state and of the education system in particular.

(ibid., p. 31)

Where priority is given to the *context* of accumulation, the state is obliged to emphasize the 'universal' aspects of education, in which the importance of personal development and equality of opportunity are central principles. For Dale, these count as two of the 'basic myths' which the state is obliged to promote in order to retain public support for its other – more divisive – policies.

Tensions of this kind have been much in evidence during the past two decades as the state has tried to demonstrate its commitment to universal education by claiming to be raising standards of education for all while, in the name of 'parental choice', supporting the mechanisms of the assisted places scheme and charitable status for private schools in order to promote the growth of the independent sector. It has also committed itself to national training targets while devolving responsibility for meeting them to the Training and Enterprise Councils at the same time as reducing their budgets (Bennett *et al.*, 1994). The importance of a highly qualified workforce is often proclaimed, but alongside a minimal response to criticisms of the low quality of National Vocational Qualifications (NVQs) and their low standing with employers (Smithers, 1993; Field, 1995). Perhaps the most convincing test of the political commitment to education and training is whether it is regarded as a cost to be contained or as a social investment, and on this the evidence for the former has been overwhelming.

In the period since the publication of *Schooling in Capitalist America*, the relationship between education and capitalism in the UK has undergone a profound transformation. What has been achieved by four Conservative governments in reforming the culture and governance of education around the central principles of free-market capitalism has far exceeded anything envisaged in the wave of reaction to Bowles and Gintis's book.

As the debate at the time made apparent, educational practitioners were far from happy with the argument that in some of their professional practices they were affording legitimacy to the capitalist wage-labour system. A professional ethic founded on the enhancement of individual potential was generally perceived as having little to do with the values of business and the wealth creation of the nation, and the suggestion by Bowles and Gintis that there was a degree of 'correspondence' between educational practice and the capitalist system met with vigorous rebuttal in certain quarters. Supporters of the thesis, while acknowledging that there were important areas of educational culture which were not reducible to 'capitalist relations', argued that the dominant political forces of capitalist societies would always subordinate the socially progressive aims of education to the necessity for supporting the economic system (Brosio, 1988). However, as the events of the subsequent two decades have demonstrated, radical at the time though it was, the Bowles and Gintis thesis did not prepare people in either Britain or the United States for the establishment of a much more overt relationship between capitalism and education during the 1980s. The suggestion then that educational institutions would be obliged by law to incorporate elements of business culture and management into their organizational practice, and that education would be subject to the demands of marketization, would have been regarded as far-fetched in the extreme.

Historically, the publication of *Schooling in Capitalist America* coincided with a major turning point in Western industrial economies. Although the implications were not altogether clear at the time, by the beginning of the 1970s, the international economic system established by the 1944 Bretton Woods agreement was unravelling at a rapid rate. The costs to the American economy of the Vietnam War posed the first major threat to stability, leading President Nixon in 1971 to devalue the dollar and thereby end the long post-war policy of fixed exchange rates (Keegan, 1992). A further 10 per cent devaluation in 1973 intensified the financial instability just as the OPEC states quadrupled oil prices between October and December of that year. The raging inflation precipitated by these and further oil price rises during the 1970s undermined the economic stability of most of the world's major economies at the same time as there was growing evidence that the industrial performance of Britain and the US was losing ground to both European and Japanese economies.

As Keegan and other commentators have pointed out, the oil shock helped to trigger the first serious recession (1974–75) of the post-war years. Nation-states struggled to bring down double-figure inflation levels by reducing demand or, as was the case in Britain, borrowing from the International Monetary Fund. Industrial relations deteriorated as trade unions struggled to maintain the living standards of their workers faced with high levels of inflation. Some on the left talked of the 'crisis of capitalism' (Gamble and Walton, 1976) and the right was able to claim that Keynesianism had failed. As Keegan puts it, 'these were the breeding grounds for a revival of classical economics, *laissez-faire*, and the "counter-revolution" to Keynesianism, known as Monetarism' (1992, p. 51).

What was not anticipated by Bowles and Gintis was the election, first in Britain and then in the United States, of right-wing governments determined to lead a national revival based on the principles of aggressive free-market capitalism. At the heart of this process was the quest to identify the causes of economic failure, accompanied by a growing economic nationalism. It was as part of this process that, in Britain especially, education came to be targeted as one of the main causes of the problem, and the charge that it was culturally hostile to the interests of wealth creation in Britain began to be widely circulated by politicians and employers. It mattered not that in 1974 the Department of Industry, with Tony Benn as Secretary of State, had published a White Paper entitled *The Regeneration of British Industry* in which the main problem area identified had been the low level of industrial investment in Britain. There had been no mention of the role of education in Britain's economic decline.

The main tenets of that White Paper had all been forgotten two years later when, in October 1976, James Callaghan made the speech at Ruskin College which was to begin the process of overtly linking education and Britain's economic performance. In the so-called 'Great Debate' which followed, a DES[1] Green Paper included the then-startling recommendation that schools should 'help children to appreciate how the nation earns and maintains its standard of living and *properly to esteem* the essential role of industry and commerce in this process' (DES, 1977, p. 7, emphasis added). Writing in 1984, Ranson commented that

The Treasury in particular took the view that education should serve the economic needs of the country: 'we took a strong view that education could play a much better role in improving industrial performance. The service is inefficient, rather unproductive and does not concentrate scarce resources in the areas that matter most. The economic climate and imperatives are clear; the task is to adjust education to them.'

(Ranson, 1984, p. 223)

The Ruskin College speech opened an agenda which has continued to run for two decades. As far as Callaghan (1987) himself was concerned, we have it on record from his autobiography published eleven years later that he had no subsequent cause to regret his unprecedented intervention in the running of the nation's education system. Indeed, it was a matter of some satisfaction to him that he had stirred up what he saw as a complacent community of educational professionals. Bernard Donoughue (1987), his political adviser, took a similar view, commenting particularly on what he felt to be the negative influence of the teacher unions.

The Labour Prime Minister had been supported in 1976 by his civil servant advisers in both the Treasury and the Department of Industry, each of which produced discussion papers proffering their diagnoses of Britain's ailing economy (DI, 1977). Although other factors were mentioned, much of their criticism focused on the education system, where the essential problem was perceived to be a cultural one: the world of education was seen as being too preoccupied with its own social agendas based on equal opportunities issues, and of being committed to a soft-centred, 'progressive' ideology of learning. At the micro level of institutions and practitioners, the problem was seen to be the inadequate attention paid to 'skills' and 'attitudes'. Young people were not being educated sufficiently in basic skills and were failing to 'esteem' business and industry as the mainspring of national 'wealth creation'. Educationists were tartly reminded by politicians and major employers that their priority henceforth should be the country's economic future and that without the profits from business and industry there would be a declining future for education. The goals they valued so much would have to take second place to the task of helping Britain regain its national profitability.

One of the remarkable features of this political intervention was the speed with which its message acquired status as folk myth. Within a very short time the nation's economic weakness had become defined as a cultural problem whose solution was going to require a fundamental redirection of educational effort. Between 1977 and the late 1980s countless conferences heard countless industrialists restate the Wiener (1981) thesis that Britain's economic problems stemmed from the fact that it was a nation of anti-industrial values, and that the persistence of a landowning aristocracy had been a principal cause of a cultural bias which embraced the public schools, Oxbridge and the City-based professions. The state mass-education system established at the turn of the century had simply reproduced this value system through the grammar schools which based the education they had to offer on the already established curricula linking the independent schools with the university system. It was but a simple step to identify teachers, with their supposed ethical rejection of capitalist materialism and their idealistic notions of the importance of children's self-expression, as being responsible for national economic failure.

The wide circulation given to this analysis of Britain's failing economic performance had the effect of driving many educational practitioners on to the defensive. Teachers had little evidence with which to refute the charge and there was sufficient plausibility in the culturalist explanation to induce a failure of intellectual nerve. Added to which, there was little possibility of those on the left in British education mounting a defence of the *status quo*. They themselves had long been critical of what they saw as the persistent élitism and exclusiveness built into educational curricula and assessment practice, and also at what they perceived to be structural biases in relation to class, race and gender.

During the 1980s other nation-states came to take up positions similar to that of the UK with regard to their own education systems. Australia, New Zealand, Canada, the United States and a number of European states each began to reinforce the relevance of education to their national economic effort. In Britain, the Thatcher government of 1979 saw education as one of the main institutions requiring major reform. Even without the assistance of the Labour government it displaced, the incoming Conservative administration would have pursued its educational reforms, but the events of the previous three years had made that task much easier in view of the fact that there was little agreement as to what the role of education should be at a time when unemployment had broken through the one million mark and was set to rise much further.

Even at the time, the 1976 speech was seen as a defining moment; but in retrospect its significance if anything seems greater. For the first time in the history of mass education in Britain, the state set out a clear priority for the economic purpose of education, thereby establishing an explicit connection between education and economic nationalism. In the international struggle for economic supremacy, the education and training systems were to be responsible for equipping the new model army of entrepreneurs and 'captains of industry' with the skills of economic success.

One of the cautionary observations made by Dale in his analysis of the capitalist state is that 'state policy-makers do not possess perfect knowledge of the state's needs or of how to meet them, through education or any other means at their disposal' (1989, p. 29). This comment seems particularly apposite in respect of the abrupt change in education policy made in 1976. The agenda begun by Callaghan was in our view seriously misconceived in terms of both education and training and national economic policy: a baleful intervention which has continued to legitimate a narrow, utilitarian and superficial view of education based on a seriously flawed analysis of Britain's economic decline. It reinforced a polarization between vocational and non-vocational forms of education and wrongly cast 'progressive' teaching methods as the villain of the piece in the drive to improve basic skills. The ill-informed attack on experiential learning for young people gave rise to one of the more bizarre paradoxes to come out of the Great Debate. Within a very short time, the methods which had incurred prime ministerial disapproval when applied to young people were being widely adopted as the most appropriate and 'user-friendly' for industrial training and the education of adults (Avis, 1991d).

POLITICAL AGENDAS FOR EDUCATIONAL REFORM

When the first Conservative government under Margaret Thatcher came to power in 1979, the education system, along with trade unions, was already part of the demonology of the New Right. Henceforward education became a major instrument in the campaign to reassert and rehabilitate the values of capitalism. As the extract from

Norman Tebbit's autobiography quoted at the beginning of the chapter indicates, even in 1991, after twelve years of educational reform, the New Right's long-standing antagonism to the educational community remained undiminished.

It is evident that the educational and training reforms enacted by the Conservative governments since 1979 have had two different but related objectives. The first, an *economic* objective, has been to make some attempt to meet the demands from employers for a more vocationally relevant curriculum and assessment system as part of the task of preparing young people for the 'flexible' workforce of the 1980s and 1990s. The second, and, from the New Right's viewpoint, arguably the more important *political* objective, has been the necessity to attack and replace the cultural and ideological basis of education in order to destroy its potential for undermining the free-market economic system it wished to install.

The problem for the New Right has been that in principle these objectives are in conflict with one another. In order to meet the demands for the higher-level skills required by a genuinely knowledge-based, competitive economy, the state is obliged to invest heavily in the provision of an education capable of generating innovative, experimental and critical thought, while being able to transcend national cultural boundaries and be sufficiently open and expansionist to allow rising levels of participation. If the priority is to restrict and control the input which educational professionals are able to make to the nation's educational capital, then this can be most effectively achieved by severe cost-cutting, the tight regulation of professional training and practice, a highly prescriptive curriculum and a definition of education which disallows critical, experimental thought. If such a system of education can be devised in which the emphasis is moved from teaching to student self-regulated learning, from knowledge acquisition to information-gathering, from critical investigation to demonstration of practical competence, the objective can be met all the more easily. The problem for the New Right has been to appear to be meeting the economic objective while in reality being more concerned with the political objective. By the recession of 1990–92, the illusion that the state was committed to moving Britain towards a high-skill, high-wage economy had become impossible to sustain, and – virtue being made out of necessity – the Major government made no secret of its support for the trend towards a low-wage, low-cost, unprotected, 'flexible' workforce, a stance which formed the basis of Britain's opt-out from the Social Chapter of the Maastricht Treaty in 1993.

Notwithstanding the unintended consequence of uniting parents, teachers and governors in opposition to cuts in educational budgets (particularly apparent in the public expenditure rounds of 1994–95 and 1995–96), it is difficult to deny that with regard to their objective of limiting the influence of educational professionals, Conservative governments have had a measure of success. The legislation introduced since 1988, bringing changes in the governance of schools as well as that of further and higher education, has substantially redrawn lines of responsibility and accountability which have led to greatly increased regulation of professional workers and intensification of workloads. At the same time, the introduction of a marketized system of course provision and output-related funding has heightened competitive relations between different institutions. The widespread adoption of the managerial and public relations practices familiar in the world of private industry has been a logical progression from these developments. How lasting these reforms will prove to be is not at all clear. Faced with a different political–educational agenda, they may prove to be shortlived. It has to be recognized, however, that the managerial structures designed to implement and maintain New Right reforms had by the mid-1990s become firmly institutionalized, their discourse dominating educational debate even within the Labour Party.

With regard to its economic objectives for education, we shall argue that the Conservative experiment has singularly failed to deliver the improved economic performance that was expected. This failure has resulted not simply from inherent weaknesses in the policies themselves, but because the policies have been expected to run alongside macro-economic policies which have rendered them ineffectual and irrelevant. In spite of the claim that the supply-side reforms introduced during the 1980s and 1990s were necessary to produce an economy based on enterprise and higher-level skills, the evidence is that these have been peripheral to the interests of the major economic institutions – particularly those of the City – and the more powerful forces of a 'monetarist' macro-economic policy which have led to further intensification of Britain's economic weakness. Instead of the high skills, high value-added products and services promised in the rhetoric, we have seen instead the continuing loss of industrial capacity, the de-industrialization of former industrial strongholds, low levels of investment in new equipment, infrastructure and research and development, and a deregulated labour market which has brought rising levels of redundancies and casual employment (Buxton *et al.*, 1994; Hutton, 1995a). In short, the 'reinvention' of education for Britain's so-called economic revival was founded on a set of beliefs which have led not to economic improvement but to further economic decline, bringing with it social fragmentation and exclusion – all within a national culture dominated by a regressive authoritarian state determined to suppress alternative views and values (H. Young, 1994).

It is clear that a central feature of the education and training policies of the past decade and a half has been the subordination of whatever economic purpose they may have had to the political demands of the broader ideological project of the New Right. Although there has been some acknowledgement of the importance of the relationship between Britain's skill base and its future economic prosperity, successive Conservative governments have shown a much greater concern for securing the compliance of education and training provision to the political ideology of the market than they have with genuinely addressing the qualitative improvements in vocational preparation required by changes in the international economy.

The consequences of the New Right's emphasis on implementing its political principles through education and training have been the further weakening of the British economy and the serious under-investment in the qualitative upgrading of the nation's knowledge and skill base. In almost every essential, the route taken by Conservative governments from 1979 in establishing their vocational education and training programme has been misconceived to the point where it has actually undermined Britain's capacity for national economic regeneration – this at a time when the main drive of economic policy should have been towards effective participation in the new global trading networks.

NEW RIGHT ECONOMIC POLICIES AND BRITAIN'S CONTINUING ECONOMIC DECLINE

The contradictions which surround education and training provision derive from the fact that in trying to meet their political objectives, successive Conservative governments have failed to address the inconsistencies between their policies for the economy and those prescribed for the education and training system. Once the parameters had been set by the first Thatcher government in 1979, divergencies between the two spheres of policy became inevitable.

We can identify at least four dimensions to the problem:

The substitution of technology for human labour

A globalization process premised on the infinite pursuit of efficiency and competitiveness is likely to see a continuing rise in structural unemployment in the most advanced economies as companies seek to cut labour costs through the substitution of technology for human labour. This is to be expected, given that the underlying rationale of globalization is to encourage the growing concentration of production in order to generate economies of scale in supplying world markets. Employers in a deregulated labour market will be able to shed labour with relative impunity, and the greater the avoidance by the state of Keynesian interventions designed to promote investment in the public infrastructure the higher unemployment is likely to be.

Limited demand for high-level skills within the economy

In any economy it is unlikely that highly skilled work could constitute more than 25 to 30 per cent of the jobs available; but the additional aspect to the problem in the UK is the absence of policies (other than a faith in the market) capable of generating investment in highly skilled forms of employment. The majority of jobs in the British economy fall into the category of intermediate and lower-level skills, but these are particularly vulnerable to the casualization process referred to below. They are also notoriously prone to the practice of 'poaching' by one employer from another, widely seen as a particular problem in the UK. Expanding those labour-intensive areas of the economy which *are* capable of utilizing large numbers of highly skilled people – the health and education services, for example – is not considered an option by a state determined to cut back on public-sector employment.

A deregulated labour market which encourages employers to substitute lower-cost, 'flexible' workers for the more highly skilled and therefore 'expensive' labour

The pursuit of a deregulated labour market has been one of the main objectives of the New Right since 1979. According to Hutton (1995a, p. 94), with the exception of the US, Britain has the most deregulated and unprotected labour market of any of the OECD economies. During a period of a persistent surplus of labour in the economy, government references to the importance of training for skilled workers can easily be ignored. At a deeper level, however, is the effect of the antagonism shown by politicians and employers to the importance of workers' rights in the employment contract. The general hostility to trade unions and the preparedness of Conservative governments to see the break-up of industries and the fragmentation of labour markets in order to maintain the supremacy of management increases the sense that workers are simply commodities to be hired and fired as and when the need arises.

Conflicting policies in relation to macro- and micro-economic management

This has been a major factor in the widening gulf between the reforms in education and training and the directions taken by the economy itself. The high value of the pound and high interest rates during the 1980s, coupled with the credit boom brought about through the deregulation of bank lending in 1980, helped to bring about the two recessions of the decade which were critical in causing severe loss of industrial capacity which has persisted into the 1990s.

In the remainder of this chapter we shall be exploring these and related issues further. They are particularly important at a time when the relationship between national education provision and employment is becoming increasingly problematic. In spite of the political emphasis on the necessity for 'a highly motivated and well qualified workforce' (White Paper, 1995, p 78) in supporting Britain's international competitiveness, it is clear that the provision of education and training is a second-order problem. The first-order problem concerns the number and quality of jobs available. Such phrases as the one from the White Paper above are mere rhetoric if they fail to address either the scale of the problem facing Britain's economy or the unwillingness of sufficient employers to take on and make effective use of highly skilled and motivated workers if and when they employ them. Indeed, after two decades in which education's economic value has ostensibly been given overriding importance over its other objectives, there is increasing evidence that the global market will lead to even higher levels of structural unemployment than have existed hitherto (Rifkin, 1995).

The promise on which Mrs Thatcher came to power in 1979 was that her government would revitalize the nation's economy through the promotion of individual enterprise and wealth and by freeing it from the 'dead hand' of 'dependency'. Public expenditure on welfare provision would be reduced as it would on public-sector activity generally. Trade union power was to be curtailed and managers would be given the 'right to manage'. The main instruments by which these goals were to be accomplished were the mechanisms of 'the market' – to be installed wherever possible in public-sector institutions – and a form of managerialism founded on the efficiency and financial disciplines of the private sector. Where these mechanisms were not immediately available, they would be created by legislation. In short, what was promised was the assertion and revitalization of a form of capitalism which had not been seen in Britain since the inter-war years – and which bore within it the spirit of Victorian values of economic liberalism and *laissez-faire*.

On the economic front, the main commitment was to 'sound finance'. 'Bearing down on inflation' was to be the mainspring of economic policy and the use of both the exchange rate and interest rates in order to maintain the value of sterling was to be the chief mechanism by which this goal was to be achieved. A counter-inflation policy would have the secondary beneficial effect of causing industry to be more 'efficient' in that it would be inhibited from handing on to the consumer the costs of pay rises and the wages of 'surplus' employees. The control of inflation at once imposed a disciplinary framework on employment and a brake on the expansion of public expenditure. As Hutton puts it,

> This 'monetarist' philosophy neatly dovetailed with the long-standing prejudices of the Conservative right, because it provided a heaven-sent justification for the crusade against collectivism in all its forms. The best way to lower public borrowing ... was to reduce public expenditure rather than raise taxes ... and reducing public expenditure would entail shedding the responsibilities that the state had undertaken in the fruitless attempt to make Keynesianism work, along with endlessly expensive social contracts with trade unions. Low inflation and the attack against the red menace became intertwined.
>
> (Hutton, 1995a, p. 69)

Education and training institutions have been tightly boxed in by this agenda. They have been subject to the cutbacks in public services expenditure and expected to absorb the market and managerial regulations progressively introduced during the past decade. They are expected to espouse – or at least not to challenge – an economic vision based on the values of individualism, enterprise and 'flexibility' in work. And they are obliged to tailor their curriculum and teaching methods to an ideological, financial and organizational structure in which professional opinion is substantially qualified and monitored by external agencies. At the same time, they are often asked to associate themselves with an economic scenario in which high standards and high skills are deemed to be essential to Britain's social and economic future. This is well captured in the opening paragraph of the White Paper *Competitiveness: Helping Business to Win* (1994):

> The UK faces a world of increasing change; of ever fiercer global competition; of growing consumer power; and a world in which our wealth is more and more dependent on the knowledge, skills and motivation of our people. These changes present both opportunities and challenges.
>
> (p. 6)

Later in the same paper this is spelled out rather more fully:

> Hard working people with high skills and the knowledge and understanding to use them to the full are the lifeblood of a modern, internationally competitive economy. We have to aim higher than in the past. We have to develop the self confidence and self esteem which make good citizens and good workers. We have to demand respect and rewards for vocational education and training as well as academic study. Above all, we have to give all our people – not just some of them – every opportunity to give of their best, from their very first day at school to the end of their working lives. A fulfilled workforce meeting individual targets, driven by the will to perform to their individual best, will be a world class workforce.
>
> (p. 30)

These high-sounding phrases are typical of many government pronouncements directed towards education and training institutions since 1979, but they bear little relationship to reality. Both in supply and demand terms there is every reason to question their validity. The fact that they are platitudinous is immaterial. They still constitute – as they have since 1979 – one of the main ideological rationales for education and training in Britain (and also in a number of other states where the New Right's views have been adopted). And it has to be said that at no point has the education community been invited by government politicians to consider or debate such statements – indeed, educational professionals are frequently patronized by the message that they lack economic awareness and are in need of direct, 'real world' experience. (This was the case, for example, in 1989 when the Department of Trade and Industry launched its Teacher Placement Scheme under its Enterprise Initiative.) Where educational professionals have challenged the New Right's concept of the economic future, there is little evidence that their views have been taken seriously.

On the demand side there are two problems with the kind of statements about education, training and employment made in the 1994 *Competitiveness* White Paper. The first is its presumption that the globalized, high-tech economy will necessarily generate large numbers of jobs requiring high levels of skill. The second is that where highly skilled jobs *are* created, those providing them will be persuaded to locate them in the UK simply by virtue of the availability of an indigenous skilled workforce. Both presumptions are problematic and raise fundamental questions about the complex of factors which influence the distribution of skilled jobs in an increasingly international division of labour.

On the supply side, the question not considered in government education and training policy is whether the kinds of vocational education and training provided in the UK are likely to enhance or depress the skills of its workforce. Again, the presumption of Conservative governments has been that their vocational education and training policies are the right ones, but there is now increasing doubt as to the adequacy of the vocational education and training (VET) system that operates in the UK – particularly its dependence on a behaviourist view of competence (Hyland, 1994).

The issue as to whether global economic changes are likely to lead to an increase in the proportions of highly skilled work in the labour market is a complex one, and it cannot be assumed that simply because the systems of co-ordination, production, marketing, distribution and management are themselves becoming more complex, those employed to operate them will be required to work at higher levels of skill. Reich's (1991) depiction of the labour market as falling into three broad bands – routine production workers (25 per cent), in-person servers (30 per cent) and symbolic analysts (20 per cent) – underlines the fact that only a small proportion of the population will be employed in work where problem-solving, problem identifying, and symbol manipulation skills are necessary. If one includes a proportion of the residual 25 per cent (where Reich includes workers such as farmers and miners, and state employees such as teachers), there is still nevertheless room for only a small minority of the working population. It may well be true that the demand for intermediate skill levels required by Reich's 'in-person' workers (for example, communication, information technology and report-writing skills) have risen as this category of employment has expanded, but there are countervailing tendencies towards 'de-skilling' which also have to be taken into account.

It is becoming widely accepted within the sociology of work that over any particular timescale there will be a tendency for skill levels to rise and wane and that the notion of 'polarization' best describes the dual process of 'upskilling' and 'de-skilling' which occurs in a fluid labour market. As new skills are identified, there is an initial phase when specialist training combined with scarcity will reinforce the impression that the skill required is of a high level – particularly if it represents an advance on skills previously so defined. Over time, it is likely to become routinized and more widely shared, with the possibility of becoming absorbed within new technology. This has been the fate of many industrial skilled workers over the past century and is far from unknown among white-collar and professional workers.

A second factor in the downgrading of skills – and one which has become of considerable significance during the dominance of the New Right – is the adoption of forms of managerial control in which driving down the costs of labour takes priority over almost every other management responsibility. This may take the form of 'delayering' and 'downsizing' within organizations – methods which have received so much publicity during the 1990s; or alternatively, as is happening in some areas of public-sector management, the knowledge bases of professional workers are themselves subject to managerial attempts to delegitimize, simplify or rationalize out of existence some elements of the 'expertise' on which their skills have been based. This particular fate has been experienced by doctors and teachers among others during the past decade – and particularly by those employed in further education.

There are, therefore, technological, market and managerial factors operating on the *demand* for highly skilled workers, in which employees are themselves forced into defensive positions as the skills required from them are downgraded. Protagonists of the New Right would no doubt counter that this is fundamentally a *supply* problem in which employees have to recognize the necessity of accommodating themselves to the variations in demand, and that this is why individual employees have to take responsibility for career management and the need to constantly update their training.

This view, which has been a key element of the New Right's approach to training and employment, totally ignores, of course, the power of its macro-economic policies to influence levels of investment in industrial and commercial development, and therefore the employment opportunities available to its working population. It is here that the education and training discourse and the discourse relating to economic policy have become totally separated. Indeed, the effect of insulating educational and training professionals from debates about the nature of economic change has been to make this more rather than less likely, with the consequence that the issue of the *economic appropriateness* of vocational education and training has been seriously neglected.

MACRO-ECONOMIC POLICY AND BRITISH MANUFACTURING DECLINE

As was indicated above, the dominant feature of government economic policy during the 1980s was the concern to control inflation via the regulation of the exchange rate and the maintenance of high real interest rates (the difference between interest rate and inflation rate) which remained a feature of monetary policy throughout the decade. It is the view of many commentators that the much-vaunted 'economic miracle' about which a good deal was heard during the 1980s was in reality a mirage and that the monetarist experiment caused enormous damage both to Britain's industrial base and its employment structure.

The first indication of the industrial and employment consequences of the new 'monetarism' was the recession of 1980–82 which had a dramatic negative impact on Britain's manufacturing base. According to Hutton (1995a),

> The results were catastrophic. Facing super-competitive imports and priced out of export markets by a fantastically expensive pound, manufacturing production fell by 14 per cent in 1980 and 1981 and profits dropped by a third. National output (GDP) fell cumulatively by nearly 5 per cent and by 1983 there were two million fewer people with jobs than in 1979.
>
> (p. 70)

Various assessments of the economic policies of the eighties have commented on the fact that the overwhelming problem was the negative impact of monetary policy on Britain's industrial base. Although the pound was allowed to devalue during the 1980s, with beneficial effects on exports and productivity, real interest rates were kept high – 'much higher', according to Hutton, 'than at any time since the war'. This inevitably had a depressing effect both on employment and investment – and particularly investment in training. At the same time, the financial deregulation (which included the removal of restrictions on bank lending) introduced by the Conservative government in 1979 led to a huge credit explosion as banks and building societies fuelled the boom in house prices. According to Hutton,

> Over the 1980s private debt levels doubled, so that by 1990 households held £114 of debt, up from £57 in 1980, for every £100 of disposable income, both the fastest growth rate and highest absolute level of debt of any western industrialised country. Most of the lending was for buying houses and flats, and the stock of mortgage debt increased sixfold from £52 billion in 1980 to £294 billion in 1990. House prices more than doubled over the same period.
>
> (Hutton, 1995a, p. 71)

A good deal of the mortgage lending was used to buy imports and consumer goods and there was huge investment in the service sector – offices and shopping malls especially – to support it. However, rising inflation brought the boom to an end in 1990 and interest rates were raised just at the time the government decided to enter the ERM with an over-valued pound. The loss of consumer confidence, coupled with high levels of debt, rapidly became translated into job-shedding followed by bankruptcies and company liquidations as demand collapsed. The government was then faced with two structural deficits: a high negative trade balance (standing at £26 billion in 1989) and a ballooning public-sector borrowing requirement brought about by the costs of rapidly rising unemployment.

While the boom in the financial and service sectors had been building up during the 1980s, manufacturing had languished. As Hutton puts it, 'Britain finished the 1980s with shopping malls, banks and houses aplenty but its manufacturing base static.' In 1983, following the 1980–82 recession, Britain went into deficit in trade in manufactured goods – for the first time since the industrial revolution.

According to Wells,

> British manufacturing industry suffered even more than during the Great Depression of the 1930s: manufacturing output fell by as much as 19.6 per cent from peak (June 1979) to trough (January 1981); between one-fifth and one-quarter of the sector's equipment and capacity were destroyed and 1.7 million jobs (or 23 per cent of the 1979 manufacturing labour force) were lost.
>
> (Wells, 1993, p. 93)

In 1985, the Select Committee of the House of Lords published a report which claimed that manufacturing in the UK was in crisis, and that if remedial action were not taken it could come to constitute 'a grave threat to the standard of living, and to the economic and political stability of the nation' (House of Lords, 1985, p. 83). This view was further reinforced by a subsequent report from the House of Lords Select Committee on Science and Technology, *Innovation in Manufacturing Industry*, published in 1991, where attention was drawn to the fact that

> The failure of British manufacturing industry to remain competitive has had serious consequences. Our manufacturing base has declined. Our home market is increasingly penetrated

by imports. Our share of world markets in manufactured goods is too small. The implications for our future prosperity are grave.

The Government makes much of improvements in productivity and profitability in the 1980s. Of course these are important and welcome. But these improvements have been accompanied by a serious reduction in the manufacturing base. The small size of the manufacturing base will constrain the growth in output which we will need in the future. Only a substantial increase in output can correct the huge deficit on our balance of trade, without a decline in the quality of life in the United Kingdom.

The Government also makes much of the slight improvement in the deficit in recent years. But this has been largely the result of inward investment from abroad, which has shielded us from the full effects of our industrial decline. It has also been due to lower home demand because of high interest rates and other anti-inflationary measures. When the economy expands again and demand increases, the deficit will grow again unless industry becomes more competitive and so increases profitable sales.

(House of Lords Select Committee on Science and Technology, 1991, pp. 29–30)

According to Temple (1994), the manufacturing trade ratio, which he defines as 'the balance of trade in the output of manufacturing industry expressed as a percentage of the value of total trade', 'deteriorated by about 12 per cent between the periods 1975–9 and 1986–90' (p. 83). As Table 2.1 shows, of the 'high-tech' industries, only aerospace made a positive contribution to the trade ratio in UK manufacturing. All the others are on the negative side. What also comes out of Temple's analysis is confirmation of Porter's (1990) assessment of Britain's industrial and market strengths – that with the exception of chemicals, pharmaceuticals and aerospace, Britain lacks large companies in the high technology sector, with high investment in research and development, and a substantial science base. Much of Britain's tradable activity lies in relatively low-skill sectors such as food products, alcoholic beverages, packaging and household goods.

The structural failures of Britain's economic policy during the 1980s are chiefly attributed by Hutton to the dominance of finance in its economy, where industrial investment and employment are left to the market. It has been argued by Cain and Hopkins (1993) that unlike Britain's industrial centres, the City has been able to benefit from the Thatcherite policy of deregulation. Having captured much of the Eurodollar and Eurobond business during the 1970s, it was able to weather the global competition of the 1980s more easily than other parts of the economy. As it has done so, however, it

> has become much more of a centre for multinational business and finance than a British financial market, and the most powerful institutions are now based on American, Japanese or German capital. ... Consequently, the present generation of City people must act increasingly on behalf of interests whose central decision-making processes lie outside Britain.

(Cain and Hopkins, 1993, p. 294)

One of Hutton's most telling points is that as a consequence of its global role in the capital markets, the rates of return to shareholders expected by the City are much higher and the pay-back times on investment much shorter for British companies than for those of its competitor countries – particularly Japan and Germany – where there is a more organic and long-term relationship between companies and institutional lenders. The restrictions which this policy places on investment have been among the most important factors in the failure of UK companies to develop long-term strategies for product and process innovation. Fears of over-extended credit in combination with a stagnating market act as a powerful deterrent to major capital investment. According to Hutton

Table 2.1 *Largest contributors to change in manufacturing trade ratio: 1975–79 to 1986–90 (in percentage points)*

Animal slaughtering, meat processing	0.993	Motor vehicles and engines	−2.224
Aerospace	0.652	Motor vehicle parts	−1.734
Extraction of other minerals	0.626	Other machinery	−1.103
Milk and milk products	0.526	Mining machinery	−0.867
Sugar and sugar by-products	0.480	Agricultural machinery	−0.680
Non-ferrous metals	0.392	Basic electrical equipment	−0.588
Sawmilling, planing	0.326	Other electronic equipment	−0.539
Pulp, paper, board	0.296	Hand tools	−0.521
Iron and steel	0.214	Electronic components	−0.455
Wood semi-manufactures	0.181	Plastics processing	−0.452
Organic oils and fats	0.167	Clothing	−0.354
Fruit and vegetable processing	0.148	Miscellaneous industrial machinery	−0.329
Animal feeding stuffs	0.128	Office machinery, data processing equipment	−0.309
Miscellaneous foods	0.125	Shipbuilding	−0.307
Leather	0.041	Rubber products	−0.302
		Total manufacturing	−12.003

Source: Buxton *et al.* (1994), p. 83.

(1995a), the structural deficits which built up before, during and after the 1990–92 recession have forced Britain into a series of dilemmas at the centre of which is the fear that any indication of a consumer-led economic expansion will precipitate a rise in inflation, a rising negative trade balance, a fall in the value of the pound, raised interest rates and a tightening of the vicious spiral once again. The inter-relatedness of the various elements of this vicious spiral is set out in Figure 2.1. Seen in a context where the main drivers of economic policy are financial rather than industrial or social, the vulnerability of education and training provision becomes clear. Counter-inflationary policies which drive up interest rates also lead to falling industrial investment and domestic consumption. Together with a highly valued pound which weakens exports, such policies lead to unemployment, cuts in training and increases in the Public Sector Borrowing Requirement (PSBR) through a combination of falling revenues and increased benefits payments. In order to contain the expanding PSBR, taxes have to be raised, thereby further restricting domestic demand and industrial investment. Such a scenario broadly represents the situation pertaining to Britain's economy during the 1990s. Although education and training programmes continue, albeit with reduced resources, they can of themselves do little to reverse the process. The state may use the device of the 'flexible worker' and low wages to help kick-start employment in low-skill sectors, but the most likely outcome is the build-up of a classic reserve army of unemployed – or as one commentator put it, a 'much better qualified dole queue' (Robinson, 1995).

There is now a substantial literature attesting to Britain's continuing relative economic decline, made particularly apparent in the aftermath of the 1990–92 recession (Healey, 1993; Coates, 1994; Buxton *et al.,* 1994). The contraction of the manufacturing sector during the 1980s has continued further through the 1990s. UK companies, having lost market share in a number of sectors during the 1980s, have had little success in replacing the business that has been lost. Investment in new production has been severely affected by the recession of the early 1990s and companies have continued to struggle with the cripplingly high rates of return for shareholders demanded by the City (Hutton, 1995a). A further factor is that the economic consolidation taking

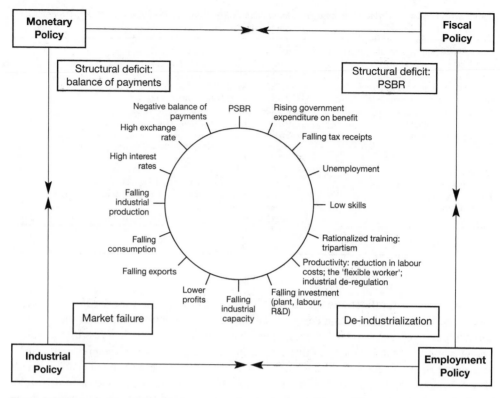

Figure 2.1 The cycle of economic decline

place within the European Union is leading to high levels of company rationalization as production is concentrated in the geographically favoured regions of mainland Europe (Benington and Taylor, 1993).

Although unemployment is running at high levels in many European countries, it is arguable that in Britain the situation is particularly unfavourable in that many of the newly created jobs are in casual and insecure forms of employment, and infrastructural weaknesses compound Britain's economic status as a peripheral state within the European Union. This underlying economic weakness is underscored by the fact that, in the spirit of making a virtue out of necessity, British governments of the 1990s have made much of the supposed economic benefits of a low-wage, under-protected and 'flexible' workforce which the labour reforms of the 1980s were designed to bring about. Britain's decision to opt out of the Social Chapter of the Maastricht Treaty was a logical consequence of the policies it had been pursuing. The fact that this was then hailed as a model of employment practice to the rest of Europe is a measure of how far the British government has been prepared to see the quality of work further degraded.

In spite of their importance to economic regeneration and success, the skills produced through education and training are not in themselves sufficient for the generation of new jobs and the growth of industrial capacity. Other important agencies within the political economy have a more direct and powerful impact on decisions as to whether and where investment is to be located. An obvious illustration of this point is the level of unemployment among graduates. Drawing on figures provided by the DFE in its 1994

Annual Report, Andy McSmith, Political Correspondent of *The Observer,* reported that up to Christmas 1994 graduate unemployment was still rising:

> At the latest count, 16,240 former students spent their first Christmas after graduation out of work. At one-seventh of the total, this is the worst percentage ever recorded. Even during the 1981–82 slump, under 13 per cent of students were still unemployed weeks after leaving university.

Drawing on the student loan repayment figures, he went on to say that 'Many who find work stay for years in relatively low-paid jobs. Almost 176,500 young people who left university in the past five years earn under £14,000 a year' (*Observer*, 12 March 1995).

In a global economy, where capital is footloose and where the measures of optimum return bear no relationship to national sentiment, it is the dominant political and economic interests which are likely to prevail. However, there is little doubt that, other things being equal, a well-educated workforce and a substantial training culture are a necessary condition for strategic investment in new forms of production. As Thurow puts it,

> Consider what are commonly believed to be the seven key industries of the next few decades – microelectronics, biotechnology, the new materials industries, civilian aviation, tele-communications, robots plus machine tools, and computers plus software. All are brainpower industries. Each could be located anywhere on the face of the globe. Where they will be located depends upon who can organize the brainpower to capture them.
>
> (Thurow, 1992, p. 45)

The contraction of Britain's industrial base and the growth of casualized forms of employment are in many ways a consequence of the agendas pursued by the New Right supported by a discourse for education and training which bears little relationship to reality. The surprising feature of this phenomenon is that the negative targeting of the education system has persisted since the mid-seventies and has powerfully legitimated a set of reforms in education and training which will do little to promote economic regeneration and will most probably do the reverse.

It might be argued that an emphasis on deficiencies in education and training as a major cause of economic decline has been a necessary condition for the scale of the institutional reforms carried out by the New Right. Having attacked educational professionals for having subverted the values of capitalist accumulation through purveying 'anti-industrial' attitudes, it is much easier to attack the basis of that professionalism and install new managerial structures of control. However, this interpretation of economic decline has both profoundly distorted the debate and prevented the serious development of a more systemic understanding of the problem. Any serious analysis of Britain's economic position, as well as its options for the future, has to include consideration of industrial policy in a broad sense and the geo-political movements of capital and labour which underlie so much of the present distribution of production and employment opportunities around the globe. Solutions to whatever new 'structural imbalances' occur (not forgetting that there are already existing structural imbalances which have long favoured the Western industrialized nations) are likely to be forged through international agreement between rival trading blocs.

GLOBAL FREE-MARKET CAPITALISM AND THE FUTURE OF WORK

It is becoming increasingly apparent that after a decade and a half, the policy of *laissez-faire* economic management favoured by the New Right has given rise to a growing divergence between the reality of structural unemployment and the positive rhetoric of education and training policy. Although the official line remains that economic growth is capable of generating new employment opportunities, even if it falls short of bringing back 'full employment', the persistent high levels of unemployment in the UK are confounding those optimists who, at the end of the 1980s (DE, 1988), were predicting serious labour shortages for the forthcoming decade. The so-called 'demographic time-bomb' (in which the falling birthrate of the 1970s was expected to produce a reduction of about 25 per cent in the numbers of school-leavers coming on to the labour market) which featured in the 1988 White Paper has quietly disappeared from view even as its effects were being felt in the falls in unemployment between 1992 and 1995.

While the UK has intensified its employment problems – particularly in the quality of the jobs available – by leaving much of its economic activity to the free market, other Western European states also continue to experience high levels of unemployment. To an extent this has been due to the collective commitment to low levels of inflation as part of the membership terms of the European Union, but it has also been due to the power of the global financial markets to dictate the terms of nation-state economic activity. There is, however, a growing belief that structural unemployment is inherent in the globalization process itself, and that in its commitment to the global market, Britain, along with other nation-states, will experience growing social dislocation.

One of the central issues of the globalization challenge is the long-term social and economic viability of the competitive free market. As a consequence of the deregulated nature of worldwide capital investment, a single nation-state has only tenuous influence over the direction and flow of capital investment. As one commentator put it:

> By liberalizing their trade policies, by deregulating their economies, and by privatizing their enterprises, national governments have much less control over what goes on in their own territory or what their own multinationals do elsewhere, and they no longer have the resources they had in the past to solve social problems. At the same time, multinational corporations are less bound economically, politically, and morally to nation-states.
>
> (Schmidt, 1995, p. 76)

Schmidt's observations are borne out in much of Britain's recent economic history. If a multinational company wishes to close down a production site and move it to another part of the world, there is little to prevent it from doing so. In the flurry of takeovers and mergers over the past decade there have been countless instances of ownership transfer between the transnational companies of different nation-states, many of which have resulted in loss of control by former British owners. One of the most noteworthy examples occurred in 1994, when the British car company Rover was sold by British Aerospace to the German car manufacturer BMW – an event which brought to an end Britain's indigenous car industry. During 1995, takeover and merger began to embrace the City's financial institutions. Within the space of six months four eminent British investment banks, each with a history going back to the eighteenth century, were taken over by larger European banks. One of them – Barings – was brought down by the reckless trading of an employee on the Singapore futures market, gambling beyond the limits of normal risk because of pressure to increase profitability.

Changes in the national ownership of companies may not in themselves cause an immediate problem. As Reich and others argue, they may well inject a new dynamism in the form of advanced technologies and working practices into their adoptive local economies. For decades, foreign-owned multinationals have expanded their production and distribution facilities into favoured locations throughout the world, becoming significant generators of local economic activity. In many cases, however, this does not happen. The history of takeovers and mergers provides enough instances of 'asset stripping' – in which a predator company simply retains those assets which it values and 'rationalizes' or otherwise disposes of the rest – for this to be a well-recognized outcome. Because in Britain the company is 'sovereign' in matters of ownership and control – needing formally to consult only its shareholders – it is within its rights to disregard any wider social considerations arising from its policies. Even where asset-stripping is not a motive for takeover, problems commonly arise when the agenda of a foreign-owned company runs against the interests of a local population. The centres of decision-making for major investment and employment developments usually remain in the country of origin, and during periods of economic downturn those sites located overseas are often the most vulnerable.

In its free-market form, the global market-place is a highly unstable and unpredictable environment. As companies relocate and restructure to gain competitive advantage, an inevitable consequence is the redistribution of employment opportunities throughout the global economy. But what appears to be economically rational may have serious social consequences. A community can find itself suddenly without its main employer as it either closes down through lack of orders or transfers production elsewhere. An event of this kind can bring with it a huge social fall-out with unemployment, falling house prices, damage to the local economy and widespread loss of self-esteem for those put out of work. The ripples can extend far beyond the original source of the problem, and there have been many such examples in the recent history of British industry.

The high levels of structural unemployment in Western Europe (as well as in other advanced industrial societies) raise fundamental questions as to the social costs of exclusion which are bound to arise from the dominance of a narrowly conceived model of economic efficiency. As Ormerod (1994) suggests, the failure to incorporate broader concepts of social productivity within the calculus of Gross Domestic Product, in which work is seen as having human and social value, is likely to lead to yet more poverty, polarization and social disorder than already exists. The core of Ormerod's argument is that the obsession with efficiency as the engine of 'competitiveness' will inevitably lead to the further rationalization of employment as the drive to reduce labour costs remains paramount. Through advances in information technology and telecommunications, the automation of both manufacturing and service operations will continue to increase, leading to reductions in the demand for labour – a phenomenon which already includes the so-called 'knowledge-based' industries and organizations such as universities. Unless an economy is able to generate new forms of production and service capable of absorbing the displaced labour, it will have serious difficulty in making inroads into the rising numbers of unemployed.

According to Rifkin (1995), such solutions to unemployment will not be available to governments without fundamental changes in public policy; indeed, present trends indicate that worldwide unemployment levels are set to rise even higher:

> Caught in the throes of increasing global competition and rising costs of labor, multinational corporations seem determined to hasten the transition from human workers to machine surrogates. Their revolutionary ardour has been fanned, of late, by compelling bottom line considerations. In Europe, where rising labor costs are blamed for a stagnating economy and a loss of competitiveness in world markets, companies are hurrying to replace their workforce with the new information and telecommunication technologies.
>
> (p. 6)

Rifkin's study takes an apocalyptic view of the future of work. Based on an analysis of the new technologies currently being developed across most areas of the market economy – in food production, manufacturing and service industries including finance, information processing and telecommunications – it is unequivocal in its assessment that the third industrial revolution will lead to further extensive automation and massive job-shedding during the next two decades. According to Rifkin, the potential for both technological substitution and managerial practice to displace workers will far exceed the capacity of the market to create alternative forms of employment; extrapolating from what is already current practice, he conjures up a scenario in which there will be a dangerous polarization between a minority of the population with well-paid, skilled work and a majority excluded from both employment and access to a reasonable income.

As Rifkin and a number of other commentators are suggesting (Standing, 1992; Ormerod, 1994), serious political recognition will have to be given to the probability that, on present trends, the globalized economy will continue to give rise to a progressive reduction in demand for employed labour. The imperative for greater competitiveness will inevitably lead companies to substitute machines for human labour as the power and availability of technology enable them to do so. There may well be some scope for Keynesian solutions to the problem of unemployment, and tax inducements could enable employers to take on more workers, but unless governments themselves are prepared to act as employer of last resort – a proposal which runs counter to everything the Conservative party has stood for during the past two decades – there may well have to be some form of decoupling of employment and income distribution among a nation's citizens which is more positive than the benefit system. For some commentators this would take the form of a basic or citizen's income provided to all adults as of right (Van Parijs, 1992). An alternative possibility is the extension of social entrepreneurship schemes, such as the project operated by the Wise Group in Glasgow, which provides jobs and training for the long-term unemployed based on environmental and community infrastructure development (Hutton, 1995c).

There is no evidence that scenarios such as these are seriously considered by the proponents of global capitalism – at least publicly. The underlying belief remains that, as with the first and second industrial revolutions, new technology will create new types of work. This may, of course, happen to a degree, but if so, it will be in a context where technological substitution is likely to intensify under the pressures for greater efficiency. A further problem lies in the fact that opportunities for employment are themselves more geographically dispersed as the competition for work becomes increasingly global. The transfer of data-processing tasks across the globe, for example, will become increasingly commonplace.

The problem facing Britain is that the strength of its belief in the unfettered market in goods and capital is not matched by the support structures of its 'real' economy –

particularly its manufacturing base. It is the weaknesses within it that have consistently undermined UK economic performance as market forces work increasingly against its economic interests. According to the Royal Society of Arts publication, *Tomorrow's Company* (1995, p. 3), only 2.3 per cent of the companies participating in a 1994 IBM/London Business School survey were considered to be 'world class in terms of performance', although 40.3 per cent 'had most of the practices in place to enable them to become world class'. As a number of critics of the free-market ideology have pointed out, far from being the means to economic salvation, extending the operation of the free market in both economic and social policy is likely to lead to a further hollowing out of the British nation-state and its ability to support the socially unprotected (Benington and Taylor, 1993; Gray, 1995; Hutton, 1995a). The New Right solution is to rely on the capacity of the individual to become 'flexible', 'marketable' and endlessly mobile. That will be an option for some; but if Rifkin's scenario is only half realized, the consequences of what Johnson (1995) has called the 'red-toothed social Darwinism' of the New Right are not difficult to imagine.

It is now clear that the concentration in British economic policy on supply-side reform in education and training, while leaving unchanged the systemic weaknesses of Britain's economy, has made only a marginal impact on Britain's declining economic performance. The continuing low levels of investment, coupled with the damaging loss of industrial capacity during the recessions of 1980–81 and 1990–92, have left British business with a diminishing presence in the major areas of high technology. Without substantial and long-term economic renewal, the calls for a highly skilled workforce will remain empty rhetoric if the demand and capacity to utilize those skills is not there. At the same time, the narrowing of education to match the restricted vision of a competitive free-for-all in the global market-place will in all probability leave it with little from which new growth can emerge.

THE COMMODIFICATION OF EDUCATION AND TRAINING

We have argued that the past two decades have seen the political economy of the UK dominated by the consequences of continuing economic decline alongside the growing diminution of the nation-state as a political entity. The forces promoting globalization have been welcomed by those seeking advantage from the new financial, production and distribution networks of the world economy, while the capacity of these same forces to transfer employment opportunities to overseas locations is a major factor of social – and ultimately political – instability. The problem for the UK has been that without a secure long-term investment base, British companies have seen their chances of moving into the high technology sectors of the economy substantially reduced. Apart from chemicals and aerospace (now in contraction through the 'peace dividend'), Britain has only a tenuous presence in what Thurow (1992) calls 'the key industries of the next few decades'. At the same time, the combination of trade liberalization, privatization and deregulation has led to a substantial transfer of control from the nation-state to transnational business interests – a situation exacerbated by the opposition of the British state to the creation of a coherent and co-ordinated industrial policy. There has been some compensatory inward investment from Japanese automobile and consumer electronics industries, but these have usually taken the form of assembly operations, with most of the research and development capacity remaining in the country of origin. There is also the further factor of the negative impact on the trade balance of imported Japanese parts (Hutton, 1995a, p. 78). Even the financial sector of the British economy has not been immune from takeover and merger as some of its own undercapitalized banks and finance houses have seen their assets transferred into foreign ownership.

In such circumstances, the British state has perceived its economic role as a limited one based on the optimization of existing supply-side conditions for capital accumulation – central among them being the reduction of social overheads associated with employment, as part of its commitment to 'freeing up' the market. The curtailment of trade union activity, the abolition of wages councils, the unwillingness to accept a minimum wage and the refusal to join the European Social Chapter have been the main features of a strategy designed to enable employers to take advantage of a largely unprotected labour force. As important has been the ideological task of shaping popular opinion towards acceptance of the new economic conditions. The notions of 'flexibility' and the need for responsiveness to 'change', for example, have been promoted as the inevitable features of contemporary employment, and the repeated interventions of government ministers have been calculated to habituate the population to low expectations of a 'job for life' and to acceptance of job insecurity, unemployment and increasing workloads and fragmentation in the workplace. Having failed to establish a high-skills, high-value economy with the benefit of the North Sea oil revenues of the 1980s, the Conservative establishment has consciously set out to play its global role from a low-skill, low-wage base – at least for a large proportion of its labour force.

As far as its responsibilities for creating an educated and trained workforce are concerned, despite the slogans of 'standards', 'quality' and 'choice', the role of the state has been both minimalist in resource terms and politically intransigent in the organization and management of the system. Reductions in unit costs have been a key priority throughout, and all sectors of education have experienced severe pressures on their budgets (although City Technology Colleges and grant maintained schools have received more favourable treatment). Minimalism of a different kind has also characterized post-16 education and training. The NVQ system was designed primarily to provide a framework for work-based assessment while the specification of vocational content is officially left largely to employers. Although NVQs were ostensibly set up to provide employers with the skills they required, many of them are either unhappy with the competence-based system of vocational qualifications or ignorant of its details (Field, 1995). According to a Trades Union Congress (1995) survey, only 5 per cent of UK companies are using NVQs, and 72 per cent have no plans to do so. Commenting on government promotion of NVQs, Field has suggested that 'much of the training revolution of the 1980s was in fact concerned primarily with the political management of high unemployment levels, so the NVQ initiative appears to be chiefly an attempt to provide a visible response to poor economic performance and the associated public criticisms of the British training system' (1995, p. 42). General National Vocational Qualifications (GNVQs) provide an alternative route for those not wishing to undertake A-level courses, but there have been numerous uncertainties since they were introduced as to their aims, content and the appropriate form of student assessment. In August 1995 it was reported in the national press that more than two-thirds of GNVQ students had failed to complete their courses within two years. As far as higher education is concerned, public funding has progressively fallen for over a decade and is due to fall by a further 12 per cent between 1995 and 1998, thereby exacerbating already severe pressures on students, staff and capital stock such as libraries. Commenting on this projection, the 1995 OECD Survey for the United Kingdom warned of the dangers of applying industrial models of productivity to public service provision, pointing out that 'in education, as enrolments have risen strongly, it is the quality rather than the quantity of output that bears the brunt' (p. 83).

The minimalist, pseudo-arm's-length policy, in which the state claims to restrict itself to setting up the supply-side 'delivery mechanisms' and output targets for post-compulsory education and training, allows responsibility for any labour-market failure to be devolved either to the providing institutions or to individual students (see Chapters 4 and 6) – despite the fact that the structures through which both experience education and training have been prescribed by the state itself. As Ormerod points out, the justifying logic for this approach derives from the discredited precepts of competitive equilibrium theory of neo-classical economics which decree that, provided individuals have the appropriate skills and are prepared to work for low enough wages, the labour market should clear. Thus, from this ideological position, the main responsibility for making the system work is carried by the education and training agencies and individual trainees themselves.

The contradictions which arise for the British Conservative state from trying to legitimate the different underlying rationales of its education and training policies have become increasingly transparent. Any pretence at universalism is challenged by its preference for selective education and 'opting out'; the notion of parental and student 'choice' is countered by the tendency for 'successful' institutions themselves to select their student intake; the rhetoric of commitment to raising 'standards' and 'quality' is met by the reality of underfunding and reliance on employers and work-based trainers, whose vision is often restricted to short-term goals; arguments for highly skilled workers in a 'knowledge-based' society are undermined by a deregulated labour market and the lack of an industrial policy which could help to generate such jobs; and the provision of an 'education for the twenty-first century' has to overcome both the conceptually deficient, competence-based system of vocational education and training and the prevailing emphasis on cultural nationalism within the school curriculum.

Thus, reflecting the underlying contradictions between the ideologies of global expansionism and cultural protectionism, British education policy finds itself facing in opposite directions. On the one hand, educational institutions are required to espouse the ideology of the global free market which is both reducing Britain's employment base and bringing about greater insecurity in work, and on the other, they are expected to sustain a form of national cultural identity which is increasingly undermined by the restricted programmes of education and training on offer. In order to carry out this task, schools and colleges are obliged to adhere to an enclosed, tightly regulated system consisting of a nationally prescribed, traditional, subject-based curriculum and a closely specified structure of vocational qualifications – each supported by a rigid framework of standardized testing. In spite of growing evidence that such an inflexible system is inappropriate for the uncertainties of the global economy, a succession of Conservative governments has intensified the control of the state in preserving this narrow vision.

As we suggested at the beginning of the chapter, one of the main objectives of the New Right has been to legitimate and strengthen a free-market culture and practice within education. As the memoirs of ex-Conservative ministers have shown, from its first term of office there has been an unremitting hostility to the socially progressive values of British education which has persisted throughout. Ian Gilmour (1992), one of the few dissenters from this policy, is scathing about the Conservative government's stance towards academic culture, which, he claims, was based on dogma, and 'dogmatists cannot tolerate high intellectual standards, which both depend upon and engender freedom of thought' (p. 162). He tellingly observes

> that the Thatcher government was unable to understand the concept of intellectual investment, because it does not produce immediate cash returns. An under-educated society will in due course become socially unstable and economically inefficient, but Thatcherites were too blinkered to appreciate that simple point. For them, immediate economies and tax cuts were far more important than the long-term future of the country.
>
> (Gilmour, 1992, p. 175)

A crucial phrase here is 'the concept of intellectual investment', the one element of an education policy that might be thought essential in preparing citizens for the uncertain consequences of globalization. Instead of which, the central element of the New Right's strategy has been the exercise of ideological and organizational closure over the content, practice and demand for education. The priority given to this policy has itself encouraged the further downward drift of the 'low-skills equilibrium', as the providers of education and training are compelled to work within a closed system of managerial regulation which links the state, executive agencies such as the Funding Councils and the TECs, and the employer-led bodies – a system which bypasses the professional judgements of those trying to make the system work. The intellectual resource base on which it draws is almost entirely driven by the current perceptions, concerns and requirements of employers who are themselves likely to be uncertainly positioned in the global market, who may not understand the complexities of the social and economic changes taking place and whose insights may well be based on one company's experience of the domestic economy.

One of the more questionable features of the education and training policies of the New Right has been the presumption throughout that business and industry constitute the most appropriate source of knowledge and understanding – whether for students or teachers – of Britain's future economic development. Two decades of industry–education liaison have been founded on the belief that British companies constitute the ideal providers of the essential elements of economic and industrial understanding. Work experience for young people, teacher placements, local Education Business Partnerships, and numerous liaison and 'enterprise' projects have been promoted on the assumption that local business and industry 'know best' and are the agents best suited to the task of fostering 'economic awareness' and an understanding of the 'world of work'. Furthermore, British companies – particularly those in the private sector – are often held up as exemplars of management practice that might be considered for adoption by schools and colleges. One of the main justifications for the emphasis given to such a 'pedagogy of the workplace' is the widely held belief that educational professionals are ignorant of conditions in industry and commerce, and that direct involvement with business culture will enable them to become more aware of the 'realities' of economic life. The limitations of such a policy are not, however, difficult to see. Not only is it often paralleled by a failure to recognize the importance of the broader analytical context, which would bring into play more complex and critical perspectives towards employment under global capitalism, but it has also promoted what Ahier calls 'a persistent, shallow optimism' about the functioning of the British economy (Ahier, 1995, p. 155).

Some of the dangers of relying uncritically on British companies as a major source of information about vocational skills and economic understanding are underlined by the Royal Society of Arts (1995) report, *Tomorrow's Company*. In it, the authors draw up two sets of contrasting characteristics which distinguish their ideal world class 'company of tomorrow' from what they describe as 'yesterday's company'. According to their typology, 'yesterday's company' gives priority to financial returns over other aspects of company performance, is indifferent to stakeholders other than shareholders, is 'locked in adversarial relationships', sees its employees as labour costs to be cut, expects conformity from them, and 'views environmental concerns as peripheral'. Above all, it fails to develop an *inclusive* approach to the different stakeholders involved. Implied in the report is the view that these are the characteristics which predominate in British companies. In summarizing the results of their company survey, its authors are unequivocally critical of their respondents, observing that 'there is a large gap between what most business leaders claim is important and the priorities they set for themselves and their companies' (p. 11). Quite clearly, any attempt to reverse the 'low-skills equilibrium' through vocational education will require broader and more critical perspectives on current practice than are currently on offer.

The acceptance of British business practice as the principal – and often exclusive – resource base for vocational education and training, and the belief that teachers and young people simply have to experience it to understand it, is paralleled by the mechanistic and behaviourist emphasis of much of the prevailing 'training paradigm'. Some of the strongest criticism levelled at NVQs has been directed at their emphasis on behavioural competence and the absence of rigorous supporting frameworks of knowledge and opportunities for reflective learning – particularly at levels 1 and 2 (Smithers, 1993; Hyland, 1994). According to its critics, the current system of vocational qualifications both lacks the intellectual content of vocational courses previously on offer (Smithers, 1993) and also fails to educate to the levels experienced by trainees in other European countries (Green, 1995).

A central feature of the exercise of political power since 1979 has been the priority given to overtly technicist forms of analysis and management which draw their intellectual content from the precepts of neo-classical economics and the 'scientific management' movement of the 1920s. One of their dominant characteristics is a refusal to admit to the complexities and unpredictability of social behaviour, whether this be in the family, in employment or through the role of consumer, and which cannot be accommodated within the mechanistic forms of accounting and functionalist methodologies of the market. The behaviourist emphasis of the current training paradigm is consistent with this predilection for what Ormerod (1994) calls 'mechanistic modelling' which underlies much of the economic and social policy of the New Right. One of its key defining characteristics has been its reliance on a reductionist, quantitative, disaggregative methodology in which individuals are perceived as units of input and output within the market. Expertise and professionalism are disaggregated into 'competencies' and skills; the work process is broken down into identifiable and measurable tasks, and 'quality assurance' is rendered as a set of accountability procedures. Above it rides a managerial system through which the regulation of incentives and deterrents – output-related funding, performance measures, assessment, inspection and audit – preserves the appearance of efficiency and order. Thus it is as an aspect of *managerialism* that this combination of measurement, accounting and the disaggregation of social attributes fits together as the dominant apparatus of institutional control.

It is this sterile and dehumanized system, founded as it is on behaviouristic concepts of 'competence', which has led to the increasing commodification of education and training, and which, somewhat ominously, is increasingly seen as an appropriate model for professional education and development (particularly for teachers). In his condemnation of the intellectual basis of the 'competence movement' Hyland (1995) has drawn attention to the parallels between the philosophy of the NCVQ and the 1920s 'social efficiency' movement in the United States, pointing out that

> All the essential ingredients of NVQs are present in the early American model: a conservative ideology, a foundation in behaviourist psychology and a determination to link vocational education to the specific requirements of industry. Little wonder that a movement which was constructed out of a 'fusion of behavioural objectives and accountability' (Fagan, 1984, p. 5) should come to provide the ideology for the neo-behaviourism of the NCVQ system which was to have such an irresistible appeal to those seeking control, accountability and input–output efficiency in the new economic realism of the 1980s.
>
> (Hyland, 1995, p. 49)

Notwithstanding their 'irresistible appeal', it is quite extraordinary that this primitive and manifestly inadequate set of managerial principles should have been given such an unwarranted restoration in the face of the weight of refutation and criticism they have received since their original inception. In consequence, it is probable that the promotion of a narrow and superficial economic instrumentalism, founded upon a dehumanizing and asocial managerialism, will continue to inflict serious damage on the British education system. Moreover, the resulting intellectual impoverishment is likely to have increasingly negative effects on Britain's capacity to participate in the globalization process. The state's resistance to anything other than mechanistic instruction and the imitative learning of subject matter determined by itself or its nominees is likely both to undermine democracy further and to confine the experience of citizenship to the level of material consumption. As Pring (1995) has argued, the 'community of educated people', holding to a belief in 'serious reflection, critical scrutiny of others, testing against the evidence, corroboration within a tradition of enquiry' (p. 126) as well as 'moral deliberation and exploration of values and beliefs' (p. 130), has shown itself to be particularly vulnerable to a political party determined to eliminate the values it wishes to deny from the process of education:

> This idea ... of a community of educated people is a fragile one – fragile because threatening to those who, in positions of power, wish to control, cannot brook criticism, cannot face uncertainty. They, therefore, see the curriculum in a different way from that which we have been considering. They impose a different language – the language of inputs and outputs (not of transactions or explorations), of performance indicators and audits (not of professional responsibility or judgement), of commodities to be delivered (not of a conversation to be engaged in), of producers and consumers (not of teachers and learners), of skills and competencies (not of understanding, judgement or imagination). And under the new reality shaped by such language, a comprehensive system of curriculum outcome is created – of attainment targets, behaviours, competences – which embraces every aspect of learning from the cradle to the grave, all recorded in a National Record of Educational Achievement, to be presented when one dies to St Peter in the hope that one may finally share in the heavenly banquet.
>
> (*ibid.*, pp. 141–2)

Pring then goes on to conclude that 'It is a mark of the fragility of that community of educated people, that this Orwellian nightmare should have been accepted so meekly' (*ibid.*).

CONCLUSION

We have set out in this chapter to explore the political and economic agendas underlying the New Right education and training reforms in the context of the increasing globalization of production, trade and investment. We have suggested that the dominance of nation-state protectionism in the UK with regard to cultural and political values has taken precedence over the construction of an economic and employment policy appropriate to participation in the emerging international labour market. Although the explicit linking of Britain's economic weakness to the failures of the education system was a seriously misconceived analysis at the outset – even if its secondary purpose was to destabilize the educational community – its inadequacies have become more apparent with the economic failures of the 1980s, which have left Britain with a seriously depleted manufacturing base. The most important contribution to these failures has been the dominance of Britain's financial sector in determining the country's economic policy and the failure to integrate the priorities of the City with the needs of manufacturing for long-term investment in research and development. Through the combined demands of 'global competitiveness' and the removal of employment rights for British workers, there have been enormous opportunities for employers to reduce labour costs through various forms of casualization and 'downsizing', so that long working hours and job insecurity have now become the dominant features of contemporary employment.

In spite of the lip-service paid to the importance of education and training to the British economy, the political reality has been one of underfunding, ideological containment and a fundamental indifference to the quality of vocational provision – despite the apparatus of performance measures and quality audits that have been set up. In view of the political energy that has been devoted to specifying an increasingly narrow set of cognitive inputs in both pre- and post-16 education, it could be expected that any resulting outputs in relation to student learning and understanding themselves run the risk of being unable to rise above the low levels set down – a situation that some would characterize as one of 'garbage-in-garbage-out'. The expectation that education and training should remedy economic underperformance has provided a basis of legitimation for reforms which will have precisely the reverse effect, in that they have reduced the capacity of the system to provide genuine intellectual investment in meeting the social and economic uncertainties of further globalization. At the same time, those same reforms have seriously reduced the democratic potential of education and fostered a form of 'citizenship' which promotes individualist values of material consumption above all others. By suppressing debate as to the implications of globalization for education, training and citizenship, and by installing a divided, minimalist, instrumental system of learning and training for the majority of school leavers, there has arisen a policy shortfall which it will take a major political effort to reverse.

NOTE

1 During the recent past, there have been several changes to the title and function of the government department responsible for education in England and Wales. For many years, it was the Department for Education and Science (DES). In 1992, science was removed and it became the Department for Education (DFE). In 1995 this changed again, as the DFE was merged with the Employment Department to form a new Department for Education and Employment (DFEE). This final change has both political and symbolic significance, given the central arguments of this book.

Chapter 3

The Myth of the Post-Fordist Society

James Avis

In the middle of the twentieth century Clark Kerr and others (1973) coined the term 'industrialism' to suggest the convergence of advanced capitalist societies with those of the Soviet bloc. As we move towards the twenty-first century, post-Fordism has assumed the mantle of industrialism – all societies are becoming part of a global economy in which the fluidity of capital and swiftness of information flow lead towards the homogenization of labour across national and fiscal boundaries. The cost of skilled labour will tend to converge and increasingly competition will be based upon the skills of the working population. Value addedness, continual improvement and constant innovation become the key to economic success and survival. The previous chapter considered the way in which the New Right in Britain has tried to come to grips with globalization and the decline of the nation-state. It illustrated both the contradictory tensions within New Right policies, and the social, economic, educational and human cost incurred by them. This chapter focuses upon how these changes are reflected in debates about post-Fordism and post-compulsory education within Britain.

Central to the current settlement over post-compulsory education and training within Britain lies a particular conceptualization of the economy and the role of people within it. The language of post-Fordism is often used in this conceptualization, as are terms such as flexibility, multi-skilling and so on. Some writers have linked forms of post-Fordist employment to transformed social relations which are seen to herald the move towards a new form of society (Brown and Lauder, 1992a). In other formulations capitalist social relations are taken for granted and yet within this constraint we are offered the vision of a learning society in which everyone can be fulfilled (CBI, 1994).

A key tenet of Thatcherism was the notion of an enterprise culture (Hall, 1988; Hall and Jacques, 1983; Johnson, 1991b). The self-reliant individual was set against the dependency culture supposedly spawned by the policies of the social democratic state. The enterprising individual would transcend these limitations and be in the vanguard in the creation of a dynamic and thrusting economy and society (Keat, 1991). A series of factors precipitated changes in the nexus between the individual, economy, society, the state and post-compulsory education and training. These included the fiscal crisis of the state, the collapse of state socialism in Eastern Europe and changes in the world economy, as well as the perceived success of Japanese companies and management styles (O'Connor, 1973). Advances in production technology, developments in computerized systems in terms of stock management, 'just in time' systems, as well as the increased ease with which machines could be tooled up to handle small-batch production heralded a break with Fordist systems of mass production. These changes facilitated the move towards product diversity, niche marketing and so on. Such production innovations require, it is claimed, a different type of worker, one able to be a team member but at the same time capable of exercising responsible autonomy (Friedman, 1977). Post-Fordism is a term coined to describe these changes and sits readily alongside the debates on flexible specialization (Piore and Sabel, 1984; Murray, 1987; Pollert, 1988; Tomaney, 1990).

Enterprise culture and post-Fordism are intimately connected, both having arisen as a response to similar conditions. The terms differ with respect to their political orientations, the former deriving from the Right and the latter from the Left, or at least from modernizing currents in society. Enterprise has a resonance with traditionalist conceptualizations of the self-reliant entrepreneur of the nineteenth century whereas post-Fordism is part of a modernizing discourse that anticipates the twenty-first century. Both relate to the material and social conditions faced by Britain in the latter part of the twentieth century. In many respects, enterprise culture and post-Fordism embody similar conceptions of the person – an enterprising individual is after all an empowered person, and post-Fordism espouses worker empowerment. Both conceptions stress individual responsibility, autonomy and a form of citizenship organized around the empowerment of the consumer. This can be seen in educational discourses concerning enterprise and core skills in which 'team work' is seen as the sum of separately identifiable parts. Thus, the worker contributes to the activities of the group as an individual, thereby developing skills that enhance their employability and stock of human capital. However, enterprise and post-Fordism differ in that the latter has the apparent potential to be developed in collective and socialist ways. The centrality placed on team work, flattening of hierarchy and so on provides the space in which this can develop.

Brown and Lauder (1992b) offer a useful comparison between Fordism and post-Fordism (see Table 3.1). Post-Fordist models reflect an increasingly globalized view of the economy. It is argued that if Britain is to compete effectively in the twenty-first century, a high-skills, high-trust society/economy will need to be created. Such an argument is reflected in the policy framework within which post-compulsory education is placed. The abiding assumption is that the reversal of economic decline can only be brought about by an upskilling of the labour force and a reformation of post-compulsory education and training. C. Ball (1991) in a rather kitsch way reflects this line of argument. In *Learning Pays,* he constructs what he calls the vicious and virtuous circles of the twentieth and twenty-first century, which are used to illustrate the low- and high-skills equilibria (Figure 3.1).

The assumptions embedded in these arguments presuppose a general direction for the development of the economy. Other writers have called for a break with the low-skills equilibrium that has beset the English economy and its replacement by one based on high skills (Finegold, 1993; Finegold *et al.*, 1990; Cassels, 1990). The argument is sometimes couched in terms of choice, viewing the economy as being at a crossroads. However, in essence there is no real choice but to pursue the high-skills route, for the failure to do so would lead to an exacerbation of the general decline of the British

Table 3.1 *Characteristics of Fordism and post-Fordism*

Fordism	Post-Fordism
Economy, competition and production process	
Protected national markets	Global competition
Mass production of standardised products	Flexible production systems / small batch / niche markets
Bureaucratic hierarchical organisations	Flatter and flexible organisational structures
Compete by full capacity utilisation and cost cutting	Compete by innovation, diversification, sub-contracting
Labour	
Fragmented and standardised work tasks	Flexible specialisation / multi-skilled workers
Low-trust / low-discretion; majority employed in manufacturing sector / blue collar jobs	High-trust / high discretion; majority employed in service sector / white collar jobs
Little on the job training; little formal training required for most jobs	Regular on the job training; greater demand for knowledgeable workers
Small managerial and professional elite	Growing managerial and professional service / class
Fairly predictable labour market histories	Unpredictable labour market histories due to technological change and increased economic uncertainty
Politics and ideology	
Trade union solidarity	Decline in trade union membership
Class-based political affiliation	Declining significance of class-based politics
Importance of locality / class / gender-based lifestyles	Fragmentation and pluralism; global village
Mass consumption of consumer durables	Individualised consumption / consumer choice

Source: Brown and Lauder, 1992b, p. 4.

economy and with it living standards (see CBI, 1994). Absent from this upskilling rhetoric is any understanding of uneven development. This is illustrated by two claims deriving from different political standpoints. In the first, there is some acceptance of mass unemployment, although the move towards upskilling would serve to ameliorate these conditions. In the second, the assumption is that a dynamic economy would be able to resurrect patterns of full employment and restore the welfare state to its former glory. However, both claims have a tendency to collapse into one another and are predicated on the existence of capitalist social relations. Interestingly, both arguments have recently become tempered by a concern with social solidarity and the restoration of societal values of care and responsibility (Blair, 1995). It is assumed in both trajectories that economic, and therefore national, survival and well-being depend on the high-skills, high-trust route. Once this post-Fordist strategy is adopted, the accompanying work forms and relations would permeate throughout society.

It is here that there is a conflation of real changes in the global/national economy with interpretations of these which take on a particularly ideological hue. Post-Fordist production processes do not necessarily lead to the increased skilling of the workforce. Indeed the notion of a high-trust, high-skill workforce can be fraudulent. The Nissan car factory in Sunderland provides a case in point where the language of upskilling sits alongside the degradation of labour (Garrahan and Stewart, 1992). Garrahan and Stewart's work suggests that what is crucial is not so much changes in skills level but rather the development of new ways of regulating labour in which worker self-discipline is developed through the formation of workers' subjective experiences which are central to the labour process.

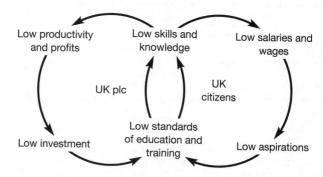

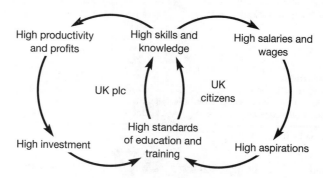

Figure 3.1   Vicious and virtuous circles of the twentieth and twenty-first centuries
Source: C. Ball, 1991, p. 2.

There is another difficulty surrounding the optimism of the policy frameworks which take for granted post-Fordist development. There is an assumption, which echoes forms of nationalism, that sees the economic future of this country residing in the skills of its people. It is as if there is an innate potential for technological skill and inventiveness. Tony Blair reflects these ideas:

> Our country's future depends upon our ability to release and fulfil the innate talent of all our people. *The British are one of the most innovative and creative nations in human history.* Education and training hold the key, not just of personal fulfilment and advancement, but also to economic prosperity and a good society. Investment in education is investment in the here-and-now of our children, but it is also investment in the skills and minds of the future which will rebuild our national wealth and social fabric.
>
> (1994, pp. 12–13, my emphasis)

There is the assumption that new educational forms will liberate this potential and the British economy will be able to regain a leading edge. However, there must be serious doubts as to whether this will be the case. Hutton (1995a) reminds us of the secular failure to invest in industry, training, research and development within Britain. This failure means that Britain, even if it had a world-class education and training system, would not be well placed to compete in the global economy. This is important, for it implies that in itself the development of education and training is unlikely to generate economic rejuvenation because the manufacturing base has been weakened by both New Right market-based policies and the long-term failure to invest.

But what are the educational consequences of post-Fordist arguments? Superficially there are clear resonances between explanations of economic change and the demands being placed on post-compulsory education and training. Hickox and Moore (1992) suggest that for the first time a loose correspondence is being forged between the needs of the economy and post-compulsory education. Such a correspondence was assumed to be the case by earlier Marxist reproduction theorists but was not sustainable under close examination (Bowles and Gintis, 1976). The outlines of such a correspondence can be seen in policy documents and in the literature emanating from curriculum bodies such as the Further Education Unit (FEU) (1991, 1992) and other curriculum modernizers. In such reports one meets the well-rehearsed calls for student-centred learning, the transmogrification of the student into a learner, a terminological shift of rhetorical importance – a shift which is supposedly to counter both the élitism and infantilization of being a student, thereby opening up and democratizing learning for adults. This move breaks the link between scholarship and learning. Learning becomes refracted towards learning 'to do' and the achievement of a technical competence (Hyland, 1994). In these policy documents one also meets the well-rehearsed calls for:

- flexibility
- adaptability
- problem-solving skills
- the development of core skills
- action planning
- summative and formative profiling
- the development of interpersonal skills that facilitate team working
- lifelong learning

and as a linchpin to the whole, the empowerment of the learner (Burke, 1995). The learner is to take control of and responsibility for learning; there is to be a break with the stultifying restrictions of traditional curricula and pedagogy. Yet these processes and arguments are lodged within an educational system that is deeply conservative, in which the academic–vocational division is paramount and in which class-, race- and gender-based divisions are endemic. Although some of these difficulties arise from the transitional nature of change, others derive from the desire to maintain traditionalist curricular and pedagogic relations by conservative constituencies. Green (1990) has argued that the dominance of public schools hindered the development of English education and skewed the educational system so as to reflect the interests of a narrow class- and gender-based constituency. However, the move towards a modernized post-compulsory system, it is claimed, will deliver a labour force suited to post-Fordist conditions and thereby undermine these structural inhibitions. But what are these post-Fordist conditions?

To paraphrase Tom Peters (1987), post-Fordist firms thrive on chaos. Continuous improvement is the order of the day. In such conditions, organizations need to be adaptive to change. Some years ago Burns and Stalker (1961) coined the term 'organic organization' to describe such firms. These were set against mechanistic organizations. The latter were bureaucratic, rigidly hierarchical, with clear organizational structures and fixed division of labour. The former were characterized by a flatter hierarchy, a less clear division of labour, team working and greater flexibility. It is the organic organization that is to be generalized in post-Fordist economies, since it is this which provides for quick responses to changed circumstances. The move towards team working and the development of problem-solving skills is to be pushed further down the organizational hierarchy and ultimately to be located on the shop floor. The traditional autonomy of the professional is to be passed to the generic worker. We are all to become self-regulating enterprising subjects who will 'give of their all' and are committed to the values and goals of the organization in which they work. The corollary of these changes is that labour needs to be developed to work in such organizations and to acquire the requisite attributes and 'skills'. It is here that post-compulsory education and training is to play a key role.

However, there are other consequences of these changes. For some writers these new conditions and emergent work patterns are the pre-conditions of a more equal, even socialist, society. Brown and Lauder's (1992b) work provides a case in point. Here the argument is akin to Marx's claim that capitalist social relations carry the seeds of their own destruction. In the Brown and Lauder argument, post-Fordist organizations encourage participation and the democratization of work relations. In order for such organizations to be successful they require the development of collective intelligence.

> Skills and talents are concerned with solving problems within already existing paradigms and systems of knowledge. Intelligence has to do with understanding the relationship between complex systems and making judgements about when it is appropriate to work within existing paradigms and when it is appropriate to create new courses of action or avenues of thought ... Collective intelligence [is] defined as a measure of our ability to face up to problems that confront us collectively and to develop collective solutions.
>
> (Lacey, 1988, pp. 93–4)

Such relations are antithetical to capitalist social relations and are therefore transformative. The contradiction between these two sets of relations will be transcended by the democratization of work relations, which represents a higher stage of development. Whilst the last statement goes further than those made by Brown and Lauder, it represents the logical consequence of their argument and illustrates its modernist roots. Foucault (1983) reminds us that all discourses are dangerous. The affinity between these types of arguments, management theories and the quality debate illustrates the point (see Chapter 5). There has been a long tradition within management theory which attempts to appropriate the creative energies of labour. This can be seen in the work of Elton Mayo and the human relations school, in Maslow's and Herzberg's notions of self-actualization and in the more recent work of Peters and Waterson, all of whom attempt to engage variable labour power and to colonize the meanings that workers attribute to wage labour (Mayo, 1945; Herzberg, 1966; Maslow, 1954; Peters and Waterson, 1982; Peters, 1987). The aim is to create a committed and self-motivated labour force, a labour force that has a stake in the company and that broadly shares its goals.

Garrahan and Stewart (1992), in their study of Sunderland car workers, illustrate the commitment that some workers have made to Nissan. This commitment derives from the apparent autonomy that work relations offer as well as a stake in the wider quasi-family relations that characterize the company, as demonstrated in a sense of belonging engendered by team working and company ethos. For Garrahan and Stewart such a stake serves to gloss over the underlying exploitative relations that surround a production regime in which post-Fordist forms have been grafted on to Fordist relations. Nissan should more properly be understood as an expression of *neo*-Fordism, at least in terms of the experience of those working on the shop floor. The regulation of workers' beliefs becomes crucial to sustaining their compliance and commitment. Knights and Willmott (1989) echo this in the stress they place on the importance of shaping beliefs in ways that align with the needs of employers. Clearly, in neo-Fordism, we are not discussing a functional relation but rather one that is struggled over, offering both gains and losses. Such contestation also needs to be placed in its material context. However, the central point is that post-Fordist visions do not challenge deep-seated capitalist relations.

Yet it would be wrong to assume that post-Fordist work relations are without progressive possibilities. The danger is that these become collapsed or incorporated within a capitalist logic. Post-Fordist labour processes are predicated upon levels of commitment and motivation from the workforce. These can be contrasted with those found in Taylorist and Fordist forms as seen in the tyranny of the assembly line. The Nissan study is important. It illustrates the way in which an argument lodged within the post-Fordist rhetoric of worker involvement serves to gloss over the continued existence of Taylorist forms in which workers connive in their own self-regulation through participating in processes of continuous improvement. The sharing of knowledge about production is fed back into work processes with the resulting intensification of labour (see Chapter 5).

Clearly, the ways in which changes in the labour processes are experienced vary both between and within industrial sectors. However, a central theme revolves around self-motivation, commitment and attachment to the core values of the organization. It is at this juncture that the contradictions of post-Fordism become evident and in which its radical possibilities lie. Thus, we are to be self-empowering and regulating on a terrain that is set by others and on the basis of interests that may be antithetical to our own. We are to become enterprising subjects operating on a terrain characterized by a turbulent environment in which we act in competition with others, albeit across different teams/organizations, and are concurrently subjected to individualized appraisal and target setting. Our flexibility and involvement allow us to take advantage of the opportunities that become available. The entrepreneur acquires surpluses by operating in those spaces in which consumer/provider ignorance provides the opportunity for exploitation. This is essentially an exploitative relation which is antithetical to socialist and collective interests. It may appear to engender more effective and efficient action but this again is framed by particular and specific constructions of the terms. Efficiency, effectiveness and value-addedness are held uneasily under the sway of a managerialism that is lodged within a capitalist logic.

So far this analysis has been overly pessimistic and has played down the radical possibilities for a socialist appropriation of terms such as post-Fordism. There are a number of reasons for this. In the debates over the economy and post-compulsory education there has been a tremendous slippage. We find apparent agreements between a range of constituents who in the past held diametrically opposed views. Socialists and industrialists now share a common agenda calling for the reorganization of education (see, for example, CBI, 1994; M. Young, 1993). It would be easy enough to view these links as representing a qualitative shift in social relations heralding progressive possibilities. But there is an alternative formulation that sees these developments as representative of varying interests operating within changed conditions in which the New Right hegemony has gained ascendancy. This ascendancy is nevertheless vulnerable, having to be continually resecured. It should not be read in a crude Thatcherite sense as representing a victory gained in the 1980s. Rather, it should be understood in terms of a post-Thatcherism that is attempting to secure a dominant position by drawing upon theories of human resource management and the development of human capital. Such a shift brings together a range of constituents who have stakes in the evolving organizational and social relations. Such constituents range from those academics offering MBA degrees to currents within liberal feminism.

The shift towards management and work practices informed by human relations is read by some as offering a socialist potential, albeit dependent upon struggle (Brown and Lauder, 1992b). These and similar types of argument represent in some sense a departure from class analysis and politics by the Left (Webster, 1994; Westergaard, 1994). Politically it is here that the decline of the grand narrative, the collapse of socialism and the new realism of the Labour Party come into play (Norris, 1993). Harvey (1993) has used the case of a factory fire in the southern states of America and the resulting deaths to illustrate the way in which the developments in social theory and leftist politics have played down the significance of social class. He contrasts the Left's silence over this fire with the furore surrounding the appointment of a black Supreme Court judge accused of sexual harassment. Harvey suggests that by taking on board class issues one is able to articulate accompanying concerns about gender, race and so on. The shift away from class-based analyses carries the danger that capitalist social relations are left in place or become theorized only at a superficial level. Part of the problem lies with the Left and its difficulty in seeing alternatives to the current discourse. Thus it becomes trapped by an illusion of a reforming and more humanistic capitalism (see Hutton, 1995a; Hampden-Turner and Trompenaars, 1994). This is deeply misleading – the fire that Harvey discussed is a case in point, as are the activities of transnational companies in the Third World and variable practices found within our own society. After all, the aim of industry is to accumulate capital and extract surplus value – activities which sit uneasily with the empowerment of all workers. These tensions become most apparent when economic activities are placed within a global context.

We have criticized Brown and Lauder's post-Fordist argument for its modernist underpinnings. The same form of criticism could be levelled at this chapter, its use of the term socialism and our willingness to draw on neo-Marxism as a form of critique. Post-modernist arguments question claims to universal truth as well as grand narratives of progress such as Marxism and social democracy, spelling out the totalitarian and oppressive consequences of these (Ross, 1988). Where, then, is the space for political intervention? One response is to move away from the sphere of grand narrative and focus on the local and specific. The particular sets of relations surrounding, for example, specific teaching relationships or managerial practices, which are seen as neither inherently oppressive nor emancipatory, become sites of political intervention. In part those who wish to exploit the progressive possibilities offered by post-Fordism and managerialism could operate within this terrain. But the notion of complete closure, of the ability of any constituency to gain complete ascendancy, is untenable. There are spaces for struggle but sometimes these may be matters of accommodation and survival rather than transformation. It is at this juncture that the debate over class politics has something to offer. The suggestion is not to operate with a homogeneous conception of class and struggle but to try to unpack the relationships between class groups, social movements and educational practices. A localized politics may be able to deliver progressive outcomes within limited circumstances but these will be subject to the constraints imposed and interactively shaped by a larger politics. This is why, despite all the risks involved, the move towards a grand narrative becomes politically necessary – the move towards 'principled positions' (Squires, 1993).

There is a danger with our preceding argument. Post-Fordist analyses have been criticized for their location within a class-based politics that is focused almost exclusively on the white male. Williams writes in relation to post-Fordist discussions of welfare:

> In particular, the relevance of social relations other than class is ignored in relation to: the organisation of paid and unpaid work in welfare; the consumption of welfare; conflicts and struggles over the distribution and delivery of welfare provision; the ideological content of welfare policies and practices; and the outcome of welfare policies.
>
> (Williams, 1994, p. 57)

It therefore becomes important when considering educational discourses that use the rhetoric of post-Fordism to interrogate these for their ethnic and gender consequences. How is the person positioned and conceptualized? How is difference viewed? Within policy frameworks, difference becomes associated with unfair discrimination – and lying behind all this is the universal white, male subject. While the intention is ostensibly to remove discrimination so that we all stand on the same footing, it is a footing that is constructed in white, male terms.

NOTES TOWARDS ALTERNATIVE PRACTICES

At the risk of repetition, we want to rehearse some of the currents running through the previous analyses that point towards the development of alternative educational practices. Elsewhere in this book, we have discussed post-compulsory education within the global context. Whatever educational strategies are developed these have to be placed within such a framework. The increasing globalization of capital is a crucial facet as it constrains what is possible within a particular society. Of itself, the development of education in Britain is unlikely to be successful in transforming the economy as the technological lead gained by other societies means that the post-Fordist scenario is compromised. The skills of our people are unlikely to be liberated to facilitate economic renewal unless accompanied by a range of economic and industrial policies (see Hutton, 1995a). Such policies would need to address investment, the position of Britain in the European Union and its relation to competition from other economies. We would need to consider seriously Britain's position on the periphery of Europe and the consequences that this carries for investment.

Lipietz (1993) argues we are living through a crisis of social democracy and its manifestations within Fordism. He associates the New Right and market-based policies with what he calls liberal productivism which is seen to have failed and has engendered mass impoverishment at a societal, global and ecological level. The commitment to economic growth and unregulated capitalist competition is deemed both unsustainable and ecologically harmful. He calls for the development of an alternative to Fordism and liberal productivism. Such an alternative is based on valuing the creative capacities of workers, ecological principles and Third World awareness. In such an alternative compromise the shibboleth of economic growth is replaced by sustainability. Whilst the idealism of this position is apparent, it has much in common with leftist post-Fordism:

- Both celebrate the creative potential of labour.
- Both locate progressive possibilities as being 'determined' by the socio-economic context and the state of technological development in which we are currently placed.
- Both play down the social antagonisms that crisscross our society and therefore veer towards a notion of a socially responsible and constrained capitalism.

We have discussed the notion of a settlement over post-compulsory education and training. Whilst a number of themes are present within this current settlement, of central importance is a particular conceptualization of the economy as well as an understanding of the failures of post-compulsory education and training. There is a coincidence over the assumed needs of employers, learners, trade unionists and government. The logic of upskilling is central to such arguments, as is an assumption of an easy consensus among constituents. Absent from all of this is a sense of difference and social antagonism. However, it is these very silences and tensions that provide the fissures upon which progressive practices can be developed.

The use of post-Fordist notions in these debates is misleading. A particular reading of economic development is provided. Changes in the patterns of work, trends towards flatter hierarchies and the development of new forms of management that move away from hierarchical and authoritarian structures are all seen to be benign. These changes claim to offer workers enhanced control at the site of waged labour and therefore provide less alienating work environments with increasing levels of job satisfaction. To some extent this is the case although it sits within a logic committed to capital accumulation. Alongside these relations lie uneven development, neo-Fordist work relations, under- and unemployment. The rhetoric of post-Fordism ignores these patterns, offering in its place the development of an empowered future with increased worker control – a benign capitalism. Uneven development means that, for some at least, the link between capitalist development and enhanced life chances is compromised. Implicit within these arguments is a notion of human capital and individual development – a variant on the meritocratic myth – which is undermined by these processes (see Young, 1961; Althusser, 1972; Bowles and Gintis, 1976). The potential for the development of all, even the most able, is rendered problematic. The notion of development used is one aligned to the perceived needs of the economy. Economic needs are placed within a dominant position and the satisfaction of other societal requirements is dependent on the success of the economy. Such definitions of economic need represent the interests of dominant social groupings, namely those of capital, men and white people, and are presented as universal and taken for granted. However, it should be noted that because of the struggles involved in their construction, there are nevertheless ambiguities.

The contradictions and limitations of the arguments over post-compulsory education raise a number of issues and herein lies the potential for radical action. For example, notions of equal opportunity fail to embrace these contradictions as only a few will be in a position to take up the opportunities that post-Fordist relations offer. Because of this, notions of social justice, citizenship and difference are central to the construction of alternatives. The rhetoric of equal opportunities, social development through economic growth and good management practices offers a universalized discourse that plays down the significance of difference. The neglect of difference can arise in a number of ways, for example, the division between those in and out of employment and also by the way in which people are positioned in social relations as male or female, black or white, etc. The learner/employee is positioned within these economic arguments as a homogeneous being. There is no real recognition of difference other than through the notion of discrimination. We are effectively constituted as units of production or of labour, or even as value-added units. Once the notion of difference is recognized, a number of consequences emerge. Key amongst these is the question of the relationship between economic requirements and learners' educational experiences and needs. How do we think through the provision of post-compulsory education and training in the context of under- and unemployment? Once we recognize the differential relations people have towards employment, a rather different agenda is set in place for post-compulsory education, one in which the needs of industry and the economy become subject to debate. Economic requirements become just one of a number of concerns that post-compulsory education needs to address. The argument here is rather different from that espoused for life-long learning or education for adulthood as both these are lodged within economic hegemony. If under- and unemployment is the destiny for many people, and if the promise of post-Fordism is seriously compromised, how should post-compulsory education respond?

Clearly, institutions should be alert to the needs and demands that such constituents make. However, a concern with social justice means that the agenda becomes one of offering access to skills and knowledge that contribute to the development of an active citizenship. Such educational concerns go well beyond those embodied in the rhetoric of post-Fordism.

NEW ALLIANCES, SOCIAL JUSTICE AND DIFFERENCE

Challenging the hegemony of current economic discourse is important, for both the Left and Right are frequently constructing the demands on education within such a framework. This discursive framework is assumed to be able to satisfy human need and talks the language of new conditions in which upskilling will prove to be all-pervasive. Thus, for those on the Left the task is simply to be swept along by history. The educational preconditions for a modernized capitalism are those required by a 'Learning Society' (National Commission on Education, 1993). Such a strategy is limited. Whilst we should align ourselves with this trajectory, particularly against the low-skills, low-trust route, of itself this pathway is flawed and is unable to secure the conditions for radical democracy and an active and participatory citizenship. It is unable to secure the conditions for radical democracy because of its failure to recognize social difference and antagonism. The question, then, becomes how to build alliances that can open up the possibility for change and that could secure a political constituency to struggle for this.

The current settlement over post-compulsory education holds together a range of contradictory interests and constituents. Underlying it, however, is a construction of common interests – a happy coincidence. The notion is that the satisfaction of economic requirements can fulfil other needs. Once this connection is questioned, the basis of settlement is undermined and the constituent parts could be reworked and reformed in different combinations. It is here that the struggle over an active citizenship, difference and social justice has a part to play. This opens up questions surrounding the type of society we wish to live in and the quality of life available. Once we enter these debates we are faced with questions about the nature of education.

Donald argues that education should provide the 'knowledge(s), skills and resources ... citizens need in order to be able to participate effectively in its [radical democratic] dialogues and negotiations' (Donald, 1992a, p. 165). Later he suggests that 'literacy adequate to a radical heterogeneous democracy might need to be driven ... by the principle and skills of cultural translation, the ability to negotiate across incommensurable traditions' (*ibid.*, p. 167).

These arguments move the debate a long way from the current concerns of post-compulsory education in Britain. Earlier in *Sentimental Education*, Donald argues for the development of a critical vocationalism. Here there is a merging of the rhetoric of post-Fordism with its critics. However, the point is to avoid the conflation of economic needs with those of all. Such a conflation can be avoided by placing active citizenship, social justice, difference and social antagonism within a central position. By doing so, easy certainties and universalistic discourses are undermined. The difference between this standpoint and that of pluralism is the centrality placed upon social antagonism embodied in fundamental notions of conflict and differential interest. Pluralism sees society as criss-crossed by differential interests. However, where conflicts arise they are resolved through negotiation which takes place under the sway of societal consensus. What notions of radical democracy add is an understanding of irresolvable social antagonism. The existence of these antagonisms suggests there is no easy resolution to societal conflict. The struggle for a more humane society is therefore unending and cannot be embraced by a technical rationality that fails to consider the conditions of its own creation. Mouffe writes:

> Any attempt to bring about a perfect harmony, to realise a 'true' democracy can only lead to its destruction. This is why the project of radical and plural democracy recognises the impossibility of the complete realisation of democracy and the final achievement of the political community. Its aim is to use the symbolic resources of the liberal democratic tradition to struggle for the deepening of the democratic revolution, knowing that it is a never-ending process.
>
> (Mouffe, 1992, p. 238)

Democracy and social justice therefore have to be continually struggled over and the extension of both becomes central. The demand placed on education should move beyond the narrowly economic and the currently assumed correspondence between economic, societal and personal needs. It requires deconstructing and its tensions exposed. The following chapter grounds these concerns, focusing upon the market economy of post-compulsory education and, as with the preceding chapter, illustrates the social, political, human and educational costs of current practice.

Chapter 4

Post-compulsory Education in a Post-industrial and Post-modern Age

Denis Gleeson

INTRODUCTION

In the previous chapter it was noted that changes in post-compulsory education find expression in certain key themes and questions surrounding post-industrialism and post-Fordism. It was also argued that an apparent consensus over post-school education embodies national ambitions for education and economic reform, enshrined in such recent concepts as 'the learning society', 'skills revolution' and 'learning pays'. In policy terms, this chapter analyses how such consensus and ambition translate into the market economy of post-compulsory education. Although most post-school education and training in Britain and elsewhere remains in the public sector, a mixed market/non-market system is emerging in place of what Marginson (1993) refers to as the old municipal model of administered output. According to Robertson (1994), it is envisaged that the new post-school agenda will be held together by a credit and contract culture, allowing employers, trainees, students and institutions to 'trade' in the market-place.

What this chapter seeks to do is analyse the recent universal expansion of post-compulsory education in relation to two main aspects of the policy issues involved. The first concerns a socio-historical account of the rise of post-compulsory education, as it is mediated by economic crisis and decline. Here, questions regarding an apparent policy consensus among previously antagonistic political and economic parties are considered. So too is the fashionable assumption that market, employment and social dislocation represent inevitable features of post-modern times – increasingly defined in terms of flexibility, diversity and choice. The second concerns the relatively recent impact of post-Fordism, or more appropriately, *neo*-Fordism, in anticipating education change for the twenty-first century. We argue that the rediscovery of a *post-industrial* perspective represents little more than a distraction or gloss on inequalities generated by market and business reform. The issues here are not new. What is new perhaps is the abandonment of pretence that education and training are anything more than the servant of industrial, business and economic interests. In the title of a recent government report, education and training reform is defined primarily in terms of *Competitiveness: Helping Business to Win* (White Paper, 1994). What this chapter seeks to do is to define more broadly the framework of such debate, in favour of knowledge, citizenship and democracy in post-16 educational reform.

SKILLS FOR THE TWENTY-FIRST CENTURY

In the past decade post-compulsory education and training have attracted the interest of government, trades unions, employer representatives, educationists and the increased participation of students themselves. Moreover, international monitoring of post-compulsory education and training reform by the Organisation for Economic Co-operation and Development (OECD) and the World Bank, in terms of assessing economic growth and development, has raised global interest in post-school issues (Callan, 1994). In Britain, much recent attention has followed on the influential government White Papers (DES/DE, 1991; White Paper, 1994) which acknowledge that decades of failure to invest in post-compulsory education and training, in both good and bad times, have left Britain with a vicious circle of low skills, low wages and low productivity, and also with one of the least educated and trained workforces in the industrial world. Indeed, a new-found consensus has emerged among previously antagonistic parties (the Conservative government, trades unionists, the Confederation of British Industry [CBI], the Labour Party, the National Commission on Education and others) that nothing short of a *skills revolution* is needed to break this vicious circle and arrest Britain's downward economic spiral. In addition, a number of key factors have raised the policy profile of post-16 education and training, in relation to:

- the decline in manufacturing industry linked with the collapse of the youth labour market and traditional training routes;
- the lack of competitiveness and achievement: the vicious circle of low skills, low wages, low productivity linked with low post-16 participation, high drop-out rates, lack of universal post-16 provision, and rigid academic–vocational divisions;
- the development of new technology and management systems influencing work redesign and organization, further affected by replacement of traditional labour, changes in industrial relations and organized labour (from Fordism to post-Fordism);
- the geo-politicization of education and training: in response to global, political, international and multi-national, industrial and commercial developments (with implications for national and local systems of education, training and work);
- the demographic trend: the bulge in the youth population and change in the 'binary divisions' between school, college, work and higher education, including increased student participation in post-16 education and training.

In various and often contradictory ways, such apparent new realism has placed post-compulsory education and training at the centre of policy debate in Britain and elsewhere. Once viewed as the Cinderella or handmaiden of British industry, post-compulsory education has increasingly become an integral part of mainstream education itself. In recent years, improvements in General Certificate of Secondary Education (GCSE) and A-level results, the take-up of vocational qualifications and increased student participation rates bode well for the passage of post-16 education and training reform. Despite the lack of enthusiasm for science, there are encouraging signs that more young people are taking advantage of the broadening post-16 curriculum framework, with its promise of parity of esteem between academic and vocational qualifications, credit transfer, improved higher education access and job opportunities. Moreover, with General National Vocational Qualifications (GNVQs) now on stream, there are signs that post-compulsory education is, at last, opening up the range of opportunities first envisaged by the Crowther Report (1959). From an all-time low of less than 20 per cent of school leavers participating in post-compulsory education and training in the 1950s, there has been a steady increase with more than 70 per cent of school leavers now going on to some form of further education and training (Smithers and Robinson, 1993). Yet, despite this statistic, in recent years the expansion of post-compulsory education has passed virtually unnoticed, except for those students and staff working within it.

Diverse influences at home and abroad, unemployment, changing technology and work organization, marketization and global and geopolitical factors suggest that mass post-compulsory education is becoming a universal phenomenon. Such factors, increasingly associated with post-industrial and post-Fordist changes in society and production, have brought into question traditional distinctions between school, education and work, including those associated with academic and vocational education. Two other related factors have also placed post-compulsory education high on the political and policy agenda. The first concerns the transition from an élite to a mass system of further and higher education, which involves changing values, hierarchy and differentiation in the emerging new system. Here, policy matters to do with progression into higher education, course development, student recruitment and employment, organization and resource management feature significantly. The second concerns funding control and costs as unpredicted student numbers become absorbed into post-compulsory and higher education (Ainley, 1994; Brown and Scase, 1994). Not only has this attracted government interest in further and higher education policy, but it has also raised new questions about the relationship between post-compulsory education, economic growth and efficiency.

Whether or not new openings in further education and improved school results account for increased student participation, or whether it is the result of collapsed youth labour markets, remains a contested issue (Gleeson, 1989). Either way, Maclure (1991) argues that dire economic crises of the late 1980s and early 1990s have led to an emerging policy assumption that all young people should continue in education and training to at least 19, and be linked with the planned expansion of further and higher education. Four basic policy assumptions are, according to Maclure, deemed necessary to drive the new reforms, and include: two routes for 16–19-year-olds (academic and vocational); two modes of provision (full- and part-time); overlapping qualifications (A-levels and GNVQs); two sets of destinations (higher education and work). However, in order to be successful these policy assumptions must, according to the government (DES/DE, 1991; White Paper, 1994), be linked to nationally agreed training priorities, targets and standards, encompassing:

- centralized reform of national vocational qualifications in more systematic and competence-led fashion, linked with national and international training targets;
- supporting progression between school, college, work and higher education, linked with access, training credits and vouchers;
- giving more attention to post-16 provision, self-governance participation and retention,

including student choice, curriculum flexibility, modular and credit-based learning;
• sustaining local, regional and national, industrial and commercial partnerships, legislation designed to create and sustain an education and training market associated with consumer choice and 'new managerialism' in schools and colleges.

Given the post-16 policy vacuum pervading since the Crowther Report (1959), such acknowledgement of the guidelines necessary to achieve national post-16 reform would seem to represent a significant step forward. Are there grounds for optimism that recent legislation will translate such new-found consensus into a more coherent post-16 policy framework? In addressing this question, two interrelated issues are worth considering: the first is that apparent notions of consensus, though appealing, are rather more difficult to discern in reality; the second is that the present preoccupation with investment in training (enshrined in contradictory rhetoric about, on the one hand, workfare and on the other, reskilling the economy), obscures deeper inequalities within British society itself. Before taking up these issues, we first look at the central ingredients of the Further and Higher Education Act (1992) which has an important bearing on post-16 policy issues.

LEGISLATING FOR CHANGE

The Further and Higher Education Act, which transferred funding and control of further education, tertiary and sixth form colleges from Local Education Authorities (LEAs) to the institutions themselves, took effect from April 1993. The principle, first envisaged by the Robbins Report (1963) for higher education, and now extended to the colleges, granted independent corporate status to institutions, with responsibilities for their own budgets, staffing, marketing, personnel, course planning and provision. Essentially, the mechanism of funding and control of further education passed from LEAs to the Further Education Funding Council (FEFC), a central body with delegated Regional Advisory Committees and with funding formulae driven primarily by student numbers and courses offered. However, the funding formula is not quite that simple and also involves colleges in a bidding process linked with various corporate requirements laid down by the FEFC, including adherence to total and strategic quality management – issues we turn to in more detail in the next chapter. Following on the government White Paper (DES/DE, 1991) which expressed concern about declining skill levels, the Further and Higher Education Act set out to deliver a more integrated pattern of post-16 education and training provision. It was envisaged, for example, that traditional distinctions between further education, sixth form and tertiary colleges, and between academic and vocational curricula, would decline as institutions, free from LEA influence, competed for customers in the market-place. In making colleges more responsive to market forces (specifically by providing top-up funding for enrolments over target), the new funding mechanism was seen to provide an incentive to colleges to recruit additional students and reduce unit costs.

Translated into practice, the legislation envisaged that self-governance, together with other related initiatives, would have a major impact on changing post-16 provision, making it more client-focused and responsive to commercial and industrial needs. According to one college principal, the new arrangement of post-compulsory education would redistribute the subsidy from the supplier (the colleges) to the customer (most likely industry or commerce) and the consumer (the student) (Temple, 1991). Yet, given that colleges have always operated in the market-place, does recent legislation do any more than confirm arrangements that were already in place? There is more to it than that. The Further and Higher Education Act retains two ideological objectives. The first is *political*, reflected in government attempts to break the public service element of further education, enshrined in its historical and local democratic links with the 1944 Education Act, LEAs and the Crowther Report (1959). The second is *administrative,* in placing further education in new market arrangements, apparently unfettered by bureaucracy and more responsive to market needs. Thus, if granting corporate status is ostensibly to do with making colleges competitive, independent and entrepreneurial, it also has much to do with deregulating post-16 arrangements, making them more responsive to a business, industrial and commercial infrastructure which they are expected to serve. Viewed from this perspective, the legislation is less concerned with providing a policy or curricular framework for post-16 education and training than with radically *repositioning* post-compulsory education within new administrative, organizational and accounting arrangements. It seeks to do this in two interrelated ways: first, by creating an *internal market*, lumping together sixth form, further education and tertiary colleges, linking institutional survival with unit costs, student numbers and strategic funding; and second, by encouraging a new competitive infrastructure involving schools, post-16 institutions and a wide range of other organizations and quangos.

The way private enterprise and market forces find expression in post-compulsory education and training is not a new phenomenon, the ethos of the latter being rooted in voluntaristic and entrepreneurial traditions. Unlike the growth of mass schooling, further education has taken a highly individualistic path, its expansion depending much on the patronage of industry, business and commerce and the ability to attract greater student numbers. Yet, despite its resilience and resourcefulness in the market, post-16 provision has, over the past thirty years, been patchy, operating against a national background of under-funding, low participation and policy neglect. Almost by default, further education and tertiary colleges have been left to their own devices; their curriculum development reflecting anomalies in both the labour market and the qualifications jungle. This has not only led to growing disparities between academic and vocational curricula, but it has also resulted in considerable curricular replication, duplication and waste, including confusion over the meaning and value of post-16 qualifications, across school and college provision. Viewed alongside the catastrophic national picture of piecemeal and half-hearted attempts at industrial training, and the subsequent run-down of Industrial Training Boards, Skills Centres, youth, community and adult training programmes, it is curious then that Conservative government policy should view voluntarism and market principles as the means of igniting the post-16 reform process: or is it?

Following the Education Reform Act (1988), the Further and Higher Education Act (1992) and the Education Act (1994), post-16 policy in the mid-1990s in England and Wales has been driven by market principles and deregulation. Effectively, the three Acts have combined to break a municipal or public service view of school and further education which linked schools and colleges with LEAs within the spirit of the settlement which followed the 1944 Act. Institutional autonomy and corporate status now place institutions in the market-place apparently freed of external constraint. This, together with TECs, Training Credits, Business Partnership, new rules of governance, strategic funding and corporate management, now has a major impact on school and post-16 provision, rendering education and training more market-led, client-centred, entrepreneurial and responsive to industrial and commercial needs. It is envisaged that this will be achieved in two interrelated ways: first, by post-16 institutions becoming less course-led and more student-centred and, second, by schools and especially colleges anticipating new markets and funding arrangements with FEFC, Training and Enterprise Councils (TECs) and business, industrial, commercial and related bodies. In this way, recent legislation seeks not only to promote centrally an expanded post-16 education and training system, driven more by private than public enterprise, but also to ensure delivery of National Targets for Education and Training, associated with improved skill levels, GNVQs and increased student participation and better value for money. In so doing, reduction in unit costs, competition and responsiveness to market needs are seen to encourage efficiency and flexibility of both choice and provision.

Viewed optimistically, the impact of such factors will radically alter the traditional base of post-16 education and training. Increasingly, the shift in resource towards the student challenges conventional patterns of course and curriculum development, creating new pathways and patterns of provision. This, linked with the gradual erosion of binary divisions between polytechnics and universities, including distinctions between academic and vocational education (Dearing, 1994), is likely to have a significant impact on teaching and learning in the 16–21 sector and beyond. Thus, despite the fragmentation and diversification associated with the recent 'massification' of post-compulsory education and training, there is, according to Robertson (1994), a discernible policy thread running through the reform process. Evidence for this, Robertson argues, is reflected in a growing awareness that reform can be held together by an emerging credit culture which allows students and institutions to 'trade' in the market-place. However, such a view would seem to be out of step with developments on the ground in schools and colleges, for two reasons. First, despite apparent increased student participation, evidence of greater school-leaver choice – between dole queue, Youth Training, A-level and full-time vocational education (now GNVQs) – remains much the same as a decade ago. And, second, everyday life in schools and colleges, according to S. J. Ball (1994) and others (Whitty *et al.*, 1993), is not experienced in terms of diversity, choice and flexibility, but in relation to conflict over curriculum assessment, contracts, budgets and *jobs* – students who cannot get them, and teachers who are in fear of losing them! As important is the way the current preoccupation with vocationalism, markets and credits masks any real understanding of how students learn. The assumption that changing the mode of *delivery* of the curriculum will automatically bring about change in learning is erroneous. As Clark (1994) reminds us, the danger here is of replacing one inflexible structure with another, without addressing the nature of the learning process involved:

> the theoretical discourse arising from the ideas of *social constructivism* in respect of children's learning or the concept of *androgony* do not appear to have been applied to the study of the young adult learner. The insights of Vygotsky, for instance, into the nature of adolescent consciousness where *imagination* is *'make believe play without action'* (in contrast to the make believe play of young children which is *'imagination in action'*) have

relevance to the learning process post 16. Such ideas sit uncomfortably with discussion of 'performance criteria','competency' and 'outcomes'.

(Clark, 1994, p. 5)

We return to this theme of learning in Chapter 7.

If, on the surface, a market approach to post-16 reform appears radical and student-centred, there remains tension between prescription and openness in the education policy–practice process. The underlying tension between the two, together with divisions between academic and vocational education, has been a persistent feature of the English education system (Reeder, 1979) which arguably reflects Britain's lack of competitiveness (Wiener, 1981; Barnett, 1986). Such tension also has its roots in the struggle between old humanists, industrial trainers and public educators which has characterized the history of state education in England (R. Williams, 1961). If recent official recognition challenges such tensions, contradictions in the way government policy has sought to implement markets in education has tended to reinforce them. This has arisen in two interrelated ways: first, by curbing the influence of the professions, trades unions, LEAs and health and safety bodies, including the abolition of Wages Councils, Industrial Training Boards and training levies; and, secondly, by centrally and prescriptively defining the content of the school and college curriculum via quangos representing different dimensions of the academic and vocational divide. Such policy has, in practice, ensured institutional and individual adherence to central state control. It has also involved transferring the knowledge base of the curriculum from professionals to others, such as government agencies like NCVQ, employers, TECs and FEFC. Moreover, reducing the role of LEAs, teachers and unions to residual functions, creating managerial systems charged with accountability and establishing institutions as financially autonomous (within formula driven limits), effectively ensures deprofessionalization and the compliance of schools and colleges to the requirements of external agencies and agendas. As we have seen in Chapter 2, such factors, reinforced by teachers working to predefined content, assessment and contracts, reflect the pervasiveness of the *political* in support of economic agendas in education.

While the primary focus of government legislation remains one of placing institutions in the market-place, little thought has been given to how different facets of the learning and competitive process hang together beyond self-regulation. Missing too is any coherent analysis of the effects of markets in terms of upgrading or downgrading knowledge and skills in the curriculum, particularly in relation to fluctuations in the fortunes of local and national labour markets. Left unregulated, for example, the education market does not necessarily operate or effectively redistribute skills and resources in the interests of producers, customers or nation. The danger here is over-production of some courses where student demand is high but local and national demand in terms of job opportunities is low. Courses that sell today may not sell tomorrow, resulting in over-production of some skills and under-production of others. In such circumstances, it remains unclear how market-driven post-compulsory education and training will respond to local and national skill requirements, and how the balance between local need and national provision will be regulated, by whom – and in whose interest?

Linked with this is the danger of institutions working to their own market agendas and survival instincts, leading to greater institutional parochialism, including curriculum protectionism. In such circumstances, where do new questions and ideas about skill and knowledge in the curriculum come from? Moreover, preoccupation with unit costs, cost-effective courses and student numbers may radically affect the responsiveness of colleges and employers in meeting special education, adult, community and multi-racial needs in the face of more lucrative 'earning courses'. In terms of national skills short-ages, how market forces will respond to skill shortage or support envisaged principles of post-16 integration of provision, qualification and progression remains in question. It may well be that without some form of *planning*, replication, duplication and waste will continue to prevail. For Evans (1992), this represents a salutary reminder to employers and college principals alike that when recession ends they will discover the difficulty of recruiting skilled and able students and staff if they base their forecasts and contractual arrangements entirely on market forces – a view endorsed by Austin:

> You cannot turn the supply of plumbers on and off like one of their own taps. It is a certainty that when the recession finally ends and orders for new homes pick up, there will be a painful, immediate and familiar shortage of skilled labour. Angry customers, frustrated contractors and embarrassed politicians will sound off once again about how badly the supply side of the system works, while those who have been trained have their wages raised by the competing employers, and more tenders will be won by firms from France or the other EC partners ... if you have a product for which demand is so irregular, which is expensive to provide (think of the costs of all the materials which trainee builders get through) you might advise your governors that you should pull out.
>
> (Austin, 1992)

This view brings into sharp relief the often tenuous relationship between long-term requirements of curriculum planning and the short-term interests of market needs. The question arises, how do employers and post-16 institutions avoid the market trap in responding to the demand and supply side of important skills? In addressing this ques-tion, the government response has been to match market-led post-16 education with the flexibility of a competency and outcomes approach based on work (NVQs) and college-based training (GNVQs). In contrast to the European tradition of time, knowledge and skill-based training, Britain has adopted the American model, essentially defining the content of training in market and occupationally derived terms. Transported into the British context, a question remains about the commitment of employers to this educa-tion and training reform. In Britain, the evidence of employer funds flowing into such a system has proved highly disappointing, reflecting Jallade's (1992) view that there is little chance to win at local level a battle over training reform, grant levies and student grants that has not been fought nationally. In other respects, it is doubtful whether corporate status, new rules of governance and competition between colleges is an appropriate response to low skill levels and post-16 recruitment and retention.

Already, changing labour-market conditions, demographic trends, skill shortages and disenchantment with government education and training initiatives have led many LEAs, schools, colleges and students to search for alternative solutions in the absence of policy. There is, in the present economic climate, a growing recognition that market- and employer-led reform has failed to meet the needs of the majority of 16–19-year-olds. New qualitative questions about familiar quantitative problems are now being asked. Though staying-on rates have risen sharply, so too have drop-out rates, raising questions about the appropriateness of much of the curriculum on offer for increasing numbers of young people staying on in Britain and elsewhere. Provision, including grant entitlement, requires that more regard is given to their wider educational needs, their future progression and the skill requirements of a much broader range of occupations (Raffe, 1990). The question is, how might such characteristics better inform, and find expression in, future policy thinking?

The official answer to this question is that recent legislation will provide a framework in which corporate status and tripartite funding (from FEFC, TECs and LEAs) will drive the new market mechanism, ensuring its coherence. Following the Education Reform Act (1988), there has been a heightened belief among all parties that the survival of the British economy depends on real and lasting education and training reform. Yet the question remains, can the inevitability of this momentum be left to voluntarism and markets alone? In terms of the history of post-compulsory education, the answer to this question is a big 'IF': 'if only young people, educationalists, government, unions and employers come together to make it happen' (CBI, 1989). Unfortunately, in the absence of any visible signs of consensus operating in practice, this fragile conclusion returns us to the question: whose responsibility is it to bring people together, to initiate real and lasting change, to monitor progress and to hold the ring?

The erroneous assumption is that self-regulating market influences or some form of credit framework will resolve this policy problem (Robertson, 1994). In fact, funding by recruitment, retention and achievement brings forward the necessity for schools and colleges to make uncomfortable decisions about how to allocate resources and how to compete, rather than co-operate, with other establishments. Essentially, the process is inward looking. In such a climate of doubt and uncertainty about the future of education, it is perhaps not surprising that much energy is expended on institutional competition: on vying for students who come with a price on their heads, as opposed to developing quality schools and colleges designed to serve the best interests of their students. This, coupled with the return to an examination-based GCSE, continued conflict over education cuts, contracts, deregulation of LEA control and government hegemony of teacher education and continuing professional development, has placed retrenchment over change on the agenda. Alongside this, the failure to reform A-levels adequately and provide a unified system of post-16 provision ensures that 'parity of esteem', rather than equality, represents a real challenge to New Labour – an issue which we take up further in Chapter 8. Currently, the situation is complicated by existing tripartite divisions in post-16 education and training, between the academic (A-level), the broad vocational (GNVQ) and the workplace (NVQ). Regarding the latter, NVQs have been widely criticized for their low quality and knowledge base. Compared with the French and German apprenticeship systems, where breadth is demanded in the interests of nationally assessed standards, NVQ levels are determined by loose contractual arrangements, connecting TECs, training providers and employers with unpoliced National Targets for Education and Training. If the introduction of subsidized work-based training has, nevertheless, attracted the interest of employers in meeting their specific training needs, there is evidence that it has done little to influence long-term thinking about work organization, skill progression or the economy's needs (Hyland, 1994). Here, two competing perspectives circumscribe the debate: the need to provide young people with high quality education and training to improve their job prospects; and the question of whether employers have an equal need to plan for or employ highly educated and trained young people.

It is here, as in the past, that consensus and voluntarism often evaporate in inter-agency wrangles over funding, accountability and control. For this reason, breaking the vicious circle cannot be left to chance, autonomy, credits or market forces, which of themselves do not assure quality or equality of provision, or guarantee delivery of the skills necessary to industry, employer and society. As we have sought to argue, the chief concern of government legislation is not primarily with improving the quality of education and training but with regulating labour markets and driving down costs. It is, therefore, misleading to assume that current rhetoric associated with quality control and quality assurance has anything to do with improving the quality of provision: rather, the opposite – an argument that we will develop further in the next chapter. Though official training policy is apparently concerned with improving skill levels and staying-on rates, its real effect is to strengthen the bureaucratic control of institutions, to ensure their compliance to business principles (Brown and Lauder, 1992a). Fascination with the market obscures wider structural inequalities and masks uneven developments in the economy, some of which are, ironically, generated by training policy itself. Moreover, such inequalities, associated with unemployment, class, race and gender issues, have become redefined and appropriated as problems of audit, access, participation and equal opportunities – as dysfunctions to be overcome by more training. In so doing, a colonization and co-option have taken place of progressive and left arguments, which have become subsumed within notions of post-16 educational reform, consensus and market ideology. Yet, if we are to treat seriously the qualitative improvement of post-16 education and training, there is a need to establish *a discourse of change* which both informs policy, practice and provision and also goes beyond the limiting confines of legislation and market rhetoric.

INTO A POST-MODERN AGE?

An inevitable conclusion from the discussion so far is that it reflects a peculiarly 'in-house' British policy phenomenon: an historic failure to establish high-quality post-compulsory education reform in line with major industrial competitors. One argument is that the experiment with markets simply represents a parochial response to 'dogged sloth' (Maclure, 1991) – a bid by government to capture politically the post-16 education and training agenda, and little else. There is, however, more to it than that. Another way of looking at the issue is in terms of broader social and economic agendas, which find expression in what is sometimes referred to as the transition to a 'post-industrial' and 'post-modern' age. From this perspective (and looking beyond the immediate and parochial in British society), market dislocation may represent a global symptom of wider post-modern trends, characterized by institutional pluralism, variety, contingency, ambivalence and consumerism. According to Halpin (1994) the post-modern condition is one of constant mobility and change, but with no clear direction or development; it finds expression in the world-wide collapse of Fordist production methods and, with it, old truths associated with full employment, the transition from school to work and the concept of career itself. For Whitty *et al.* (1993), the fascination with such post-modernist thinking is not a peculiarly British phenomenon. Policymakers in the United States, Australia, New Zealand, Sweden and elsewhere are working within similar global frames of reference and are producing parallel policy initiatives rather than directly borrowing policies from one another (Callan, 1994). However, there seems to be a pattern. Deregulating expensive state education systems in favour of market-led reform serves a number of functions. First, in saving money (though there is some debate about this) and, second, in celebrating difference and diversity as an antidote to the 'one best' school or college system. The appeal of such policies, particularly 'new' or quasi-independent schools or colleges (such as the City Technology Colleges in Britain), is twofold. In the first place, a variety of types of privatized school or college is seen to be more responsive to the pluralistic needs of particular markets, communities and interest groups, which have now replaced traditional class divisions and once gave rise to the common state institution. And, secondly, the comprehensive common school or college smacks of the 'determinism' and uniformity of a bygone age, now in contradiction with the needs of a (post-)modernizing economy and society. The attractiveness of such niche development suggests that British market-led policies are not such isolated examples as they may seem, but reflect deeper social, ideological and economic shifts emanating within and beyond nation-states, and are linked with secular consumerism.

These changes, argues Hutton (1995a), reflect a radical break with earlier forms of capitalism, defining new conditions of production, consumption and pluralism, variously defined as post-industrial and post-Fordist. In economic terms, old Fordist regimes are being replaced with new forms of production characterized by flexible specialization (Piore and Sabel, 1984), as 'one best' models of schooling, work and post-school education and training give way to diverse modes of production, consumption, market and consumer choice. Not surprisingly, a close affinity can be discerned here between the rhetoric of post-Fordism, markets and curriculum reform, and developments within contemporary social theory associated with post-modernism (Green, 1994). Essentially, such theory offers new ways of understanding social fracture and economic fragmentation as virtuous: not so much as dislocation, or as inhibitors of *real* change, but as part and parcel of the inevitably shifting nature of pluralist society and of popular culture itself. According to Hargreaves (1994) the issue, in policy and curriculum terms, is to recognize that the conditions of post-modernity are both dangerous and emancipatory, the challenge being to go beyond traditional beliefs in systems, values and policies and to embrace new principles of equity, knowledge and skill development. Here, the affinity between post-Fordist and post-modernist thinking is compelling for two reasons. First, in encouraging new thinking – 'thinking the unthinkable', in facing up to the failure of post-war liberal democratic reform, and in recognizing that there was no golden age of education policy, schooling or employment. And, second, that conventional social-democratic approaches in education, which favour the common school or college, now face a need to respond to increasing specialization and diversity in modern society. Thus, instead of relying on conventional structures and institutions to deliver teaching and learning, there is a need to develop new forms of pedagogy which both anticipate and reflect the changing nature of markets, production and society itself. The question arises: can such sociological interpretation be taken seriously, or is it another form of 'new age travelling' (Ozga, 1995)?

While there remain disagreements about whether a shift from Fordism to post-Fordism has taken place and whether post-Fordism offers adequate insight into current trends in industrial societies, there are those who see radical potential for education in the post-Fordist claims (P. Brown and Lauder, 1992b; M. Young, 1993; P. Brown and Scase, 1994). Despite evidence of its uneven development within Britain, the argument runs that increasingly hierarchical systems of managerial control and surveillance are being replaced by flexible organizational structures, involving adaptable machinery, flexible workers, flatter hierarchies and the breakdown of the division between mental and manual labour. It is also argued that in the twenty-first century new skills of thinking, learning, abstraction, team-work, independent thinking and experimentation will be required by increasing numbers of workers. This is supported by a commonly held belief that new technology provides the potential to enable young people to become multi-skilled and flexible, and that if young people become better skilled and qualified, they will be able to acquire better jobs. And so the argument runs. Moreover, with the gradual collapse of the Fordist assembly-line school or college (in favour of the self-managing corporate institution), modernizers of all political persuasions anticipate a progressive and humane redefinition of learning in school, college and workplace. Thus the post-Fordist vision of society not only offers a progressive interpretation of the relationship between work, learning and society, but also the creation of new forms of knowledge implied in radical shifts both in the content and form of the curriculum. For Young (1992, 1993) such change necessarily involves challenging divisive specialization associated with academic and vocational divisions, insulated subject boundaries and the separation between education and training.

> It is suggested that in future changes in industrial economies will be expressed in terms of moves from divisive to flexible (or organic) specialisation. In curriculum terms flexible specialisation is a way of describing a curriculum for the future which would need to be based on the following principles:
> – flexible relationships between core and specialist knowledge;
> – opportunities to connect knowledge in different areas and relate theory to practice in a variety of contexts;
> – clearly defined and inter-connected pathways.
>
> (Young, 1992)

For Young, this represents as much a cultural as a structural shift in the curriculum, embracing new principles of integration, core skills and flexible specialization which mirror those flexible principles associated with change in the emerging post-Fordist workplace. In support of such analysis, Brown and Scase (1994) maintain that bureaucratic organizations are being superseded by alternative structures, often labelled 'flexible' and 'adaptive', which have implications for work, curriculum and learning on lines advocated by Young. From school to corporation, it is argued, organizations are being restructured in ways that challenge conventional assumptions about the nature of work, management and professional careers, with flatter, leaner and more participative systems becoming the order of the day. Increasingly, modern organizations (including schools and colleges) require managerial and professional employees with a range of skills and competence that extends beyond the present confines of academic, educational and technical expertise. In Britain, two government White Papers (DES/DE, 1991; White Paper, 1994) both endorse this assessment by identifying deep-seated failures in school and post-compulsory education. These failures include overly behaviourist models of training, lack of investment in intermediate skills and an inability to translate knowledge and innovation into economic growth.

Such factors, overlain with traditional suspicions about theory and thinking skills, have maintained often narrow and arbitrary distinctions between academic and practical modes of thought (Bourdieu, 1971). Increasingly, it is argued, there is a need to challenge the dependency culture engendered by instructional discourse in favour of a pedagogy of work and self-learning (Frykholm and Nitzler, 1993), embracing what has recently been described as the predeterminants of a knowledge-based or learning society (Reich, 1991; Ranson, 1994). The question arises, will adaptive, flatter and leaner organizations necessarily bring about a change in the learning culture of individuals, groups and institutions? Equally important is the question whether 'new' managerial changes under way in British schools, colleges and universities (modularization, semesterization, credits, access, accreditation of prior learning) reflect progressive changes in work or represent a reinvention of Taylorist principles. Similarly, is the changing market relationship between school, further and higher education a feature of growing national competitiveness, or is it a knock-on effect of collapsed labour markets? Though the conclusions to Brown and Scase's recent book, *Higher Education and Corporate Realities* (1994), are tentative on such questions, their work challenges the celebratory rhetoric of widening access, opportunity and social mobility harboured in the official discourse concerning further and higher education expansion and labour market flexibility. Their major argument is that wastage of talent, which had been an endemic feature of British society in the nineteenth century, shows little sign of being eradicated in an education system and labour market that continue to favour higher socio-economic groups. If, however, their study provides convincing evidence and argument to support this claim, their position wavers between both adopting and unmasking the rhetoric associated with the 'adaptive' post-industrial paradigm.

A problem with their analysis is that, despite the disclaimers, its key questions are ultimately premised on an acceptance rather than an interrogation of economic rationalism. It is argued, for example, that 'as organisations move from bureaucratic to adaptive models of organisation, managers, administrators, and professionals need to be more flexible, creative, innovative and socially skilled' (p. 164). Whether flexible specialization at work and in the curriculum will correspond or follow on in such fashion (or is even desirable) is open to question. The danger here, as with Young's position, is one of causally linking changes in curriculum with assumed technological changes in production. It is premised on a challenging but seductive economic rationalism which implies, almost inevitably, that new curricular arrangements in the twenty-first century will find their expression in progressive changes in work, and vice versa. Our concern here is that evidence supporting the assertion that corporate institutions are becoming less bureaucratic and more flexible is mixed and contradictory. Perhaps another way of looking at this is in terms of the transformative potential of critical education and political action as a means of challenging organizations, including post-compulsory education and higher education, to be more adaptive, innovative and open (Ainley, 1994).

It is not difficult to see how such radical and universal conceptions of the post-Fordist knowledge worker appeal across a broad and diverse spectrum including educationists, government, opposition, CBI, trades unions and examining bodies. Though the Conservative New Right have sought to retain traditional hierarchies in work and education, a whole string of major vocational education and training initiatives in the last ten years confirm confusion in government ranks over the skills envisaged for the twenty-first century. For different ideological reasons, educationists, the Labour Party and trades unions retain different interpretations of what post-Fordism and market reform will bring in terms of innovation, profit, change in work organization, labour and self-development. Such is the flexibility of the post-Fordist vision of society that it has become 'all things to all men'. For New Labour, it legitimates critiques of old models of hierarchy which offer false promises of choice, classlessness and freedom. For the New Right it legitimates market-led reforms in modernizing Britain's work and education institutions on more flexible and competitive terms. In so doing, both perspectives are able to idealize education and the quality of teaching and learning as necessary co-determinants of economic change, enshrined in concepts such as the 'learning society'. The danger, according to Green (1994), is that what we are left with in the end is a 'free market' in classroom cultural politics, 'where the powerful dominant discourses will continue to subordinate other voices and where equality in education will become an ever more chimerical prospect' (p. 81). Perhaps not surprisingly, such rapprochement has found favour with politicians and policy-makers of different political persuasions, as offering cost-effective solutions to rising costs associated with ever-expanding national education and training systems.

In Britain, these interpretations of post-Fordism have been used effectively to support greater deregulation of education and training while, at the same time, allowing mainly industrial and business interests to dominate the education and training agenda without delivering tangible skills or real employment. The official argument runs that core and periphery workers require higher levels of core skill and flexibility compared with the past. This is, however, debatable. In Clark's (1994) view, the constant features of high expectations and high respect for learning–training–education and, to some extent, for qualifications, do appear to be common attributes in 'high-performing' nations. It would also seem to be a near-truism that high standards of *technical education* are based upon good *'general education'* across the school and college curriculum. What is needed is a much more detailed and sophisticated analysis of the precise requirements of the *curriculum content* and the *curriculum process* necessary to develop learners who can be self-directed in a rapidly changing global economy and uncertain social context (Clark, 1994).

It is also the case that successful 16–19 education and training provision is dependent on a buoyant youth labour market, rather than being a precursor to it. Currently, the reality of recession and high youth unemployment in Britain, including growing disparities between wealth and income, contrast sharply with the rhetoric of post-industrial perspectives. In practice the supposed transition to post-Fordism in Britain and elsewhere has been associated with decline in manufacturing and expansion in the service sector – a form of neo-Fordism which is hardly evidence of any significant shift towards flexibility. The process, coupled with market deregulation and lack of industrial investment, has resulted in widespread unemployment, casualization and low pay. Traditionally, industries such as engineering, construction and energy have had the highest concentrations of young people with formally recognized qualifications. With the decline of such traditional industries the need for formal training has been increasingly determined by the demands of an expanding, mainly low-skilled, service sector, and to a lesser extent by a minority recruited into high-tech information based industries for whom NVQs are not relevant. Not surprisingly, the recent mass expansion of post-compulsory education and training reflects this trend, revealing stark contradictions between the rhetoric of upskilling expressed in government reports and the reality of segmented labour markets. For Hutton (1995a) the combination of New Right thinking, markets and post-Fordist assumptions has not only destroyed the post-war social and economic settlement, but it has also brought about a segmented '30, 30, 40' British society. The first 30 per cent he describes as *disadvantaged*, the second 30% are made up of the *marginalized* and insecure; and the last category is that of the *privileged* whose market power has increased since 1979. From this viewpoint, he argues, judgements about the appropriateness of youth and adult training provision have to be revisited in both economic and educational terms if they are not simply to replicate such segmentation. According to Ranson (1994), an internal education market which postures around the fringe of such stratification does little more than ensure selection to match a pyramidal, hierarchical society:

> It is underpinned by a political system which encourages passive rather than active participation in the public domain. A different polity, enabling all people to make a purpose of their lives, will create the conditions for motivation in the classroom. Only a new moral and political order can provide the foundation for sustaining the personal development of all. It will ensure individuals value their active role as citizens and thus their shared responsibility for the common-wealth. Active learning in the classroom needs, therefore, to be informed by and lead towards active citizenship within a participative democracy.
>
> (Ranson, 1994, p. 129)

Thus, while the concept of the post-Fordist knowledge worker operating in flatter and leaner systems may appear radical, its empowering assumptions need to be viewed with caution. They have become confused with people controlling their own labour and with making them personally responsible for their own quality management and, hence, social and economic reproduction. As Avis (1993a) argues, this may have more to do with shaping subjectivity, deference and demeanour, than with skill development or citizenship. Elsewhere, Bates and Riseborough (1993b) point to the ways in which 'flexibility and adaptability' have come to represent buzz-words of the new enterprise state, in which proletarianization and poverty have become replaced by individualism, flexibility and choice. In this respect, progressive interpretations of post-Fordism may have much in common with earlier post-industrial visions of society, embracing the end of ideology and equating changing technology and work practices with a new technology of social control and classlessness (Bell, 1974). However, the problem with this sort of economic rationalism is that it retains a limited view of education as driven by the inevitable and neutral imperatives of technology. Increasingly, the rhetoric is one of *delivering* and *managing* learning without real definition of what constitutes the nature of that learning and who it is for. This also conveys an instrumental message about knowledge and the learner, including teachers and organizations whose teaching and learning duties are defined in terms of national training and curriculum targets, tests and outcomes. Here, preoccupation with improved participation, qualification and skills, though ostensibly to do with improved productivity and employment, has little to do with enabling young people to think critically about themselves, their community and society. Thus, if the prevailing market model of pedagogy emphazises individualism and competitiveness, it has, in practice, little time for 'the self as persons in a relation to others' (Ranson, 1994). Yet, taken seriously, Young's (1993) and Brown and Scase's (1994) view that new technology provides the potential to enable young people to become multi-skilled is important. However, it needs to be tempered with the realization that it is *knowledge combined with democracy* which provides the substantive basis for a learning society (Ainley, 1994). It is to this issue that we now turn.

PROPOSITIONS: BEYOND NEW RIGHT PEDAGOGY

The principal argument so far is that real and lasting educational reform cannot be subordinated to the causal determinants of economy, or traditions of hierarchy and exclusion. Genuine alternatives must embrace an active view of *citizenship* which links partnership and empowerment in personal education and economic relations, beyond market, qualification and employer-led considerations. In the 'free market' arena in which education now finds itself, what incentives will there be to pay more than lip-service to the complex issue of providing for more equitable opportunity? Will competition be the single motivating factor? Where will new ideas and thinking about the curriculum come from? What new conditions will encourage the development of professional judgement? The current dogma is that quality education can be achieved through competition. It is difficult not to see that this conflicts with and contradicts equal concern for all young people's academic, vocational and career development.

Principles of democracy and social justice are involved here, in terms of how education and training help shape, rather than passively reflect, the changing nature of industrial society. This involves embracing broader views of the student as a *learner,* rather than as a customer or skills carrier. Moreover, the crucial importance of the quality of teaching and learning as the precursor to (rather than the appendage of) outcomes, targets, competence and performance indicators needs to be recognized. It also involves principles of inclusion rather than exclusion of key partners in education and training, giving greater voice to youth, teachers, unions, parents, local authority and community concerns. Though any alternative curricular framework for post-16 education and training is likely to be bounded by markets, it is important that markets do not dictate provision, *since markets themselves are increasingly dependent on the quality and supply of educated and trained labour.* Central to the reform process must be recognition now that it is not just markets or even legislation and structures of access and provision that need to be changed, but also the content, context and control of post-compulsory education and training, including the kinds of assumptions about teaching, learning and work which underpin them (Johnson, 1991b). It is perhaps time to recognize that the post-compulsory education and training debate is not about ends but *means*: the automatic association of the efficient with the unregulated action of markets has been taken too seriously for too long.

The necessity for addressing this question is compelling. With mass post-compulsory education and training now coming on-stream, training without work is likely to be politically unacceptable and represents an even more insidious prospect than in the 1980s, when the first wave of mass youth unemployment hit. If the first generation of training programmes exposed historical weaknesses in early leaving (as well as controlling the sudden collapse of youth labour markets), it will be more difficult to sustain public support for post-16 reform this time round if it simply represents another extension of schooling. The question arises: under new post-16 curriculum structures, will young people continue to be divided, on lines of class, gender, ethnicity and region, into different and diverging career trajectories (Roberts, 1993), or will greater flexibility between routes be achieved? Most current research on the transition from school to work stresses the stratification of inequality (Furlong, 1992; Banks *et al.*, 1992; Bates and Riseborough, 1993a; Kerckhoff, 1993). This contrasts sharply with optimistic policy assumptions based on diversity, individualism and free choice (CBI, 1989, 1993;

Bennett *et al.*, 1992; DES/DE, 1991; White Paper, 1994). The danger is that in the rush to increase staying-on rates (effectively raising the school-leaving age to 18 or 19 for most young people), we fail to revisit the difficult problem of past educational failures. From the 1960s onwards, study after study indicates the educational system, be it based on grammar and secondary modern schools (D. H. Hargreaves, 1967; Lacey, 1970) or on comprehensive schools (S. J. Ball, 1981; D. H. Hargreaves, 1982), failing large numbers of young people, especially the less advantaged of working-class origins. More recently, the focus has shifted to problems for young women and young people of ethnic minority origins (Arnot and Weiner, 1987; Troyna, 1987, 1994).

Contributors in Bates and Riseborough (1993a) paint graphic pictures of inequality in post-16 provision just prior to the introduction of GNVQ. Though we are in favour of expanding educational provision post-16, it is important to recognize that more does not necessarily mean better. It is interesting that in the United States, where staying-on rates are much higher than in Britain, similar concerns about poor quality provision are frequently expressed (Brause, 1992). The issue here is not one of dilution: a favoured argument of the New Right. Rather, in Britain, as Lee *et al.* (1990) point out, leaving youth training to market forces, voluntarism and employers has resulted in under-provision and a lowering of standards, including skill shortages and a waste of young people, tantamount to their civic exclusion. This phenomenon, recently associated with cuts in benefit, homelessness and poverty, has further marginalized some young people in both societal and educational terms. The result is that alienation and anomie become overlain, effectively creating an underclass linked with increasing levels of poverty (Rowntree Trust, 1995).

Such factors not only reinforce and reproduce wider principles of social and occupational inclusion and exclusion associated with tripartism, but they also underpin a political system which encourages passivity rather than active participation and learning in the public domain. Thus it is necessary to address a broader vision of citizenship and learning – in fact a different polity – which will sustain the personal development of all (Ranson, 1994). In addressing this issue, four preconditions are essential (Gleeson and Hodkinson, 1995). First, the professionalism of teachers and lecturers needs to be enhanced rather than destroyed, as a combination of school-based initial teacher training, growing centralized government control of education and, ironically, repressive neo-Fordist school and college management approaches threaten. Secondly, there is a need to re-examine the funding mechanisms for post-16 education and training in terms of the broader educational issues addressed here. The current obsession with performance-related funding (focused on student numbers and completion rates) reinforces a narrowing of choice, removal of flexibility and loss of unfunded 'curriculum extras' such as non-examination, adult and general education studies. Thirdly, educational purpose must range beyond economic performance and markets. This is not a matter of either/or. Paradoxically, the much-cited evidence from Britain's European partners suggests that a broader, more general education will bring the nation closer to the wider agenda advocated here, and may also better fit the economic imperative of a skills revolution (Green, 1995). Even some advocates of a three track system (Smithers and Robinson, 1993) see a need for a broader, general technical/vocational education with a greater emphasis on mathematics and science education to underpin practical skill development. And, finally, the issue of inclusion and exclusion which has bedevilled British education must be abandoned in favour of a unified approach to 14–19 education and training. A common certification for years 14–19, along the lines minimally outlined by the National Commission on Education (1993), is a necessity. In this respect, the introduction of a General National Diploma in Education will make parity of esteem between A-levels and GNVQs (as 'alternative routes') a redundant concept (Sweetman, 1994). It may also bring forward realization of the need for a common post-16 core curriculum on the lines advocated by Young (1993), providing a general education entitlement which is less divisive and more broad-ranging and, at the same time, allows for flexible specialization.

In all this, however, there remains the neglected issue of *values* in education (S. J. Ball, 1994): what is taught and whose values are to be represented in the curriculum and how. According to Tomlinson (1993), any such response to this issue must necessarily offer the development of intellectual capacities, economic skills and personal qualities that every individual has a right to acquire, and the 'obligation to put these to the service of society'. This not only demands rethinking teaching and learning, but also the content and process of the post-16 curriculum as it affects knowledge, adult learning and development in a civic rather than market-driven society. Genuine alternatives, therefore, must embrace an *educationally constructed* view of citizenship on the lines advocated by Clark (1994), which interlinks partnership and empowerment in personal, education and economic relations. For example, Hodkinson (1994) suggests that education for all young people should include three overlapping dimensions: personal effectiveness, critical autonomy and community. By personal effectiveness he means the ability to do things for oneself and with others. The emphasis is on doing, and being pro-active, be it running a playgroup, making jewellery, raising funds for charity or producing a newspaper. Critical autonomy refers to the importance of thinking for oneself, including the ability to analyse and critique common assumptions. Community is about developing one's place in a diverse community, about understanding conflicts of interest and struggle, about recognizing and respecting the rights and opinions of others, and about contributing to community and society through individual, collective and communal effort. Too often, in the past, educational provision has fallen well short on some or all of these – particularly vocational courses which have been typically uncritical, and where important issues of social justice and inequality are not even addressed. Analyses such as this clearly demonstrate the narrowness and sterility of basing a curriculum exclusively on the economic and ideological agenda. Redressing the impact of what gets left out of the curriculum suggests that it is important for schools, colleges and policy-makers to make decisions on firm *educational* grounds, beyond markets and what Evans (1992) calls the private governance of public money.

As the 1990s progress it would be naïve to harp back to some golden age of post-compulsory education and training or of democratic local control as the answer to this question. New rules of governance and democratic engagement are called for, which both bring unaccountable quangos to heel and also reconstitute debate about the meaning, governance and purpose of post-compulsory education and training: essentially addressing *who* it is for. Greater attention needs to be given both to the wider educational needs of young people, including progression and job opportunities, and to ways in which qualitative consideration of the curriculum, particularly teaching and learning, informs the post-16 policy reform process. This necessarily involves education becoming a more critical and self-critical process. In Beck's (1992) terms, self-criticism is not some sort of danger, but probably represents the only way that the mistakes which threaten education, democracy and people's lives can be detected in advance.

> What kinds of regulations and protections this will require in individual cases cannot yet be
> foreseen in detail. Much would be gained, however, if the regulations that make people the
> opinion slaves of those they work for were reduced. Then it would also be possible for
> engineers to report on their experiences in organisations and on the risks they see and
> produce, or at least they would not have to forget them once they leave work. The right to
> criticism within professions and organisations, like the right to strike, ought to be fought
> for and protected in the public interest. The institutionalisation of self-criticism is so impor-
> tant because in many areas neither the risks nor the alternative methods to avoid them can
> be recognised without the proper technical know-how.
>
> (Beck, 1992, p. 234)

To date, education and training reform in Britain has failed to blend such critical know-
how into a broad academic–vocational education. Despite the prevailing rhetoric of
diversity surrounding its recent expansion, such reform has been largely bounded by
lack of choice and opportunity in the labour market. In this, the central problem of
raising young people's levels of achievement and expectation has been hampered by the
maintenance of tripartite divisions dressed up in new vocational nomenclature. Though
the range of vocational initiatives appears innovative, it represents key features of New
Right economic and political thinking which, according to Dale (1989), entails freeing
individuals for economic purposes while controlling them for social purposes. This and
the marketization of self-managing schools and colleges is, according to Whitty *et al.*
(1993), more readily understood in Dale's terms than as a clear expression of post-
modernist or post-Fordist enlightenment. In questioning such libertarian interpretations,
Whitty *et al.* (1993) and S. J. Ball (1994) view market reform of education and training
as still conforming to Archer's (1984) definition of a modern state education system,
where overall direction and supervision remain government controlled and whose
diverse fractured parts continue to be centrally determined. The message here is that
any new thinking about reform will need to go beyond both the 1944 and current New
Right inspired and dominated settlements, the challenge being to generate a new 'third
education settlement' beyond markets, which combines conceptions of social unity,
justice and community with economic competitiveness and productivity (Donald,
1992b). Here, a key feature will be the transition from a receiver to a learner (rather
than customer or consumer) oriented pedagogy which critically redefines the relationship between learning, earning and economic growth. This process will not occur
automatically and is contingent upon a redefinition of *public education* which is neither
condescending nor paternalistic. The optimistic view that the disparate aspects of post-
compulsory education and training policy and practice can be held together by a
contract and credit culture looks increasingly untenable. What is called for is a commitment to the concept of *universal provision*, based on entitlement and equity rather than
on elusive notions of choice and diversity. Once established, the principle of a unified
system of post-compulsory education and training need not necessarily preclude new
thinking about access, credits and markets – *but neither should it be replaced by them.*
The irony is that unbridled diversity may yet prove to be a post-modern condition which
the 'mandarins of modernity will find difficult to contain' (Hartley, 1994).

If the picture we have presented here looks grim, there is growing optimism that
many parents, students and professionals have seen through current government strategies. Following recent industrial action in schools and colleges, there is also wider

recognition that future education and training policy which fails to engage with young people, teachers and the culture of the school or college is unlikely to achieve meaningful reform. Looked at on a comparative basis, though most industrialized nations have been affected by global economic change and recession, they have not all capitulated to nationalism and market realism (Hyland, 1994). Countries and economies with strong commitments to growth, social policy and investment (Holland, Germany, France, Belgium, Sweden, Denmark, Switzerland, Singapore and Japan) have been relatively more successful than those (America, Britain, Australia, New Zealand and Canada) which have 'downsized' their economies in a panic response to recession. The difference, perhaps, is between those countries which have fought to secure full employment and investment in public and private domains, including state intervention in labour-market policy, education and training, and those which have retreated, leaving markets to sort out the winners and losers in both education and the economy. According to Yeatman (1993), the current obsession with markets and managerialism finds its expression in the ways in which new types of private transnational capital and foreign competition are now setting the public policy agendas for nation-states. Thus, despite the apparent progressive rhetoric associated with 'enterprise in education', 'flatter, leaner systems' and 'credit culture', such concepts have, in reality, become associated with cost-cutting, downsizing and deprofessionalism. In schools, colleges and higher education, the movement is associated with, on the one hand, fewer teachers handling more students with fewer resources and, on the other hand, professionals working to nationally prescribed curricula and conditions of work. Despite the resistance shown by teachers, health and other public-sector workers to such encroachment, its deeper effect, according to Yeatman (1993), is to break the power of professional advocacy: 'giving power to the defining determinants of the market over knowledge, thereby displacing professionals' (p. 91). In professional terms this has been described by one further education teacher, who recently took early retirement, in the following way:

> I have friends still working in FE who say it is like being owned, body and soul, by management. Corporatism has replaced and stifled democratic debate, and so compromised working conditions that there has been a mass exodus of previously committed and experienced teachers. Staff are no longer respected, just told to shut up and get on with it.
>
> (Macleod and Beckett, 1995)

The reality for many teachers currently working in post-16 institutions contrasts markedly with the progressive images of the 'new managerialism' presented by its advocates (Robertson, 1994). In the period 1994–96, colleges were in the process of imposing new contracts which substantially increased teachers' workloads – in circumstances where funding was withheld from colleges which failed to do so. As we have argued throughout, there are no quick-fix solutions here, since New Right policies have downsized economy, education and welfare to protect the diminishing capital base of what Mills (1971) calls the 'power élite'. The first necessary policy response is, of course, premised upon an improved education and training system, not least in encouraging critical awareness of what New Right ideology stands for in protecting this power élite (Hutton, 1995a). Importantly, the nature of such reform should be underpinned by new thinking about teaching and learning, beyond the social pedestrianism and dogma of managerialism and vocationalism. It involves reconstructing the conditions of a genuine learning society beyond markets (Ranson, 1994) which are rooted in and nourished by the civic virtues of active citizenship, as opposed to the chimera of consumerist rights and citizens' charters. However, if we are to build greater coherence into a common 14–19 curriculum based on education, training and work for all, there is a need to couple this with specific community, economic and policy reforms, including:

- a commitment to full employment both as a political priority and as the dominant ethic of economic policy;
- state intervention geared to productive investment, both public and private, favoured over boosting consumer demand;
- active labour-market policy measures including public works, vocational training and special employment in public services;
- the creation of part-time jobs with full social rights in co-operation with trade unions favoured over a general reduction in working time;
- a tax structure which reflects a trend away from pay-roll taxes and social contributions toward taxes on capital assets and consumption;
- a labour movement committed to technological change and job flexibility under conditions of full employment;
- a consensus decision by all parties not to use high unemployment as a means of securing other policies.

(Shirley, 1991, quoted in Hyland, 1994, pp. 126–7)

The question arises: how should education policy respond to and critically partner such propositions? In institutional and curricular terms, any response will require caution in avoiding past mistakes made under similar conditions. According to McCulloch (1989), if we are to make use of the Crowther concept of further education for all in the twenty-first century, we should also be aware of its unresolved difficulties. First, he maintains, it is necessary to decide whether to opt for separate technical routes within schools and colleges, or for integration of technical, vocational and academic routes within a unified system (see Finegold, 1991). At the same time, McCulloch argues, it is crucial to revise Crowther's original notion, to replace its tripartite connotations of 'three types of mind' with rehabilitation of 'the practical' for all pupils and students. Equally, it still remains important to clarify the nature of the Crowther concept in curriculum terms, with regard to challenging academic and vocational divisions and the proliferation of 'initiatives' which support them (Gleeson, 1989).

According to Raffe (1990) this argument can be taken one step further: debates about education and training for 16–19-year-olds are often premised on the assumption that economic and labour-market objectives necessarily conflict with social and economic ones. In redefining the relationship, he suggests that the long-term needs of the labour market may be for a more general and less differentiated system of education and training for this age group. Such a view, also endorsed by Finegold and Soskice (1988), has important longer-term curricular, institutional and policy implications, not least in encouraging desired developments within the education system rather than reactive responses to the previous demands of outside market forces. This has significance for rethinking the qualitative base of post-16 education and training in two ways: first, by giving more attention to the organic criteria of teaching, learning and curriculum, mentioned earlier; and, second, by encouraging genuine partnership between education, business and industry, beyond the present rhetoric. According to Finegold and Soskice (1988), a more effective solution is to balance the interests of those involved in education and training (educationists, employers and government) in a partnership to achieve change. What supports this argument is that countries with successful economic systems devote substantial resources to research on education, training and labour-market development. In Britain today, policy-making has become replaced by highly centralized legislation and control, based on limited information and research on curricular and labour-market practice. Successful countries also place great reliance on employers' organizations, local authorities, professionals and unions. In Britain their role in the governance of education and training has been progressively reduced. Thus, if radical reform is to be successful, it will be important to build up expertise and involvement of the various social partners (Cassels, 1990). There is more to it than that. Serious attention needs to be given to *educating* (as opposed to training and keeping off the dole) a majority of working-class people who have hitherto been denied access to post-compulsory and adult education (Wymer, 1993). The message is clear. If the post-compulsory education reform process is to achieve a distinctive ethos and philosophy for *all,* it must stress values for the future rather than simply reproduce those of the past.

The current climate of markets, competition and rampant new managerialism impacts on students and teaching staff alike, but in different ways. In the next chapter, we critique the growth of the new managerialism, with its ubiquitous mantra of 'quality'. In Chapters 6 and 7 we turn explicitly to the experiences of young people in this brave new world of market-led post-compulsory education and training.

Chapter 5

The Enemy Within: Quality and Managerialism in Education

James Avis

The new conditions facing education in the 1980s and 1990s have generated an emphasis upon the effectiveness and efficiency of educational institutions. Whether these be schools, colleges or universities, all are to become accountable and cost-effective. In Britain the Thatcherite right has been a key force in shifting the terrain on which education operates. The Reaganite right served a similar purpose in the United States and we can discern similar currents in Australia, New Zealand and Canada. However, these processes should not be seen as simply reflecting the ideological work of the New Right. In many senses, there is a move beyond the New Right and this is intimated by the shift towards managerialism and the stress currently being placed upon human resource management. This chapter is concerned with post-compulsory education in Britain. However, the arguments developed here have a wider currency and the debates considered move beyond a narrow concern with post-compulsory education, touching on a whole range of issues.

The narrow agenda for this chapter is to explore a number of themes and questions dealing with quality, managerialism and the development of alternative practices within post-compulsory education and training. However, these concerns should be seen as part of a much larger and broader canvas.

> The need for FE colleges to look to efficiency and effectiveness, and the need to improve participation and attainment, are inescapable. Educational ideals and economic realities are not necessarily mutually exclusive, as long as appropriate changes in organisational and curricular management, and in teaching and learning, can be effected.
>
> (FEU, 1991b, p. 3)

QUALITY

Thatcherism generalized market relations across society. Areas which were formerly seen as separated from market influence became increasingly tied to its logic. The language of the consumer figured in much of this discussion and is an ever-present feature in the quality discourse. In this discourse, no matter what our location, we are all consumers and producers.

Few teachers will object in principle to the notion that their customers should have the same rights as they enjoy as consumers. However, there is a substantial difference between complaining about a badly serviced car and complaints about literacy rates or GCSE results. The principle is the same but the measures to be applied and the variables operating are very different.

(West-Burnham, 1992, p. 4)

Market relations are generalized not only across sites but within them (Funnell and Muller, 1991). Such relations are deemed equally well suited to the further education college as to the car plant. For example, at Nissan in Sunderland the next worker down the line consumes the preceding worker's product (Garrahan and Stewart, 1992). Similarly the lecturer produces a lecture for students who become consumers; the print room produces photocopies to be consumed by managers or lecturers; cleaners produce clean working environs and so on. In *Quality Matters*, the centrality of consumer relations is raised:

> The concept of customers and their requirements is applied inside organisations as well as outside them ... Everyone is at times a supplier, and at others a customer, and this applies to all levels in the hierarchy. Internally, therefore, it places equal accountability in all directions and means that both internal and external customer requirements, needs and expectations must all be clarified, negotiated and clearly understood.
>
> (FEU, 1991b, p. 7)

A number of mechanisms have been proposed to deliver quality and among these the British Standard (BS 5750) or ISO 9000 (International Organization for Standardization) have been used. However, such mechanisms are widely seen as overly bureaucratic and of themselves unable to deliver quality.

> However, the emphasis on documenting procedures is not in itself the introduction of a total quality approach. Inherent in ISO 9000 is the danger that documentation will take over the process and that the organisation will become committed not to quality management, but to the production of quality documentation ... ISO 9000 ... only facilitates changes in procedures not people.
>
> (Funnell and Muller, 1991, p. 8)

Such procedures can actually form a distraction from the delivery of quality, becoming bogged down in red tape. However, alongside these mechanisms sits a complementary view of the delivery of quality which sees it not so much as concerned with an eventual output but rather as being embedded in the production process. In this case quality becomes a dynamic process of continuous improvement. At all stages of production there is, or rather should be, a keen commitment to the delivery of quality. It is within this context that the marketization of work relations plays a part with its consumerist model of employees being both producers and consumers located in internal and external markets. It is here that the notion of ownership is pivotal – that is to say, ownership of one's own labour and of the organization's mission. This idea parodies the Marxist call for worker control and ownership of the means of production as a means to overcoming alienated labour and capitalist exploitation. In the context of quality, ownership becomes rhetorically refocused. It is about the responsible worker controlling his or her own production process, being attentive to consumer requirements which supposedly have been set by the dictates of the market. This market is effectively a gloss for management strategies in the case of internal markets and for capitalist ones externally.

The level of autonomy facilitated by production processes varies. For teachers in further education it is relatively wide, albeit constrained by the development of tighter curricular models such as NVQs and by the move towards appraisal, team teaching and the like – all of which represent incursions into teacher autonomy. It is important to note that the quality model which derives from industrial practice is claimed to be generalizable to all sites. Ozga reminds us of the importance of placing teachers' work within a labour process context and suggests that

> The education literature ignores debates on industrial relations and power that surround these issues in the literature on management and organisation theory. These debates continue and are supported by detailed case studies. Work that attempts to disclose what is really going on in the new industrial relations of post-Fordist, post-modern business and managerialism.
>
> (Ozga, forthcoming, p. 20)

Central to models of quality is the notion of ownership, and sitting alongside it is the concept of continuous improvement or *Kaizen*. Garrahan and Stewart (1992) suggest that *Kaizen* is concerned with appropriating workers' knowledge of how to do the job, in which 'knowledge of the task is divested of its private, or specific skill content' (p. 76). They write: 'The *Kaizen* process represents the institutionalisation of this appropriation of workers' knowledge, by means of an internal job evaluation process which is compulsory for all workers' (p. 76). Thus, problem-solving and continuous improvement become a part of everyone's job, becoming 'an apparatus of surveillance and control that by definition excludes the *framework* for other world views' (Garrahan and Stewart, 1992, p. 76).

These elements enter into the notion of responsible autonomy and play a part in shaping the conceptualization of empowerment. The worker/lecturer is to be empowered so as to contribute to processes of continual improvement. Personal empowerment thereby ensures the delivery of quality. There are, however, a few impediments that may hinder the process. An appropriate culture needs to be generated that can handle continuous improvement. A dimension of this would include a culture of change which attempts to secure suitable attitudes and values among employees. It is here that leadership and direction are required: leadership that facilitates or enables empowerment, allowing workers to fulfil their potential.

> This change of climate [culture] is led by senior managers following an awareness and training programme which is designed to harness their commitment to continuous improvement and equip them with understanding and skills of TQM [Total Quality Management] principles and practice.
>
> (FEU, 1991b, p. 6)

> It is through the empowering of individuals that organisations change, but it is through the leadership qualities of individuals that the culture for change is created.
>
> (Funnell and Muller, 1991, p. 11)

> Leadership is enabling others to work towards long-term goals and seeing through the long term implications of institutional change.
>
> (*ibid.*, p. 173)

We are all to be empowered but on a terrain that is set by others and according to a logic that presupposes it is meeting human needs but which may in fact be antithetical to this. Where resistance is met, it is interpreted in a number of ways. One of these is to put it down to the holding of an incorrect organizational culture – one rooted, for example, in an earlier decade. As Sallis and Hingley (1992) write, 'Many people, particularly in middle management, may find total quality difficult to accept and to implement' (p. 16). This is because they have failed to appreciate the benefits of quality for themselves, the organization and their clients. The solution to this problem is through training and education to encourage a change in attitudes whereby, for example, middle management redefine themselves as facilitators rather than simply being in charge. Flowing through all these discussions is the notion that consensus is easily obtainable – that all of us through rational processes can and will be able to see quite clearly the benefits of such a management regime organized around quality. We should all be able to see the benefits of increased organizational efficiency, effectiveness and sensitivity towards clients. Within this type of discourse, critical debates are sidestepped. What, for example, are the politics of efficiency, effectiveness and consumerist relations? In place of such debate we are offered vision, culture and empowerment.

To the extent that we are empowered, it is to control our own labour process and to accept uncritically mission statements and notions of quality derived elsewhere. These debates have far more to do with shaping subjectivity than with skill development. However, they also provide spaces for subversion, as reflected in Brown and Lauder's (1992b) arguments which point to the radical potential of post-Fordist work relations. In Chapter 3 we argued that the radical potential of post-Fordist forms has been overstated. In some organizations these developments may offer progressive possibilities but these are inevitably constrained. On a localized level the limits and possibilities need to be explored. The rhetoric and practice of quality may not only offer control of one's own labour power but may also provide a stance from which to influence a particular institution. There is no necessary relation here and the spaces provided will be dependent on workplace struggle and management strategies. Hatcher (1994) argues forcibly, when writing about managerialism and schools, that the notion of a common consensus, a shared vision within particular schools, is bound to fail. This failure derives from the endemic conflicts present within work relations and additionally represents the play of antagonisms present within the wider society. A parallel argument can be made with respect to post-compulsory education. Calls for consensus can at best create a contrived collegiality (A. Hargreaves, 1994) and at worst be solely rhetorical.

It is easy enough to argue that the quality debate is a gloss for the increased control and surveillance of labour and represents, in Foucauldian terms, a technology of the self. In other words, these debates are concerned with moves towards self-control. Such discourses generate a particular truth about society and relations within it. Unsurprisingly, assumptions held by curriculum modernizers, policy-makers, political parties and the champions of the quality movement are similar. They are all located within the rhetoric of post-Fordist arguments, seemingly accepting unequivocally the possibility of a high-trust, high-skill society (see Chapter 3). Stanton's (1992) paper, 'The contribution of Further Education colleges to delivering NVQs', provides a case in point. Here, a clear link is made between notions embedded in the quality discourse and those held by curriculum modernizers. Table 5.1 illustrates some of the conceptual affinities between the two discourses.

While a number of these terms have been explored earlier in this chapter, it is important to recognize their individualized construction. This can be seen in the understanding given to empowerment and ownership, in the construction of the employee/

Table 5.1 *Key notions: quality compared with curriculum modernizers*

Modernizers' discourse	Quality discourse
Ownership	Ownership
Empowerment	Empowerment
Process	Process
Learner-centred	Employee-centred
Learner responsibility	Employee responsibility
Problem-solving/action planning	*Kaizen*/continuous improvement
Teamwork	Teamwork

learner, in action planning and, paradoxically, in conceptions of teamwork. Teams are rather less collective than might otherwise be thought. Individuals act in teams in pursuit of their own individualized action plan. This can be compared to socialist constructions of collective work which attempt to transcend individualized difference. Ownership and empowerment are placed on terrains which have been set by others but do nevertheless represent some gains over Fordist work relations. At the same time they illustrate the appropriation of progressive/radical language by conservative forces (Fielding, 1988). *Kaizen,* action planning, continuous improvement, learner/employee-centredness/responsibility all represent the generation and encouragement of greater reflection by the learner/employee on the process of learning or production. The form of reflection encouraged is a technology of the self. A form of confessional is developed which promotes an exploration of the self with a view to overcoming its flaws and improving the processes of learning and production. In the quality movement, the banalities of Thatcherism have been applied to all relations. In whatever sphere we operate, we are all consumers and producers. Similarly social and work relations have been set on a technicized basis. A notion of technical rationality is present, the concern is to enhance performance without engaging in a critique or in reflection around the social relations in which work is placed. It is through this silence that the quality debate becomes appropriated by a conservative logic. The way in which a technicized logic is taken for granted becomes apparent in the affinity between quality and managerialism. Quality represents a particular manifestation of the new managerialism in education.

MANAGERIALISM

The quality debate within post-compulsory education and training reflects the significance and growth of managerialism. In industry, managers have struggled to secure their right to manage, and within the public services this process has been reflected in the transmogrification of administrators and senior professionals into managers (Pollitt, 1993; Clarke *et al.*, 1994). Hoggett (1994) writes:

> It seems to me that the new strategy of control [in the welfare state] is quite different to the previous bureaucratic one: rather than try and control professionals by managers, you convert professionals into managers (i.e., by giving them budgets or by setting them adrift as quasi-autonomous business units).
>
> (Hoggett, 1994, p. 43)

These processes have served to redefine work relations and definitions of professionalism within the public services. Power has been shifted away from the professional towards management. Pollitt (1993) suggests there are a number of features of managerialism:

- the main route to social progress now lies through the achievement of continuing increases in economically defined productivity;
- such productivity increases will mainly come from the application of ever more sophisticated technologies. These include information and organisational technologies as well as the technological hardware for producing material goods ...
- the application of these technologies can only be achieved with a labour force 'disciplined in accordance with the productivity ideal' (Alvesson, 1987, p. 158).
- 'Management' is a separate and distinct organisational function and one that plays the crucial role in planning, implementing and measuring the necessary improvements in productivity. 'Business success will depend increasingly on the qualities and professionalism of managers' (Reid, 1988, p. i).
- to perform this crucial role managers must be granted reasonable 'room to manoeuvre (i.e. the "right to manage")'.

(Pollitt, 1993, pp. 2–3)

These managerial themes have impacted upon post-compulsory education, being reflected in concerns with efficiency, effectiveness, customer responsiveness and in allied issues surrounding performance-related pay, appraisal and accountability.

Clarke *et al.* (1994) argue that a new settlement is being formed over welfare in the 1990s that is organized around managerialism. Managerialism represents a shift in the relations of power between professionals and managers with the latter being placed in a dominant position. It also carries in its wake changes in the relation between the state, welfare and professionalism. The way in which these changes impact on different welfare sectors will be variable. Within post-compulsory education, administrative/managerial power has historically been held by non-teaching principals. Colleges have often been engaged in marketing their courses, with some form of entrepreneurial activity being a recurring feature – the development of GCE O/A-level teaching, the involvements with Youth Opportunities Programmes, the development of access courses, etc. (Tipton, 1973; Venables, 1967, 1974; Cantor and Roberts, 1983). However, what is new about the current circumstances is the attack on professionalism, the increased stress placed on effectiveness, efficiency and customer responsiveness, and the acceptance of a quasi-post-Fordism as a paradigm for economic development.

At the centre of managerialism lies a technicist logic. It is implied that political interference within welfare organizations serves to undercut their effectiveness. Thus it follows that if managers are given the right to manage, organizations will become more effective. Political involvement provides a distraction that limits organizational effectiveness, as do bureaucratic forms endemic in local and national government. If welfare organizations are freed from such constraints they will be more effective. It becomes the role of the state to set targets for particular organizations and to allow management to manage with these in mind. Within managerialism there is an emerging model of the relationship between the state and welfare providers. The state, whether centralized or localized mechanisms, is to be a regulator and not a provider of services. Here we enter the world of quasi-markets and competitive relations, tendering and so on – all of which supposedly enhance quality and effectiveness (Le Grand and Bartlett, 1993). It is within the state as regulator that we meet with performance indicators, targets, appraisal and performance-related pay. Pollitt (1993) describes these as representing neo-Taylorism – the attempt to introduce forms of measurement in order to assess and enhance performance as well as imposing accountability. The introduction of neo-Taylorism has engendered much resistance throughout the welfare state. In further education, the ongoing struggle over national bargaining, changed conditions, hostility to appraisal and refusal to accept performance-related pay is indicative of this resistance (see issues of *The Lecturer*, 1993–95). Yet alongside this trajectory sits another managerialist current that is in apparent contradiction to neo-Taylorism – the quality debate explored earlier in this chapter. The arguments surrounding quality are rooted in management theories that are historically linked to the human relations school (Mayo, 1945). The idea here is that a committed and motivated workforce will perform well. Whilst this is clearly rooted in managerialist forms and in the transportation of ideas developed in the industrial/business sector, there are nevertheless some affinities with professionalism. These affinities have often been ignored, with professionalism and managerialism being placed in opposition to one another (see, for example, Hatcher, 1994; Clarke *et al.*, 1994). Certainly there is a power relation here, as between any occupational groups within capitalist societies in which privileges accruing to one may be at the expense of another (see Weber, 1948). The discordant feature hinges upon the question of altruism and the public service ethos which many see as inherent in professionalism (see Chubb and Moe, 1990, for a New Right critique and Illich, 1973, for a radical critique). Within teaching, this notion, coupled with the power of professional knowledge, has been part of the rhetoric used to sustain a level of independence and autonomy from the diktat of management and others. In the post-war period, this notion of autonomy and independence has been built upon legitimated teacher professionalism, with autonomy in the classroom gained at the expense of wider political engagements. Teaching was to be devoid of politics (Grace, 1987). Strangely enough, within managerialism we also see an evacuation of politics. Management is to be engaged in by those who have the skills and knowledge to manage. Holmes writes:

> Informal educational discussion constantly reveals individual values and clashes of values. *Certain of these value clashes are beyond the ambit of school-level debate. If governments and others with a statutory stake in the process and outcomes of schooling wish to legislate, direct or otherwise order changes in schooling then they may do so. To oppose such change other than through the (admittedly often cursory) opportunities for consultation is to engage in a different level of activity which is essentially political.* Of course much of the current agenda for educational change appears to many teachers to be grounded in values and visions which they find inimical; many educationalists hold values about teaching and learning which are in direct contradiction to what they perceive as being 'done' to them. *What you as the school leader can do is to lead these debates by clarifying what is beyond the school remit – and therefore non-negotiable – as opposed to what is worth negotiating.*
>
> (Holmes, 1993, p. 28, emphasis added)

In both managerialism and teacher professionalism there is the construction of technical expertise and an apparent distancing from wider political and social structures. Whilst managerialism represents the incursion of a capitalist market-orientated logic into educational relations, teacher professionalism was also prey to a form of technicism that implied the teacher *qua* professional had the skill and expertise to be an effective pedagogue. In spite of all its faults, there is a paradoxical way in which managerialism carries with it a democratizing impulse by raising questions of accountability. These also force reflection upon the conditions and framework in which managers and welfare state professionals operate.

It would be wrong to view managerialism as a management charter in which one occupational group gained ascendancy over another. Clarke *et al.* (1994) rightly assert that once the goals of managerialism are achieved there is nowhere else to go (see also Pollitt, 1993). Once efficiency gains are made and workers labour effectively, the task has been accomplished. This indicates the bankruptcy of managerialism. Managers are just that: they operate on a terrain that has been set and defined by others. Where the question of vision and mission arises it is set within externally defined constraints.

The ethos of managerialism is to apply to management as much as to any other group; the Cheshire Educational Management Programme (CEMP) provides an example (Quinlan, 1991). Whilst this scheme is organized around a trait- or competency-based model, it also contains a number of the tenets of human resource management.

> CEMP is a framework and process for management and organisational development. It is not an off-the-shelf solution and it is not a management training course. At the heart of the process is a personal review. It is through the review that the achievements and potential of individuals are recognised, learning opportunities that satisfy the needs of the individual and the organisation are identified, and regular, systematic feedback on performance is ensured.
>
> (Quinlan, 1991, p. 1)

Central to the CEMP strategy is the use of reviews which are akin to profiling or of records of achievement (see Quinlan, 1991, p. 23). The outcome of the review is to determine individual learning contracts which facilitate individual growth in line with organizational needs.

> The CEMP process is designed to:
> replace *ad-hoc*ery with planning by:
> * systematic individual needs identification
> * planned and progressive learning opportunities
> * monitoring and evaluation
>
> support the organisation by:
> * working within the existing management structure
> * emphasising organisational purpose
> * placing management learning in the context of organisational need
>
> respect the individual by:
> * recognising the unique needs of individuals
> * supporting managers throughout their career
> * empowering the individual to be responsible for personal development
>
> achieve value for money by:
> * recognising the value of work-based learning
> * targeting learning opportunities to need
> * increasing learning opportunities within budget
>
> (Quinlan, 1991, p. 1)

CEMP criticizes existing management programmes for being too far removed from the needs of specific educational institutions. The goal is to link management development to particular organizational needs. There is the assumption that some sort of consensus over organizational goals is achievable and that the creation of a learning culture within an organization is feasible. There appears to be little conflict between the needs of personal development and those of the organization. Management development is to mark out and prepare the person for progression. It is, as with staff development, an entitlement through which individual needs are respected and personal growth encouraged.

ENTITLEMENT
All managers need regular management development if they are to become and remain effective within the organisation. Management development is not just 'toolkit' or 'survival' training, which implies merely a reaction to external pressure for change. *It is to do with personal growth in a changing environment. This cannot be optional. The concept of entitlement in Cheshire therefore means that all managers have the right but also the responsibility to develop professionally throughout their career.*

(Quinlan, 1991, p. 6, emphasis added)

At the centre of this process of management development lies organizational need. This notion of need is a reification and becomes objectified and taken for granted. There is a failure to take on board seriously the struggle over the notion of need and organizational development. These are determined as a result of political processes within and outside of organizations. Once such a notion of struggle is taken on board the easy relation between the person, the organization and shared goals becomes fragmented and with it the implicit assumption that individual and organizational needs are in harmony. This policing element is recognized by Quinlan when he suggests that mentor/peer review can tend towards voluntarism and weak organizational commitment.

[CEMP] is an instrument that emphasises the responsibility of individuals for their own professional development, but also provides a means of opening up the process to management scrutiny to ensure quality and recognition of achievement.

(Quinlan, 1991, p. 18)

It is suggested that the CEMP method can be extended throughout an organization. This is mirrored in arguments about appraisal in which, in an apparently benign process, those in higher positions police those below them. This really does become a technology of the self – an attempt to shape organizational culture and forms of subjectivity. There is an affinity between this particular initiative, managerialism and the quality debate. We are all to develop our subjectivities in a particular direction and failure to do so indicates our unsuitability and unwillingness to engage in the personal development warranted in post-Fordist organizations.

Within these discussions there are common concerns about the management of labour, attempts to generate organizational effectiveness and instituting forms of labour flexibility. Handy (1989) in *The Age of Unreason* discusses the Shamrock organization in which there is a tripartite division of labour. At the centre lies a core of highly paid and qualified skilled, managerial and professional workers who are expected to exhibit high levels of commitment. They are surrounded by a contractual fringe of self-employed professionals and low-skilled, part-time, temporary workers occupying a servicing role. Such patterns can easily be seen in post-compulsory education and training; demands being placed on full-time teaching staff, the overwhelming imperative to provide quality on the basis of fewer resources carrying in its wake management by stress and the intensification of labour. Also evident is a growth in the use of part-timers and temporary contracts to provide flexibility to respond to market changes, and the low-waged rump of cleaners and caterers. The development of such labour patterns is hardly benign and for all sections of the labour force it carries heightened costs. The gendered basis of high-level commitment and the ever-present dangers of burn-out, together with the insecurities of temporary and low-waged employment, are quite apparent. The paradox is that these changes are presented in a benign form warranted by economic imperatives and the move to a post-modern world of continuous change.

MANAGERIALISM AND THE CURRICULUM

Within this section, we focus on the relation between quality, managerialism and curricular issues. There is a continuity with discussions in earlier chapters, for underpinning curricular models are assumptions concerning society, the economy and a future set within the globalization of economic and social relations. The major interventions attempting to shape the development of post-compulsory education and training are married to an analysis of the British economy that places a premium upon the development of human capital, which is seen as a means of overcoming the secular decline of the economy.

> The UK faces a world of increasing change; of ever fiercer global competition; of growing consumer power, *and a world in which our wealth is more and more dependent on the knowledge, skills and motivation of our people.*
>
> (Board of Trade, 1994, p. 6, emphasis added)

Sentiments embracing 'the skills and motivation of our people' are repeated in various guises in the policy literature. Robertson, writing of this new consensus, states:

> the pursuit of student choice and flexibility commands widespread support in principle. It conveniently unites the radicals of the Right (markets, freedom of choice) and of the Left (democratic participation, student empowerment) against the conservatives of the Right (élite participation and the preservation of standards) and of the Left (sovereignty of the academic, supremacy of the unified course, the student as apprentice).
>
> (HEQC, 1994, p. 119)

> Political differences *between* Left and Right seem to be less significant than differences *within* the various segments between 'radicals' and 'romantics' of the Left and Right opposing [the new consensus], than there is between the radicals and the romantics of either Left or Right. *In other words, there appears to be a common agenda across the political spectrum to introduce greater flexibility and student choice, to encourage markets within higher education and to expand access. This is likely to embrace student loans, a personal commitment to learning and an acceptance that professional academic sovereignty should not remain a barrier to the achievements of these objectives.*
>
> (*ibid.*, p. 334, emphasis added)

He implies that amongst 'right'-minded people of Left and Right, education is seen as the vehicle of national economic recovery. However, if this is to be enacted it calls for fundamental change in the pattern of post-compulsory education. These changes revolve around issues of *equity, participation* and *democracy* (Robertson, 1995a, 1995b). Clearly, Robertson recognizes that there are others, perhaps romantically inclined, who are attached to older educational forms which celebrate archaic and esoteric disciplines. For them, such disciplinary conventions fail to develop in students, or should we say learners, the interdisciplinarity and personal and transferable skills that are required in conditions of post-modernity. More insidious perhaps is the professional attachment of university lecturers to élitist educational practices (see HEQC, 1994; Robertson, 1995a, 1995b). While Robertson is at pains to distance himself from the accusation of managerialism, there are a number of resonances in the argument he advances. Similar tendencies are common in many of the constituents of the developing settlement over post-compulsory education.

The fiscal crisis of the welfare state highlights the importance of efficiency and effectiveness in educational provision at all levels. In order to facilitate this, new forms of educational governance have been developed, as witnessed by the FEFC and the TECs which provide funding and operate within a framework of targets and performance indicators set by the state. Incorporation has similarly offered institutions an apparent autonomy, creating a management cadre. The desire to free-up student choice through the development of training or learning credits and some form of higher education voucher is part of the marketization and commodification of education, but also, and importantly, is part of a desire to enhance student power and choice. The next chapter addresses these issues more directly. Thus, 'conservative' professional educators are pressured from two sides: first, through the increased power of management (see Hoggett, 1994, p. 43) and, second, through the extension of student choice. Robertson (1994, 1995a, 1995b) is not alone in calling for the development of credit systems (HEQC, 1994). Such systems would be embedded within a unitized or modular system of credit accumulation and transfer. In this way, students would be given the freedom to select a programme of study that suited their needs rather than those of their educators. They would be placed in a position of greater institutional mobility and the distinction between further and higher education would be eroded. A post-compulsory system developed within such a framework would thereby open up greater access. However, the full development of credit systems within modularized or unitized curricular frameworks necessitates a transformation in pedagogic and cultural relations.

Table 5.2 *Principles of a credit culture*

From	To
Exclusion	Inclusion
Teachers	Learner
Process	Outcome
Direction	Guidance
Failure	Achievement
Margins	Mainstream
Professional control	Individual choice
Structures	Culture

Source: HEQC, 1994, p. 315

This transformation carries with it changes in teacher professionalism and the balance of power between learners and lecturers – between consumers and providers. This commodification and marketization can be rewritten in terms of teacher accountability and the empowerment of learners. Learner needs are supposedly paramount, not those of the lecturer. But how are learner needs set within this discourse? Unsurprisingly, there is an affinity between the needs of the learner and those of the economy. Hayes, Fonda and Hillman (1995) in a National Commission on Education briefing paper suggest we are passing through an economic transformation towards a new form of society predicated upon a 'knowledge revolution'. Ideas such as these have been expressed by many aligned to the new settlement over post-compulsory education and training and are central to the notion of the learning society (see, for example, Walton, 1995; National Commission on Education, 1995). Yet again we meet with a happy coincidence of the needs of learners and capital. Increased participation and the democratization of education by meeting learner needs satisfies the needs of capital and the wider society. Curiously, within this discourse the democratization of education is couched in terms of increased participation and the accountability of lecturers to the learner *qua* consumer. The Commission on Social Justice states:

> the new competitive conditions of the global economy demand that we raise our productivity if we are to maintain, let alone improve our living standards and quality of life: neither protectionism, nor the low-cost, low value-added strategy offers a way forward. ... the revolution of technology, skill and organisation which is transforming the demand for and nature of work means that economic success increasingly depends upon *investment in human physical and social capital.*
>
> (Commission on Social Justice, 1994, p. 65)

Economic transformation becomes the route to a fairer, more just society. Unsurprisingly, at this stage there is a resonance with the myth of the post-Fordist society, the hegemony of economic interests, the failure to recognize patterns of antagonism, exploitation and oppressions and recognition of uneven economic development (see Chapter 3). This sits alongside changes in the labour market which herald what Ainley (1993, 1994) refers to as workless growth – education without jobs. The prioritizing of economic imperatives sets capitalist interests over and above all others, and views the modernization of capital as the route towards societal renewal. Such a standpoint is deeply flawed, as Ainley recognizes, for it ignores the necessity to develop economic patterns that are attentive to human need, third world issues and ecological sustainability (Ainley, 1994, 1995; and see also Lipietz, 1993). Issues of social justice, citizenship and the development of education systems that address these transcend narrowly economic interests. The assumption of an inherent unity of purpose between learners and capital glosses over very real points of antagonism.

The managerialist appropriation of curricular issues in post-compulsory education and training is contradictory. A settlement that draws together Left and Right can be seen to move beyond outdated political dualities but simultaneously carries within it the tensions between the two standpoints. In itself, the development of a credit culture could be progressive. However, the difficulty lies in the way in which it has been wedded to economic needs and the modernization of the British economy. This is readily discernible in discussion around personal and transferable skills. Within further education this discussion was held some years ago, but it is a current issue within higher education (see Avis, 1991b). The call for higher education to develop personal and transferable skills is almost fraudulent. The work of Brown and Scase (1994) and Ainley (1994) is central to this discussion, as they indicate the way in which these 'skills' have far more to do with class origins and cultural capital than with the outcomes of educational processes.

> [personal and transferable skills] are neither personal, transferable, nor skills; they are social and generic competences ... To present attitudes and habits detached from their cultural context as technical abilities that can be acquired piecemeal in performance not only divorces them from the cultural context that gave them their original meaning but represents them as equally accessible to all students whatever their class cultural background, gender or race. It ignores the fact that middle-class students already possess many of these competences as a result of their previous education and family socialisation. As Bourdieu pointed out, even if middle-class students do not already have all these social abilities, their previous experience lays the foundation on which to build them.
>
> For at rock bottom the real 'personal' and 'transferable' skills required for preferential employment are those of whiteness, maleness and traditional middle-classness. These are the really generic social competences that are most acceptable to most employers.
>
> (Ainley, 1994, p. 80)

This work indicates a real paradox. The move towards core skills within further education was concerned with validating the range of skills and potential that students possessed. There was a progressive interest in recognizing the achievements of those who failed academically – for the most part working-class young people – and this was not only reflected in discussion around core skills but also profiling (see for example, FEU, 1982, 1984). In the higher education context, personal and transferable skills, rather than opening up opportunity, serve as a form of closure, deepening middle-class forms of social and cultural reproduction. Whilst this reflects class-based processes of occupational recruitment which are in need of modernization, it does indicate the way in which industrial, commercial and class interests distort educational processes. Perhaps discussion of personal and transferable skills is a diversion, but it does indicate the way in which skill can never be technicized and is always social. The managerialist current has attempted to appropriate the curriculum so that it serves economic interests. This is often portrayed in terms of a curriculum modernization that is learner-centred and that enhances the power of the student to exercise greater control over their learning. However, behind this concern is a real attempt to develop in learners the skills and aptitudes required within the economic system. Personal and transferable skills, student profiling, the modernization of the curriculum and the development of a credit culture are all part of this process. It is one in which a veneer of learner control is underpinned by a desire to shape student/learner subjectivity. It is here that we have a regime of truth that portrays its singular interests as universal and as being able to satisfy the tenets of social justice. Yet at the same time this whole language can be used to subvert itself and move beyond its narrow economism into the realm of radical democracy. For, as Foucault reminds us, all discourse is dangerous and meanings cannot totally be secured.

MANAGERIALISM AND POST-MODERN CONDITIONS

Hargreaves (1994) develops an argument akin to that of Brown and Lauder (1992b) (see Chapter 3) in which he explores the progressive possibilities that inhere in post-Fordist or, more correctly, post-modern social relations. It is important to consider his argument as it is lodged within a similar framework to that posited by post-Fordism and managerialism. We are offered a vision of societies marked by continuous change, a First World in which cultural and technological skills provide value-addedness for products; a world in which the grand narratives of socialism and capitalism have been unpacked and where the local and specific is as important as the international. In such conditions organizational restructuring becomes essential. Hargreaves explores various interpretations of this and favours forms of restructuring that stress collaboration. He writes:

> Restructuring tries to address the emerging learning needs of the post-industrial, post-modern age and the more flexible structures of schooling that are required to meet those needs effectively. It seeks to create alternative learning environments to meet continuing and contemporary student needs.
>
> (A. Hargreaves, 1994, p. 242)

He views such restructuring in a post-modern age as warranting the development of cultures of empowerment and collegiality.

> If restructuring is, in some fundamental sense, about the reconstruction of school power relations, then we would expect the working lives of teachers to be organised not around

principles of hierarchy and isolation, but ones of collaboration and collegiality. Indeed, while there are many meanings of restructuring, the principle of collaboration has become central to almost all of them, be this collaboration among teachers, or between teachers and principals, parents and the wider community.

Collaboration has come to comprise a *metaparadigm* of educational and organisational change in the postmodern age.

(ibid., p. 244)

Hargreaves provides a very sophisticated and worked-out view of both the post-modern world and organizational structures and the relations that such a conjuncture requires in order to meet human needs. He stresses the contradictions and paradoxes that lie within post-modern forms. This can be seen, for example, in his discussion of contrived collegiality, or in his awareness of the danger of moral and political relativism and stasis. The solution at a school level, and by implication at a national and world level, is to reject notions of scientific certainty and move instead to those of situational certainty. Situational certainty derives not from the workings of scientific truth and knowledge, which are rendered problematic within post-modernism, but rather through open and honest discussion and dialogue that operate across a wide constituency and that respect the knowledge, skills and forms of expertise that various groups bring to the encounter. So, for example, in schools this constituency would include parents, teachers, managers, students and members of the wider community. Within such a broad constituency, conflict would be endemic or at least likely to arise over some issues. Such conflict would be resolved on the basis of dialogue, argument and by recourse to ethical principles. Hargreaves cites his own preferred values: 'From my own value standpoint, the principles of equity, excellence, justice, partnership, care for others and global awareness should be high on that agenda' *(ibid., p. 259)*.

His discussion is similar to those which have argued for a reconstituted professionalism organized around empowerment and dialogue (see, for example, Avis, 1991a, 1994). Hargreaves is well aware of the social contexts within which schools are placed and warns against forms of parochialism that can lead to limited interventions which effectively reproduce existing patterns of inequality. What then is the difficulty with his argument – an argument that is full and paradoxical in a 'truly' post-modern form? The difficulties become most apparent in his concluding chapter which, if we understand its purpose, is to bring together the kernel of his argument in order to point the way forward. The democratization of relations over schooling is important, as is the recognition of conflict and uncertainty. The tyranny of truth is rendered deeply problematic and the necessity to bring to the fore ethical principles for open contestation is stressed. Important questions about the nature of power remain. Post-modern analyses have been criticized for their relativism and in response have incorporated ethical principles (see Squires, 1993). The relativism of post-modernism derives from its attack on science and the easy certainties of the grand narratives of our time – socialism, social democracy and feminism, and now, New Right conservatism. As with post-Fordism we are offered a world in which the 'knowledge' worker is the key to economic progress. And it appears as if the economic realities of capitalist exploitation are able to be transcended. Hargreaves recognizes that education and therefore political structures and people need to engage with issues of under- and unemployment but it is as if these issues can be satisfactorily handled within a post-modern society. In other words, post-modern societies represent a higher stage of social development in which capitalism is amenable to control and in which the basis of antagonism between labour and capital has been overcome. It is for this reason that the work of organizational theorists is so appealing in that Kanter (1989), Peters (1987) and Handy (1989) celebrate the empowering possibilities of waged labour. We are offered a discourse of progress that has side-stepped the grand narrative of socialism – that recognizes its paradoxical nature but because of the way in which power is dispersed or decentred refuses a class-based politics (see Hatcher, 1994). Exactly the same form of analysis could be applied to the structures of race and gender. These absences mean we are offered a limited notion of power, conflict and struggle. All these terms are used and indeed could be argued to be at the centre of discussion, yet the logic of the argument implies they can be transcended, worked through and that a working consensus based on ethical principles can be accomplished. But there is a neglect of any fundamental sense of antagonism around, for example, class, race, gender, sexuality, and even globalization. An ethical discourse needs to handle these issues but how can we recognize our positionality, our stakes in particular social relations? Who is included in this post-modern constituency – an alliance of curriculum modernizers, big business and educational enterprisers (Mac an Ghaill, 1992)? This takes us back to some of the issues discussed in Chapter 3. How does an inclusive 'we' manage debate across incommensurate traditions? How do we handle questions of justice and citizenship? The strength of Hargreaves' argument is that it breaks the link between post-modern/post-Fordist arguments and capitalist hegemony; the paradox is that simultaneously it becomes trapped within this hegemony.

CONCLUSION

This chapter has been wide-ranging. The breadth of discussion is important as it explores the limits and possibilities surrounding managerialism and the development of new work relations. There is an affinity between post-Fordism, organizational theory, managerialism and descriptions of post-modern societies. We can see within these processes the emergence of a regime of truth. Foucault writes:

> Each society has its regime of truth, its general politics of truth: that is, the types of discourses which it accepts and makes function as true; the mechanisms and instances which enable one to distinguish true and false statements, the means by which each is sanctioned; the techniques and procedures accorded value in the acquisition of truth; the status of those who are charged with saying what counts as true.
>
> (Foucault, 1980, p. 131)

Within this emerging regime we can see many of the tenets of post-modernism:

- the end of the grand narrative in terms either of the evils of capitalism or its benefits;
- the centrality of the local and particular;
- the importance of the individual and the possibilities inherent in work for an optimistic future organized around human need.

Many of these themes have been taken up in managerialism, the quality movement and by the gurus of organizational theory. The suggestion that capitalism is based on exploitation and oppression is seen as untenable. Some capitalist organizations may indeed operate in such a way but this cannot be generalized across all. In order to succeed, an organization needs to develop the skills, motivation and commitment of its workforce. The way this is played out in particular locales will be important. Yet any organization will have to be attentive to questions of efficiency and this will apply equally to private as well as state ventures. In this regime of truth, the distinctions between the public and private sector, the state and industry and other similar dualities have been transcended. The old polarities are breaking down and with this comes much greater uncertainty and the need for flexibility. These themes constitute part of a regime of truth that is difficult to argue against.

However, against the optimism of managerialism, the quality debate and post-modernism sits the presence of capitalist social relations, patriarchal and racist structures. These structures pose a limit on the progressive possibilities that inhere in this regime of truth and the challenge is to think beyond them. Managerialism and organizational theory are concerned with the extraction of surplus labour and it is for this reason that apparently progressive management practices and rhetoric sit alongside neo-Taylorism. This is quite as apparent in post-compulsory education in the 1990s as it is in what remains of the welfare state. It is within such a framework of ideas that we are now located and which provide the terrain on which we are to struggle. Sawicki has argued: 'No discourse is inherently liberating or oppressive. The liberatory status of any theoretical discourse is a matter of historical inquiry, not theoretical pronouncement' (Sawicki, 1988, p. 166). It is also important to recognize the articulation between the global economic context, the local and the particular. The changes that have impacted upon post-compulsory education have to be understood in the light of this context. A recognition of this serves to illuminate the contradiction and presence within managerialism of a concern to generate value-addedness amongst employees through the use of strategies deriving from human resource management, yet also drawing upon neo-Fordist strategies that aim to reduce labour costs.

In part, this chapter has explored the context in which post-compulsory education is placed. There are possibilities for struggle. Many of the themes present in the discourse of managerialism, the quality movement and new organizational theory can be used to gain advantage. The humanistic rhetoric of many of these discourses can be turned back on itself and the contradictions explored to develop progressive alternatives on both a local, national and international basis. This is particularly the case with curricular arguments surrounding the credit culture. The stress upon issues of equity, democracy and participation opens up these debates for a reappropriation that undermines their economistic logic.

Up until now, we have considered the policy context within which post-compulsory education is placed. The following two chapters focus upon the lived experiences of young people in post-compulsory education and training and thus provide an essential complement to those preceding.

Chapter 6

Careership: The Individual, Choices and Markets in the Transition into Work

Phil Hodkinson

INTRODUCTION

Thus far, we have examined, and found wanting, much current thinking about education and work. A key question we have not yet addressed concerns the way in which such thinking and policy-making impacts on young people. For those believers of the fundamentalist doctrines of the New Right which underpin much of this thinking, the answer is attractively simple. Their answer rests upon unquestioned assumptions about a need to increase national economic competitiveness within a growing post-Fordist model of employment which produces a demand for cheap, flexible labour. It is primarily the responsibility of individual young people/trainees/adult workers to ensure they are trained to meet these new employment challenges, a stance justified by twin arguments: that government spending must be cut to free up enterprise, reduce the 'nanny state' and allow British industry to compete; and a belief that the fundamental unpredictability of future labour needs means that any planning is doomed to failure. The central mechanism to achieve greater individual responsibility as part of a supposed upskilling of the labour force to enhance Britain's competitiveness, is the development of an education and training market, where providers of training and educational services compete for the custom of young people and their parents.

This chapter concentrates on the workings of one of the first such markets to be created, in the field of youth training. It is based on the experiences of a small group of young people within the Training Credits[1] scheme. In this chapter, we argue that many of the assumptions of the new markets policy are unfounded empirically and that two central problems have to be faced. Firstly, even if taken at face value, current attempts to raise education and training standards are unlikely to succeed on their own terms. Secondly, the current discourse ignores and is unable to address some key questions about education and training quality, the balance between choice and constraint facing individual young people and the deeper-seated issues of inequality in society, explicitly those related to getting a job and/or training. Above all, we question the simplistic view of the nature of individualism that is implicit in almost all current thinking. Much of the argument and analysis presented here is derived from a research study recently carried out on one of the original Training Credits pilot schemes.[2] Before embarking on our critique, it is necessary first to outline briefly what the Training Credits scheme is and how it exemplifies many aspects of the new policy paradigm, together with a brief account of the actual research study upon which the analysis is based.

TRAINING CREDITS AND THE NEW SETTLEMENT

The new model of vocational education and training management in Britain assumes that the quality of provision can be improved through the measurement of outcomes and payment by results within a market context. Thus, it is claimed, if customers (parents, young people or employers) make informed choices of provision, then providers will have to improve their performance in order to sell their services (CBI, 1989, 1993; DES/DE, 1991). To create such a market, most funding for colleges or other training organizations is derived from recruitment. To mitigate the hard sell, customers are to be given 'objective' information to use for comparison, and 'neutral' guidance in decision-making. Increasingly, a significant proportion of the funding is held back until the young person has completed the course and achieved a qualification. This is intended to prevent inappropriate recruitment, reduce wasteful drop-outs (Audit Commission, 1993) and encourage higher levels of achievement.

As training providers respond to this new policy environment, management of quality is increasingly set against measurable performance indicators, within an unquestioned belief in new managerialism that we have analysed in the previous chapter. This trend is reinforced at a national level through the National Targets for Education and Training. These targets quantify a major government policy objective, which is to increase the numbers of young people achieving specified levels of qualification and thus, it is assumed, raising vocational education and training standards to meet international competition.

Within full-time education and training, markets and outcomes are reinforced by inspections of quality. There is no equivalent inspection system for part-time vocational training, possibly because this could be seen as interfering with the freedom of employers who provide most of the training, especially on the job. However, most Training and Enterprise Councils (TECs) have systems for approving training organizations.

National Vocational Qualifications (NVQs) play a key role in this new model. They are the main qualifications accepted for funding of Youth Training, and central to those National Targets for Education and Training that are quantifiable. Their focus on work-based learning and assessment is supposed to give tight employer relevance and control, though Field (1995) questions this. Their obsession with measured outcomes dovetails neatly with the drive for performance-related funding and informed markets.

Training Credits are the most complete example of this new vocational education and training model introduced thus far. Young people are issued with vouchers to spend, following provision of professional careers guidance focused on drawing up an individual action plan. All training is organized by approved trainers who have met TEC criteria. All training must lead to an NVQ, at level 2 or higher. Funding for training providers partly depends on the completion of a training programme and the successful award of the qualification.

The White Paper on vocational education and training and industrial performance

(White Paper, 1994) sets out this clearly individualist agenda. 'A fulfilled workforce meeting *individual targets*, driven by the will to perform to their *individual best*, will be a world class workforce' (p. 30, emphasis added). It goes on to commit the government to 'better careers education and guidance to help young people choose the best paths to their future' and 'greater responsiveness by providers to the needs of their customers – learners and employers – including closer examination of the learning credits approach to education and training' (p. 49). Learning credits are described as an extension of the Training Credits idea, to cover all education and training provision post-16.

Training Credits were piloted in eleven areas in England and Scotland from 1991 and in a further nine areas in a second pilot phase from 1993. Each scheme was managed by the local TEC (Local Enterprise Company in Scotland). Each pilot scheme was very different in character. This analysis is based on a study of one of the original pilot schemes, located in a predominantly rural area with a labour market dominated by small firms, with geographical variations in unemployment and an almost exclusively white population. Readers are referred to Coopers and Lybrand Deloitte (1992), DE (1993), MacDonald and Coffield (1993), Sims and Stoney (1993) and Unwin (1993) for details of other schemes. In 1991 the decision was made that Training Credits should cover the whole of England, Scotland and Wales by 1996. In the budget of 1993 the decision was announced to bring this national starting date forward to 1995.

THE TRAINING CREDITS IN ACTION PROJECT

In approaching this study, we were centrally concerned with the ways in which a diverse group of stakeholders (trainees, parents, careers teachers, careers officers, employers and training providers) perceived and made sense of the Training Credits initiative. We focused on the second cohort of Training Credits trainees, following a small group of young people from their final term in school until they were 15 months or more into their training. Sampling was in two stages. We began by interviewing 115 school pupils, mainly in small single-gender groups. Of these, 89 were in Year 11 and 26 in the sixth form, 59 were boys and 56 girls. They were attending six secondary schools, selected to give geographical spread because of the potential impact of the youth labour market on youth training (Banks *et al.*, 1992). Pupils were selected by their careers teachers as being likely to at least consider using Training Credits. We also interviewed careers officers and careers teachers from those schools.

From the 115 pupils, we selected 14 to follow through, though this was eventually reduced to 10. They were selected as interesting cases who would be using Training Credits – with a gender mix, from different geographical locations and working in different occupational areas. For each trainee we also interviewed parents, employer(s), training providers and those finding placements. All were interviewed periodically throughout the 18 months of the study, amounting to a total of 196 interviews in all.

As we analysed the data, we were struck by the diversity of experiences of the young people, and more especially by the ways in which they made career decisions and their career pathways developed. There seemed to be a marked contrast between the technically rational assumptions that underpinned the rationale and practice of the scheme, and the much more complex interactions of the young people themselves. What follows is a detailed model of career decision-making and development arising out of these data, which fundamentally challenges some of the policy assumptions of the new settlement. We have called this new model, *careership*. We hope this label signals the personal involvement in decision-making and development, and also the fundamental unpredictability of that pattern. It should be stressed that our conception of careership owes little to the CBI thinking (1989, 1993) where the term is used in a very different way. Firstly, it is necessary to outline some of the assumptions within the technical view of career development inherent in the official model.

TECHNICAL RATIONALITY IN CAREER DECISION-MAKING

The Training Credits initiative and the detailed operation of the scheme under investigation were based on a simplistic and mechanistic model of career decision-making, which Hodkinson and Sparkes (1993a) call *technically rational*. The notion of technical or instrumental rationality derives from what Habermas (1971, 1972) calls technical interests. Gibson (1986) defines it thus: 'Instrumental rationality ... is concerned with *method* and efficiency rather than with *purposes*. ... It is the divorce of fact from value, and the preference, in that divorce, for fact' (p. 7, original emphasis). In essence, life is seen as engineering, and people as machines. From this perspective, decision-making is a separated process which can be refined and made more efficient. This is to be done through providing more and better information and 'neutral' careers guidance. Another aspect of the inherent technicality can be seen in the systemic view of how decisions are taken. The decision-making process is seen as a production line along which the young person progresses, completing the decision stage by stage. In the scheme under investigation, young people had to complete a Careers Guidance Action Plan together with either a school tutor or a careers officer. This process required each young person to consider their own interests and strengths, then examine the labour market to identify the range of possible placements or jobs, and finally to draw up a training plan, specifying their training needs. The Training Credits could only be issued once this process had been completed. Such a technical view of decision-making assumes that the process is fundamentally unproblematic, beyond the engineering difficulty of improving information and guidance.

Many writers assume that decision-making is geared towards maximizing personal benefits, normally expressed in economic terms. Bennett *et al.* (1992) claimed that the key factor in career choices was the earning potential of different career routes. They write:

> We assume that, knowing their capacities and other personal characteristics, individuals form an estimate of expected earnings resulting from each education, training and labour market option, and, taking into account their taste for each, choose the stream which offers the greatest net utility.

(p. 13)

Technical rationality assumes decision-making is a conscious process which takes place in what Giddens (1984) calls discursive consciousness. By this he means the part of our thought which is made explicit and can be articulated through language. Furthermore, decision-making is normally seen as focused on long-term goals, so that a young person should identify the goal then plan out the steps towards it. Finally, intellectual notions of logic and rationality are seen as fundamental to any successful decision-making. Anything less than total rationality is seen as dysfunctional. In sum, technical rationality provides a model of idealized decision-making to be striven for, if never completely achieved, and a means to move towards it, through skilled guidance and provision of better information. It is assumed within the wider structures of a voucher-driven training market.

Many in the careers guidance community are suspicious of an overly individualistic approach. The final report of the National Educational Guidance Initiative (FEU, 1994) complained that 'the TECs and Employment Department have emphasised the individual psychological aspects of guidance rather than the social and collective. Resources are being channelled into psychometric testing but not into community-based guidance and outreach activities' (p. 12). This scepticism is reinforced and legitimated by the types of decision-making reported by young people in this study.

PRAGMATICALLY RATIONAL DECISION-MAKING

For the young people interviewed, actual career decision-making contrasted dramatically with the technical process described above. To begin with, choices were often derived from local contacts and/or through work experience.

> Body repair on cars [is what I want to do] ... Well, I got the information for work experience from my dad, and then asked them if I could work for the summer holidays, and then at the end of the summer he asked me if I wanted a job. It's interesting and you get to meet a lot of people. At the moment, I'll be doing rubbing down cars, a bit of spraying when I can ... My dad [got me into cars], he's a mechanic. She [mum] wasn't surprised because she knew I was going to end up in a man's job. It's mostly men that do it, but there's another girl where I'm working ... I doubt if I'd ever sort of go for that job if my dad wasn't a mechanic or anything. [I would have gone for] a window dresser in a clothes shop.
>
> (Helen)

Some of the pupils had particular interests which they wished to incorporate into careers and childhood ambitions sometimes survived.

> Well I've wanted to do that [caring] since I was seven. I wanted to be at work. First I wanted to be a nurse, then I was with my mum in hospital two or three weeks ago and decided I didn't want to be a nurse just in case my family was in there. So I decided to carry on with the disabled ... I've got a disabled family, disabled cousins and friends.
>
> (Jane)

Sometimes such experiences and contacts confirmed a developing choice. On other occasions the young person decided on something else.

> Mum's been a waitress for eight years. She said to me one day, 'We're really busy at work, do you want to come and wash pots?' That was about two years ago. I started washing pots as a Saturday job, and then I started like making the ploughman's in the summer, and did my work experience at a pub ... like doing kitchen staff and then as a chambermaid. And now I'm an actual waitress on Saturdays and Friday nights sometimes. ... He [my boss] said he'd be happy ... when I leave school to employ me for more days a week. I said I didn't want that. I wanted to go to college to take a two-year course then work my way up the ladder.
>
> (Sally)

Some described changes of mind:

I'm working with my dad painting and decorating ... because I enjoy doing it. I work like after school and at the weekend, at the moment anyway, and I enjoy doing it. I changed my mind 'cos I was working with my mum ... shopwork. But I changed my mind about doing that one 'cos I thought it might not suit me. So I'm doing this one [painting] now.

(Wayne)

For one 18-year-old, these changes had been frequent.

I started off doing geography and maths [A-levels]. Geography didn't work out for me, and then, the maths course, they had a half-way exam and unfortunately I didn't achieve the right result to carry on to the upper sixth. So I carried on with economics, and took up doing accountancy in my own time. I originally planned to go to university, but once I decided I wanted to be an accountant and with the geography and maths, I realised I wouldn't get in ... The main aspect was a friend of mine who works. He's actually doing his accountancy technician training with a firm in [named town]. We were talking through, I like working with figures. I like to think I'm good at maths, so I thought that would be a nice job for me to do. It appeals to me after starting the accountancy course. It's sort of become more attractive and keeping it all laid out ... I've talked through various careers. At first I wanted to go in the RAF but that went out the window when I failed the eyesight test ... So then I looked at manual work. I like engineering, I've worked as a mechanic for a year – a Saturday job. That appealed to me, but after working there for a year it made me see what it was really like. So then I moved to look at what I was really good at, what I enjoyed doing, and accountancy was the main result, after talking it through with them [parents] and my friend as well and the careers people here. I sort of talked it through and looked at all the aspects of accountancy and the best one that I thought would be for me was a technician working with the figures and numbers.

(Henry)

These, and many other examples, display two dominant characteristics.

Firstly, the pupils are describing *rational* reasons for making their choices and for changing their minds. That is, they are often choosing jobs they know a lot about and the source of information is often an insider who has no vested interest in 'selling' a vacancy and whose judgment they can trust because they know them personally. Alternatively, the information comes from actually doing some aspect of the job themselves.

Secondly, these rational decisions are *pragmatic* ... [being] based on partial information which is localised, ... on the familiar and the known. The decision making is context-related, and cannot be separated from the family background, culture and life histories of the pupils. The decisions are opportunistic, being based on fortuitous contacts and experiences. The timing of the decisions is sporadic, in that decisions are made when the pupil feels able to do so and are reactions to opportunities as they are encountered ...

Finally, decisions are often only partially rational, being also influenced by feelings and emotions. Simon (1982) calls this 'bounded rationality'. While we are not claiming that all these characteristics apply to decision making in every case, the majority of pupils we interviewed exemplified many of them.

(Hodkinson and Sparkes, 1993a, p. 250, original emphasis)

Such decision-making is neither technically rational nor irrational. In understanding the nature of the process, it is helpful to draw on a range of related intellectual ideas, drawn from Bourdieu, Giddens and schema theory. What emerges is a much more complex, interactive, culturally grounded process. We are using 'culture' to describe the socially constructed and historically derived common base of knowledge, values and norms for action that people grow into and come to take as a natural way of life. In relation to such a view of culture, Clarke *et al.* (1981) claim 'a culture includes the "maps of meanings" which make things intelligible to its members ... Culture is the way the social relations of a group are structured and shaped; but it is also the way those shapes are experienced, understood and interpreted' (pp. 52–3). In this way, people make sense of the world they inhabit.

Bourdieu uses the broader concept of *habitus* to encapsulate the ways in which a person's schematic beliefs, ideas and preferences are individually subjective but also formed by the objective social networks and cultural traditions in which that person lives. Habitus involves more than perceptions, for Bourdieu sees it as deriving from and being part of the whole person, or body (Jenkins, 1992). Habitus is 'that system of dispositions which acts as a mediation between structures and practice' (Bourdieu, 1977, p. 487). Central to habitus is tacit or practical knowledge. Giddens (1984) sees discursive consciousness as paralleled by practical consciousness. By this he means things we know and can do without articulating, in the way that one can ride a bike without being able to describe how to keep balance. Practical consciousness and discursive consciousness are linked and understanding can shift from one to the other. Both are inevitably influenced by a range of factors, which include the existing habitus derived from culture, significant others, activities and experiences, and the context (in all senses of the word) in which one finds oneself.

Both practical and discursive consciousness, and therefore habitus, change and develop. From childhood, people amass schemata which serve as tools for understanding aspects of their experiences (Rumelhart, 1980). A schema structures what a person knows of the world, by filtering out 'irrelevancies' and allowing sense to be made of partial information. In this way, two lights seen from a car in the dark can be turned into a cat or an approaching vehicle. A repertoire of schemata makes up the stock of knowledge in hand. As new experiences are gained, schemata are modified and developed and as they change so does what is recognized in the surrounding world. Brown *et al.* (1989) argue that when we learn, concepts, actions and culture are intricately inter-related and that to change one inevitably changes the others. Thus, as life progresses, though we cannot escape our past, changes in what we do or in the context within which we do it alter what we know and understand. It also follows that if our schematic view of the world changes, this in turn alters the way in which we perceive the context in which we live and the actions that we take. In this dialectical way, the life history of the individual shapes and is shaped by his/her common sense experience and *horizons for action*. By 'horizons for action' we mean what is possible. In career terms, this is determined by external opportunities for jobs and internal perceptions of those opportunities in the habitus. Job opportunities are neither objective nor subjective, but both. Habitus and horizons for action are, therefore, a result of a complex dialectical or reflexive interaction between the personal and the cultural or subcultural, and with the structures of society as they are experienced. Any attempt to separate these out, at least at the level of the individual, is so artificial as to be meaningless, except for analytical purposes.

Because schemata filter information, horizons for action both limit and enable our view of the world and the choices we can make within it. Consequently, the fact that there are jobs for girls in engineering is irrelevant if a young woman does not perceive engineering as an appropriate career. New information is constantly absorbed within an existing schematic framework, causing refinement and modification to the habitus. Thus, Helen decided that a career in a male-dominated area of car-body repairs was appropriate for her, because her experiences with her father gradually introduced the idea into her consciousness. This routinized developmental process means that it is difficult for anyone to break the mould, thus providing, as Bourdieu himself somewhat differently claims, a pattern of cultural reproduction which is not dependent on some deterministic, reified external structure.

On the other hand, schemata can be overthrown. For Kuhn (1970), this happens to paradigms of science when the amount of information which does not fit the existing paradigm is overwhelming. At the more personal level, constructivist psychologists, especially within science education, are working to develop strategies to help teachers challenge schematic views held by pupils (see, for example, Howard, 1987). Thus, habitus can change either as routinized development or radical transformation.

Laura is an interesting example of such schematic change. Originally, she set her heart on being a beautician.

> It was ages ago I thought about it [being a beautician] but I gave up hope on it, because what I really wanted to do was just be a make-up artist. And then like, the beginning of this year, my mum said something to me about it and I thought about it again, thought I'd go for it.

At this time Laura thought that she had found a route to being a beautician without going to full-time college.

> Me and my mum found it out. It was in [named paper], so we went in and spoke to her [training provider] on Tuesday, the lady in there, and that's how we found out all the information... It's retail training, like working somewhere like [named department store], and then training on retail and beautician at the same time.

However, she felt that experiences in the shop were unsatisfactory, and after a time she decided to drop out. The careers officer concerned described her meeting with Laura, after the shop placement had been voluntarily abandoned.

> She came in to see me and she was thinking of working with animals. She was also interested in mechanics and catering. So basically, had a job been there and had she been very focused, I could have done a new CGAP 3 [Careers Guidance Action Plan, part 3] with her, she could have had a new Training Credit issued and could have started on a completely new course. As it is, because she had those different ideas, and was feeling very down about it and wasn't sure, I was a bit wary of her jumping into something else very quickly.
>
> (careers officer)

The training provider Laura was referred to identified a different career option.

> It was very difficult to get anything else out of her [Laura], except that she wanted to be a Redcoat. But we looked at ... child care with a view to that being useful for when she does start maybe doing a Redcoat's job, come the summer ... and then, you know, the Redcoat disappeared. Basically, she found what she wanted.
>
> (trainer)

'What she wanted' was the placement in a nursery school, which was the nearest the trainer could get to being a Redcoat. Neither Laura, her mother nor the careers officer had any recollection of Laura previously wanting to work with children, or wanting to be a Redcoat. It appears to have been a whim that the trainer took seriously. It was an initial success. Laura herself describes enjoying working in the school and did not, at this stage, want to try anything else. Her employer was similarly impressed.

> a couple of days she was here, and I knew and she knew [she was in the right job], and she, she has literally lit up from inside. ... The children love her, she loves the children. The parents have accepted her well, and certainly the other members of staff have accepted her well. So she has just fitted in.
>
> (employer)

In this complex way, a combination of ongoing experience and sudden change had altered Laura's schematic view of herself and of a possible career, a view of career progression we return to shortly. The probably whimsical mention of being a Redcoat and the coincidence that the training provider knew of a placement in the nursery school were also important in that change. This change exemplifies several aspects of pragmatic rationality, and was very different from the technical ideal that was central to the Training Credits scheme design.

DECISION-MAKING WITHIN THE FIELD

Another weakness in the technically rational model of decision-making and of the wider economic rationalism of which it forms part, is that it assumes the young person is free to make a decision. In fact, the career decisions taken by young people are negotiated and contested, and strongly influenced by the actions of others. In this study, many other stakeholders in Training Credits were making decisions which impinged on young people's careers. Some of these decisions, such as those governing the rules for the use of Training Credits, had indirect general effect. They are excluded here for the sake of brevity, but their significance should not be underestimated. Others, on which we shall concentrate here, influenced decision-making through direct local interaction.

Clive wanted to work selling cars. He decided on this career because he had always liked cars, and because he did well on work experience and in a part-time job with a local garage. The job he eventually got was specifically created for him, because the garage owner liked Clive and liked his family.

> Our business here is obviously very localised, it's very personalised. Consequently, the people who work for me are hand picked, and we tend to take someone when someone suitable came along for what we want to do, rather than, if you like, being inundated with enquiries, or whatever. ...
>
> As he [Clive] progressed along, he became obviously higher than the average ability ... and he seemed ideal to come and work with ourselves. So I then obviously discussed this with his parents, before broaching the subject with him, because Clive, being very keen on cars, would have said 'yes' to that anyway. I'm not interested in having someone employed here just to have a dead end job. ...
>
> He's a very very nice young man, exceptionally so ... His whole family are. Which is another basis for when we employed him. Having met the whole family, and done business with them, ... giving ourselves an insight into them, they are very very pleasant, and you can see just why he's the way he is.
>
> (employer)

Both parents and employer exerted influence in this decision. In the case of Helen, whom we have already met, a similar process took place, except that her father approached an employer he knew to help find the placement.

For Laura, the training provider chose to send her to a nursery school, and the nursery school head chose to keep her on after the trial period was over. The importance of local networking in the job selection process is also confirmed in other studies (Moore, 1988; Lee *et al.*, 1990).

These examples demonstrate a further dimension to horizons for action, as the external opportunities within the horizons can be created by interactions between the young person and significant others. On other occasions, the actions of others can close opportunities down. This happened to Helen when she was suddenly made redundant. She was forced to change career rapidly and ended up working in a record shop. The story is complex. Not only did Helen enjoy her work, but when we first saw him her employer claimed she was good at it.

> Helen will be a top-flight painter and sprayer, yes, I'm sure she will ... I don't want to train people, or make use of them for sort of four or five years and then say, 'Thank you very much we don't want you any more.' Because they are no good to me if they don't progress. They have got to be able to feel confident enough to do a job that is suitable to go out of our doors.
>
> (employer)

Less than six months after this interview Helen lost her placement. She explained what had happened in this way:

> There isn't enough work. Well, that was before this week. It's packed in there this week ... Last Thursday they told me that I was leaving, and another girl, a secretary was going ... They said, 'As you know, we're not getting much business in the trade and the recession's just hit us' ... But I don't blame them really because he hasn't had much in really ... It was noticeable, it was hard to find things to do. You'd get about three people working on the same car. It was getting quite bad.

However, her employer told a different story.

> Work had got tight, but that wasn't, I wouldn't say, of great importance. It didn't reflect the fact that we got rid of her. It was merely on the pretence of that. Unfortunately, Helen was a lovely girl. Very enthusiastic to start with and then it just went. I tried all sorts of encouragements, bribes, everything, to get things moving again. Through the grapevine I heard she'd picked up with a boyfriend, or a man friend, or something. I think that was her downfall to be honest. To get Helen to walk from here to the door, it probably would have taken, exaggerated, ten minutes. She was so slow, I thought she was going to stop (laughs). Very unfortunate, because what she did she did thoroughly, but having said that she put an awful lot of time into creating that. In this business, time is against us all the time. She couldn't grasp the fact that we get a price for a job, and that price is based on selling labour, and we have a labour rate which covers everything in the workshop. She couldn't grasp that if we were getting five hours to do that, granted she was on a lower pay rate, but she couldn't grasp that she had to keep within a certain parameter. But personally, she was a great kid.
>
> (employer)

Whatever the reason, Helen was laid off, and had to find another placement. She tried hard to find a placement that would allow her to continue her car spraying training but, in the end, spread her search much wider, afraid that she would lose all financial support. At the careers centre a job advertisement for a large record shop caught her eye. 'I've always liked that shop. I wondered what it would be like to work in there ... I don't know, I like music.'

Helen's story illustrates the interplay between stakeholders with different resources and interests. She did indeed 'choose' to work in the record shop, after turning down a placement offered in a shoe shop. However, her original employer forced that change upon her, and another garage interviewed her, but then did not offer her a place.

On some occasions, young people resist the pressures from others. Laura chose to leave the shop placement and voluntarily sought something else. Mary reported resisting advice from a careers officer.

> I had one of them phoning up my house. One of them phoned up my house. 'Can she come up to the careers office to speak about it?' And I went up there and she was there going on about YTS [Youth Training Scheme] and Training Credits. I didn't want to. I just, I think it's a waste of time to be honest. My mum wouldn't let me go on it anyway ... Even if I said I hadn't a place yet, she wouldn't have let me go. ... Because she's seen people do YTS and don't get a job at the end of it. You know, now they're unemployed. If you get a job at the end of it, like firm, then you've got everything going for you. But they say they can't guarantee you a job at the end of it.

Sometimes the young people themselves initiated positive changes. Alison had happily completed an NVQ 2 in equitation, placed at local stables and working with one agricultural college. Supported by her mother, she decided to move to distant stables and a new college for her NVQ 3 because she felt she would gain new experiences, for example of livery work, that her original placement could not offer.

> I quite fancied doing another year somewhere else. I wasn't keen on going up to college yet for a year, for a full-time course, and I didn't particularly want to stay there because in a year I couldn't really learn that much more ... So I thought I might as well get myself another year somewhere else. ...
>
> They were always saying, 'Oh we're so busy – well, we'll do some so-and-so today, practise your plaiting or something.' Then when we get round to it people would turn up for hacks and they'd say, 'Oh, you have to take a hack out now.' It was always the customers first and then you fitted in when and if you could, and that was very rarely.

This happened despite assumptions by her first employer and college lecturer that she would take NVQ 3 in the same place as NVQ 2.

Once more, Bourdieu's work is illuminating. He coined the concept of 'field' to describe the 'game' in which players interact.

> We can indeed, with caution, compare a field to a game (*jeu*) although, unlike the latter, a field is not the product of a deliberate act of creation, and it follows rules or, better, regularities, that are not explicit and codified.
>
> (Bourdieu, in Bourdieu and Wacquant, 1992, p. 98)

It is helpful to see the transition to work as such a field, where different players strive for different objectives using widely differing resources. There are complex regularities which constrain and legitimate the actions of anyone involved in the transition to work field. Some are formal rules, such as those laid down to govern the Training Credits scheme. Others are regularities arising from deliberate policy-making or have evolved in the development of education and work in Britain, and the links between the two. Thirdly and most crucially, for Bourdieu, 'it is the state of the relations of force between players that defines the structure of the field' (Bourdieu, in Bourdieu and Wacquant 1992, p. 99). The 'players' are various, and include the other stakeholders interviewed in this study. Within the field, these players have differing resources and power, which make up the 'relations of force'.

This power, for Bourdieu, comes from possession of capital – economic, social, cultural or symbolic. For him, capital is relative to the field in question, not absolute: 'the value of a species of capital (e.g., knowledge of Greek or of integral calculus) hinges on the existence of a game, of a field in which this competency can be employed' (*ibid.*, p. 98). Okano (1993) explains this complex point by talking about resources, which she claims can be positive, negative or neutral. Positive resources are equivalent to Bourdieu's capital. However, the same resource may be positive, negative or neutral, depending on the context within which it is 'used'. Thus, Clive's love of cars was a positive resource in getting his garage placement, but might have been neutral or irrelevant for a job in a bank. Helen's garage employer stated explicitly that her 'working-class' family had helped get her original placement. It might have been a negative resource in becoming a lawyer. In any field, different players have differing amounts of resource, and it is generally the more resourceful players who determine the rules of the game.

All stakeholders have resources. Young people have resources based on their ability to turn down unwanted placements and to use social and cultural capital to find or create opportunities. Towards the end of the fieldwork period, Clive feared that the garage might be sold and his job lost. While in one sense this demonstrates his lack of resources to keep the garage open, he felt confident that the contacts he had made in the job would enable him to find another opening. He had acquired social and cultural capital.

However, many other stakeholders have more resources than the young people. Parents have more social and cultural capital, and many used these resources to help place their offspring. Careers officers and training providers have symbolic, social and cultural capital. They know the system well and have good connections with other key players in the field. Employers have economic and social capital. They have networks and contacts but, most importantly, they have the power to hire and fire, to determine what on- or off-the-job training the young person has access to, etc. Within the field, therefore, decisions are actually made through negotiation, struggle, co-operation and serendipitous coincidence – a complex, social and interactive process, firmly grounded in context and culture.

CAREERSHIP AS TRANSFORMATIONS

The concept of *field* contextualizes pragmatic decision-making within the wider social relations, struggles and negotiations that inevitably constrain and enable it. However, it is also necessary to locate the decision-making in a longitudinal frame of career progression. To see this clearly it is helpful to use an analysis made by Strauss (1962) on transformations of identity. Strauss presents three contrasting theoretical views of personal development. Firstly, many see it as climbing a ladder, where individuals move along predetermined paths, the nature of which can be identified, at least in broad terms, by an outsider. The second conception is of a series of changes throughout life, none of which actually transforms the central identity of the individual, just as, in Strauss's analogy, however you cook an egg it remains essentially an egg. The notion of career trajectories, as used in Banks *et al.* (1992), Bates and Riseborough (1993a) and Furlong (1992), and the current British policy paradigm, all incorporate both such views of development. For example, writers such as Bennett *et al.* (1992) assume that individuals can identify their own key strengths, interests, aptitudes, etc. as a precursor to making a 'rational' choice of career ladder, whilst researchers define young people as types, based on class, ethnicity, gender and level of educational achievement, which they see as determining future chances. Then, either through individual decision-making or due to structural constraints, individuals embark on trajectories of the ladder type. However, as Strauss writes,

> Development, then, is commonly viewed either as attainment, or as sets of variations on basic themes. In either case, you as the observer of the developmental pattern are omniscient; you know the end against which persons are matched, or you know the basic themes on which variations are composed. Neither metaphor captures the open-ended, tentative, exploratory, hypothetical, problematical, devious, changeable, and only partly unified character of human courses of action.
>
> (1962, p. 65)

Strauss, then, presents the alternative notion of development as transformation, based around key 'turning points'. 'These points in development occur when an individual has to take stock, to re-evaluate, revise, resee, and rejudge' (p. 71).

Strauss claims that these turning points are found in all parts of our lives, including job or career. In many careers, there is a predetermined structure to these turning points, many of which involve formalized status-passage. However, even within organizations where official structures resemble ladder-like trajectories, many individuals fail to match the predetermined norms. He describes, for example, problems of pacing and timing, or of mismatch between personal motivations and official structures.

This model of career development, or what we call *careership,* fitted the stories of the young people in this study (Hodkinson *et al.*, in press). Careership can be seen as an uneven pattern of routine experience interspersed with turning points, which can be of different types. Within each turning point, if career decisions are made they are pragmatically rational, and embedded in the complex struggles and negotiations of the training field. Furthermore, the turning points and routines within careership are dialectically linked, so that one can grow out of and give rise to the other.

We begin with routine. During the routine experience, of school or off-the-job training or work, schematic perceptions of the self and the job gradually develop. Three types of routine change can be discerned in the data. For some, increased experience simply *confirms* and deepens original conceptions, reinforcing existing habitus. Thus David always wanted to work on a farm. This developed when he was very young. Father was a machine driver and ex-farm labourer, and the family had always kept animals. Farming was part of his culture. When in his early teens he got work experience and a part-time job on a local farm, despite parental opposition based on doubts about the security and rewards in farming, he determined on a farming career. With parental support, he intended to be a farm manager, to escape the low pay and low status of a labourer. He got a Training Credits placement on the same farm, with off-the-job training at an agricultural college. Both experiences reconfirmed his hopes and intentions. After one year he passed his NVQ level 2 and took up a full-time college certificate course. This meant giving up his regular training allowance and relying on limited amounts of weekend work for income. His parents, who were not very well-off, made sacrifices to find the money to pay for his college accommodation. When the research ended, he was hoping to convert to a diploma course the following year, still intent on farm management.

For others, routine experience gradually deepens dissatisfaction with the current situation and *contradicts* the original or emerging identity. In this way, despite her initial enthusiasm for work in the nursery school, Laura became disillusioned and left, even though her employer had offered her a permanent job. At the end of the study she was unemployed. Her parents, also not well off, were paying for private office-skills training in an agency her mother had previously used. Laura had eventually rejected the official system and was trying to create a new identity for herself, as a secretary.

> I went to the Careers Office and they said, 'Come in for this week, this job week.' I don't want to do that, I just want to get a job. I don't want to go to other job clubs and all that lot. I mean it's a waste of ... all right, she said, 'Ooh, you'll be getting £35 a week.' But that's not what I want. I don't want to be like, try this place, try that place. I want a steady job.
>
> (Laura)

For others, routine *socializes* them into accepting a career they did not originally want. This happened to Helen, who by the end of the study had come to accept working in a record shop as a likely and satisfactory career. Talking of how she conceptualized any customized car spraying now, Helen replied, 'It's part-time now, cash on the side. I still fancy doing it for some extra cash. A bit of a hobby isn't it ... my hobby.' Bates (1990) tells a similar story of girls on a caring course who become gradually socialized into accepting the role.

Similarly, the data revealed three types of turning point. Some, as Strauss suggests, are *structural*. That is, they are determined by external structures in the institutions and schemes involved. One structural change came at the age of 16-plus, when young people had to choose whether to stay in school or leave. Another, for many, came at the end of the first year's training, when the NVQ 2 had been achieved. Decisions then had to be made about the next stage and, in some cases, new placements or jobs had to be found. At this time David transformed himself from trainee to full-time student, still within the same overall career vision. Frances completed her retail training up to NVQ level 2, and then got a part-time job working in a large department store.

Other turning points were *self-initiated*, arising in different ways from the previous routine experience. Thus, as we have seen, Alison changed placement and trainer, including a move away from home. Laura twice chose to reject careers she had embarked upon and each time transformed herself into a different career identity.

Finally, transformations were externally *forced* on some, such as when Helen lost her car-spraying job, took a placement in a record shop because it was available, and gradually transformed herself from a car-sprayer into a shop assistant.

Some transformations, as when David moved to being a full-time student, can be planned and foreseen. Others cannot be predicted and, as Strauss makes clear, some can only be recognized as significant with hindsight. This poses two further challenges for the technically rational model of decision-making. Firstly, there is a fundamental uncertainty about careership which is at odds with the emphasis on technical control. Clive was on target for his chosen career for nearly 18 months. He was getting on well at work and was valued by his employer. Both consistently talked about a long-term career in that garage as a car salesman. Though Clive always recognized that the future was not certain, neither he nor some external expert could have predicted the possible sale of the garage, for it was succeeding not failing. Because the research came to an end, we do not know whether the garage was sold or whether Clive lost his job. If he did lose the job, would this have resulted in a similar job somewhere else, or a totally unexpected transformation, as happened to Helen?

IMPLICATIONS OF CAREERSHIP AND PRAGMATIC RATIONALITY FOR VOCATIONAL EDUCATION AND TRAINING POLICY

This analysis of careership and pragmatic decision-making undermines some of the current policy assumptions, and especially the managerial and market dominated approaches to vocational education and training. Firstly, by misunderstanding the nature of career decision-making, the technically rational model deflects attention from the careers guidance needs of young people and risks the further marginalization of the careers service. Secondly, the market model of training provision and quality improvement is fatally undermined by the absence of technically rational decision-making based on informed self-interest and knowledge of training quality. Finally, the parameters of the discourse within the new paradigm exclude from consideration some very important questions about the nature of quality education and training and the progression from education to work. We will briefly examine each in turn.

Implications for careers guidance policy

At best, current policies on careers guidance deflect attention from the complex realities of pragmatic decision-making. There is a widespread assumption that if only we got the guidance right, then a majority of young people could make a single, carefully considered, 'correct' career decision, which would in turn lead to greater success and fewer drop-outs in training, because such youngsters would be square pegs in square holes. To do this, the main extra ingredients are professional 'neutral' guidance and the provision of more and better information. Our analysis suggests that such approaches are doomed to failure. High-quality careers education and guidance provide an invaluable service to many young people, but they cannot ensure that 'right' choices are made. Indeed, it is a fallacy even to consider choices as 'right', when so many variables inevitably influence careership, which is itself partly unpredictable.

A technical view of careers guidance ignores the truism that the value of professional guidance lies in the quality of counselling given, rather than the outcomes. Such guidance should be given by qualified, professional careers officers. Current approaches to guidance funding, where careers service income depends on the number of action plans produced, may be counter-productive. High-quality advice cannot be measured by whether or not a plan exists; the quality of the plan cannot be judged by whether or not it is eventually followed; some young people will need far more time than others to prepare a plan and some will need several plans.

Above all, policy-makers and practitioners must recognize the complexity of the career decision-making process. Approaches that see guidance simply as providing more and better information plus professional advice in making a single choice are naïve and unlikely to succeed. Miller (1983), writing of American college students, argues that professional guidance providers should alert young people to the significance of 'happenstance' and local networking in finding a job, rather than reinforcing the myth of technical rationality. An unintended outcome of a failure to do these sorts of things may be that careers education and guidance get a bad reputation, simply because they cannot deliver the simple, unchanging, 'correct' decision that is, in many cases, unachievable.

Choices, markets and training quality

One key assumption of the new approaches to vocational education and training management is that the quality of education or training will be improved as providers are forced to compete for the custom of young people, parents or employers. Unfortunately, the market can only work in this way if young people (and other potential customers) make choices that are largely technically rational. Thus, if young people really did carefully consider all the training options open to them and select the one that best suited their needs, then the market controls might have a partly beneficial effect. Unfortunately, as we have seen, young people did not make those types of choice. They did not know much about the training programmes they were choosing, and choices of placement were not made from the full range of available information. Furthermore, those 'choices' often amounted to little more than reacting to known opportunities as they arose. The 'choices' were the result of negotiations in the field, and influenced as much by the actions of others as by the supposed customers with their vouchers. Hodkinson and Sparkes (1994) show that the relationships in the field undermined the training market in other ways: for example, the close relationships between employers and trainers meant that employers did not act as customers either, and a training programme often followed a placement automatically and vice versa, even though both parts of the combination had not been fully considered.

Hodkinson and Hodkinson (1995) go further, claiming that other elements in the new training paradigm, such as the almost total concentration on measured outcomes reinforced by payment by results, risked undermining training quality rather than enhancing it. This was because training providers had incentives to shorten the training process, focus on minimum standards and allow borderline candidates to achieve the qualification. Similar points are also made by Smithers (1993) and Steedman and Hawkins (1994).

The deflection of attention from more important issues

The simplistic, technicist assumptions of the individualist market paradigm ignore the cultural complexity of education and training, career decision-making and the transition from school to work. The result is that several issues of central importance remain unaddressed. Those most directly linked to the analysis presented here include:

Issues of social inequality. The crudely individualist assumptions that all young people can be helped simply through a combination of advice, information and a voucher for training, deflects attention from the well-known underlying inequalities of the transition to work, based on class, ethnicity, gender and geographical location. The contested nature of job choice and social reproduction is similarly rendered invisible. The result is a simplistic version of victim blaming, where those who don't succeed even with support are implied to be responsible for their own failures.

Issues of knowledge creation. Though not directly emphasized in this chapter, the various quotations from young people and others are an important reminder that what counts as knowledge is socially created and contested between stakeholders in the field. The technicist model assumes that knowledge is unproblematic and objectively given. This renders invisible the important questions about what knowledge and whose knowledge do or should count (Apple, 1990).

Issues of empowerment. Even within an individualist perspective, the market and vouchers view of empowerment is highly impoverished. It ignores factors such as critical awareness and group action. One interpretation of this omission is that talk of empowerment in this context is a rhetorical device and that real empowerment, however that is defined, was never actually intended. As Coffey (1992) makes clear, obedience was once an explicit objective of vocational training in Britain.

The extent and nature of post-Fordism. In Chapter 3 we have mounted an attack on what we see as over-simplified assumptions about the extent and benevolence of post-Fordism. The stories referred to here contribute to that challenge. Many of the workplaces and work experiences described here are not post-Fordist, and the young people were largely powerless to influence the ways in which they were treated. Even the most altruistic employers eventually placed their own and the firm's interests before those of an individual trainee/employee. Many of the young people who formed the focus of this study were employed by small employers, and it may be argued that their experiences were consequently untypical. However, in 1991, the latest year for which figures are available, such small firms counted for 35.3 per cent of all non-government employment (DE, 1994), so in considering the extent of post-Fordism, employment in small firms cannot be ignored.

Issues of the collapsing youth labour market and the need for job creation. Similarly, by placing all the policy emphasis on market lubrication and choice improvement, attention is deflected from the very important task of the creation of job opportunities that young people might be able to 'choose'. This is partly because attention is deflected from the very many factors which constrain choice, such as unequal power resources in the training field, as well as a shortage of placements or jobs in many areas. It means that there is a failure to explore the policy consequences of numerous analyses of the shortcomings of British employers and the British labour market (e.g., Finegold and Soskice, 1988).

Issues of training quality. The assumption that quality training can be determined by a combination of markets and measured outcomes renders invisible the central question about what a quality training process is (A. Brown and Evans, 1994; Hodkinson and Hodkinson, 1995). If the quality of the British workforce is to be improved, and we have argued elsewhere that this should not be the only objective of post-compulsory education and training, then much more work is urgently needed to determine what a quality training process is, and how it can be encouraged.

Regardless of the political or ideological stance taken with regard to each of these issues, we would contend that all should be recognized as important and debated. One of our criticisms of the current discourse is the extent to which such issues remain hidden and largely unaddressed.

REASONS FOR THE DOMINANCE OF TECHNICAL RATIONALISM

Given our analysis, a fundamental question remains. Why are technicist approaches so prevalent, and why do they achieve so much support, right across the political spectrum?

The appeal of such ideas to many employers and members of the current British Conservative government is obvious. Technicist policies fall within a largely internalized ideological belief system, predicated on individualism and market forces. For those holding such beliefs, notions of individual choice, a universal desire to maximize opportunities (normally in economic terms) and the efficiency of a market as a distributor of scarce resources are assumed to be self-evident truths (see, for example, CBI, 1989, 1993; Davies, 1992; Bennett *et al.,* 1992, 1993, 1994). There is an obvious appeal to those who are personally successful in life and perhaps especially in business, for such beliefs legitimate not only their own successes but also the failures of others. Such beliefs disguise structural inequalities in society, such as those based on class, race or gender. For major employers and industrialists there is a further gain. Despite frequent analyses that many of the major problems contributing to the skills gap lie within the practices of industry itself and the financial and political context within which it works (Finegold and Soskice, 1988; Keep and Mayhew, 1991), a focus on individualism deflects attention from these areas and places it firmly within education and careers guidance – useful scapegoats if anything goes wrong.

For the Conservative government there is a further appeal. Such an ideological stance removes responsibility from the government for a whole series of interrelated structural problems, which are the subject of this book. All that has to be done is to 'empower' individual young people and employers, then stand back and await the results. Thus the use of vouchers for training, and now the proposed learning credits for all post-16 education (*TES*, 3 June 1994), are part of an overall strategy to weaken Local Authorities through the strengthening of government-controlled quangos such as the TECs (Evans, 1992; Coffield, 1990). Ironically, even some of the most fervent advocates of market rationalism see tensions here. Bennett *et al.* (1994) suggest that the TEC initiative is being strangled by excessive government regulation and control, emanating from the command and control culture of the Treasury and the Employment Department.

The potential results of such policies go further than 'blaming the victim', though that is serious enough. The growing assumption within the British discourse, that markets and individual responsibility are natural and inevitable, further marginalizes left-wing criticism and reduces professionalism to the servicing of narrow, market-derived agendas. Perhaps, above all, it hides growing central political control of education and training behind a rhetoric of freedom and choice, and thus serves the central interests of the British Conservative government.

Aspects of such technicist approaches also appeal to many progressive liberal educators and to organizations such as the Trades Union Congress and the Labour Party who would normally be opposed to market ideologies. The rhetoric of technicism appeals to managers and policy-makers across a wide political spectrum, because it offers the illusion of control over complex and possibly unmanageable processes. Professionals, such as careers officers, see technicist approaches as providing ways to enhance young people's control over their own learning and their own careers. It is also true that developments within this model, such as the Training Credits schemes, also enhance the status of those same professionals by giving more attention to their work and, in some cases, even providing more employment (Hodkinson and Sparkes, 1995a).

Finally, this emphasis on individual choice resonates with the beliefs and interests of many ordinary people – parents, young people and employers. It offers what some would call an illusion of greater choice and control over their own lives. As Furlong (1992) writes, 'the transition to work is a structured process which is experienced as "free choice"' (p. 13). Bates and Riseborough are more trenchant:

> the New Right rhetoric was finely tuned to a social context characterised by a lethal combination of growing injustice and growing individualisation. ... The 'classless' society discourse incorporated and solved the problem of social injustice, combining a frank *recognition* of inequality with an apparently graspable solution at the individual level.
>
> (1993b, p. 4, original emphasis)

One of the central themes of this book is that we need to look beyond even the most popular beliefs, in order to be able to develop better policies for post-compulsory education and training in the future. We will return to this issue in the final chapter, but first we move on to examine another central issue at the level of the individual – that of studentship and the nature of students' learning.

NOTES

1 The various names for this scheme are confusing. Training Credits was the original generic title, but different TECs invented their own names for their own versions. Then, in the summer of 1993, the Employment Department began referring to the scheme as 'Youth Credits'. To complete the muddle, the whole of Scotland agreed on yet another name – Skill Seekers. Here, we retain the original title of Training Credits, because this was the name used by the subjects of the study to be reported.

2 This study was conducted jointly by Phil Hodkinson and Dr Andrew Sparkes of Exeter University. We wish to acknowledge the enormous contribution made by Dr Sparkes to what follows in this chapter. Some of what follows has already been published, in a somewhat different format, under his joint authorship. Key references include Hodkinson and Sparkes (1993a, 1993b, 1994, 1995a, 1995b) and Hodkinson, Sparkes and Hodkinson (in press).

Chapter 7

Education for Studentship

Martin Bloomer

Centralist curriculum prescription, managerialist controls and market forces are the blunt instruments by which government is attempting to reform post-16 education in Britain. There is no mistaking the fact that they are having a profound effect upon people's lives: widespread redundancies, college closures and mergers, a proliferation of 'quality speak' and diminishing staff–student ratios are indications that this three-dimensional vice is beginning to change the shape of things. There are many voices eager to claim that the reforms are not merely doctrinaire but so misconceived that their impact upon the quality of student learning is minimal, even adverse. The blunt instruments have been wielded in ignorance of the most important considerations of all, those concerning students and their learning. In this chapter, following on from the critique of careership, we examine students' experiences of learning, their learning careers and *studentship* in order to illuminate further both the inadequacies of current reforms and the potential for human growth and development which is being stifled in the process.

STUDENTSHIP IN POST-16 EDUCATION

The term 'studentship' has been used elsewhere by Lawrence Stenhouse (Rudduck and Hopkins, 1984) to refer to a capacity for independent study and for recognizing the problematic nature of knowledge. However, we wish to use it here in a somewhat broader sense to describe the variety of ways in which students exert influence over the curriculum in the creation and confirmation of their own personal learning careers. Although it is commonplace in the 'reforming 90s' for attention to be focused on the *pre*scriptive curriculum (that which is set down in the form of plans) on the assumption that it is centrally imposed planning which determines the essential nature of knowledge and learning, evidence from Leverhulme funded research (Bloomer, forthcoming) helps to confirm the crucially significant place of studentship in the *de*scriptive curriculum (that which is experienced by students). Although passage through post-16 education for some students is marked by a relatively uncritical compliance with the requirements imposed upon them by their syllabuses and their teachers, most become distinguished in some way by a personal, critical and creative response to those requirements and expectations: they *act upon* the learning opportunities offered to them by *making* their own curriculum. It is this 'making through action' which we have chosen to describe as *studentship* and which, we claim, is wholly disregarded in the reforming process.

The Leverhulme study was carried out between 1992 and 1994 and focused specifically upon the experiences of A-level and Business and Technology Education Council (BTEC) National/GNVQ Advanced students. While the students who participated in the study were attached to a wide variety of courses, it should be noted that they were invariably among the higher achievers within the population at large. Moreover, given the localities within which it was conducted, the study included a higher than normal proportion of students of middle-class families and very few of ethnic minority groups. These points must be borne in mind as cases from the study are reported here.

The study revealed, not surprisingly, that students embark upon post-16 studies for a variety of reasons. Some of these are visibly instrumental and concern the exchange value of knowledge or qualifications, while others stress much more the intrinsic benefits attached to learning. The study also provided insight into students' conceptions of knowledge, which for some students was viewed and acted upon as a subject-specific commodity; others stressed quite different knowledge qualities, including the significance of their own part in the construction of knowledge and alluding to the place of course knowledge within the wider context of their own personal growth and development. Views of learning, too, varied considerably among students, with some laying claim to the importance of those learning activities which demanded more of their own active participation in some manner or other, and others valuing most a more receptive and passive learner role in their acquisition of knowledge. While some such variance between students appeared to be reflected in the types of post-16 course and subject which they chose to study, much was not, and it is certainly true that each of the 90 A-level and vocational course groups which participated in the research contained students with considerably varied reasons for choice of course and views of knowledge and learning. This diversity of students' dispositions to their courses and, indeed, to their life-worlds more generally, parallels that reported in the previous chapter in connection with young people using Training Credits.

The students were differentially disposed to their courses at the outset, at least in respect of the issues we have touched upon here. Some discovered that their views of knowledge and their preferences for learning activities largely coincided with those expected by their teachers and, for many of these students, transition into their new courses had proved to be relatively smooth. Routines had *confirmed* and reinforced existing habitus. In other cases, where students had held different views and expectations to those they later met with in their courses, some had come to revise their views in accordance with course expectations: they had become *socialized* by routine into new schematic perceptions. Other students, however, did not adapt in this way and some even revised their own views in such a manner that they became even less compatible with course expectations than they had been at the outset: routine and identity had become *contradictory*. Overall, it was a significant proportion of students who claimed that their own values, beliefs and expectations on matters concerning what to learn, how to learn and why to learn contradicted those which they met in their post-16 courses. Students' responses to such situations took the form of *strategic compliance* (highly visible in many students), *retreatism* (absenteeism or non-completion), *rebellion* (in the form of petty disruption, albeit in a very few cases) or *innovation* (where students devised some novel means of enabling them to achieve what they wanted from their courses). Added to the *conformism* of those students whose values and beliefs were confirmed by their course experiences or who had become socialized into accepting and sharing course expectations, this categorization of the ways in which students 'acted upon' their courses – that is, their studentship – is not dissimilar to Merton's (1968) typology of modes of individual adaptation (conformity, innovation, ritualism, retreatism and rebellion). However, we should stress here that most students in the Leverhulme study were found to exhibit properties of more than one of the five broad categories of studentship, with innovation, strategic compliance and conformity being the most visible.

It will be apparent that studentship, inasmuch as it concerns how students 'act upon' their prescribed curricula, concerns the impact of human agency upon learning. The cases of studentship to be reported later in this chapter reveal how human agency exerts itself in the face of, and even in spite of, structural constraints. They make visible some of the shortcomings in both centrally prescribed curricula and the populist assumptions about knowledge and learning which frequently underpin them. They provide for the identification of some of the principles of a curriculum *for* studentship. Before proceeding to these cases, though, it is appropriate to give some consideration to the structural conditions against which studentship in contemporary post-16 education asserts itself.

STRUCTURE, DETERMINISM AND THE PRESCRIBED CURRICULUM

Public debate about post-16 education is strongly influenced by assumptions about social structure and human agency in which the cultural and historical grounding of the latter is commonly taken for granted or ignored. Much current thinking (for example, CBI, 1993; DES/DE, 1991) is based upon assumptions that analyses of economic need provide the essential basis for curriculum planning and that a curriculum so devised provides not only for a positive response to social needs but also offers the means of fostering personal growth and development. Key elements of the debate, such as how economic and social needs are identified, are left unquestioned. They are treated as unproblematic, while the whole discourse is served by a rhetoric which deflects critical attention from centrally important issues including, for instance, the purposes of post-16 education and the contributions of teachers and learners to the creation of curricula.

Major flaws in this approach to planning have been identified in earlier chapters of this book and we do not propose to dwell on them at length here. The inadequacy, incompleteness or 'nation-state blinkeredness' of prevailing analyses of the economy, work and the labour market are particularly notable weaknesses in the chain. Moreover, as we have illustrated in Chapter 3, the surface consistency between enterprise culture and post-Fordist discourses serves only to mask the fundamentally different conceptions of individualism, autonomy, empowerment, responsibility, citizenship, democracy and society upon which they are based. Post-Fordism has idealized education as a necessary codeterminant of economic change; it is this economic rationalism which we have questioned in Chapter 4 and which has also been the subject of critical accounts of the economic benefits of expansion in higher education (Murphy, 1993). An uncritical vision of future labour requirements within the context of globalization, coupled with a failure to address the unproven assumptions of economic analyses *per se,* provides a wholly inadequate basis for curriculum planning. Failure to look beyond economic interests, however grounded, for a rationale for post-16 education compounds this inadequacy.

But curricula do not begin or end with simply bridging 'academic–vocational divides' or providing entitlement to core disciplines. There is a need to consider the content, context and culture of the curriculum with an awareness that knowledge itself is culturally specific and has different effects according to different social groups (Marginson, 1993). As Donald (1992b) points out, relationships between social inequality and the distribution of knowledge and between inequalities and the nature of 'education knowledge' have been neglected. Elsewhere, Marginson (1993) argues that economic rationalism treats people as objects, as human resources, for the economy, *as if the economy is an end in itself* – and the resonances between this claim and our earlier discussions of technicism and managerialism are clear. The effect of what Marginson calls a *master discourse* obscures an active view of citizenship which, in a democracy, is the end-point for which all systems of society, including the economic, exist. A central problem with such discourse is that it suppresses diversity and pluralism, including active conceptions of knowledge, learning and citizenship. Moreover, it limits the kinds of questions that can be legitimately asked in society by predefining the problems and, hence, framing the scope of solutions and policy options. The danger here is that notions of 'society' and 'the public good' are subordinated to the need to supply 'ideal' persons, separated off from the very social relations which sustain them. This much is evident in the political project of the New Right, confined as it is to illusory *national* rather than *global* interests. Such a rationalism rests upon a purely instrumental view of knowledge and learning in its proposals for overcoming what are seen to be essentially technical problems barring the way to national progress. Hence, due importance is attached to the improvement of skill levels, attendance, participation and behaviour. But a preoccupation with improved test scores, information and skills has little to do with enabling young people to think about their own society or to develop the knowledge and skills needed as citizens to maintain a democratic society. Real and lasting educational reform cannot be subordinated to the causal determinants of the economy, or to traditions of hierarchy and social exclusion.

Setting aside for the moment concerns about curriculum development and reform, there are equally disturbing assumptions about the impact of curriculum on students. Determinist models are frequently in evidence. These provide an incomplete account of human experience at best and a hugely distorted account at worst and, as we noted in the last chapter, underestimate the importance of agency. It is the underlying assumption of determinism that human action is solely the product of social structure and, specifically, that student learning is primarily the product of centralist curriculum planning which obscures human agency in general and studentship in particular.

A great deal of recent literature on the subject of post-16 curriculum, and particularly that published on behalf of national institutions, is underpinned by determinist assumptions. The CBI has no doubts, it appears, about the impact of curriculum upon learning, at least as far as GNVQ is concerned, and has even been moved to suggest that a public statement of A-level course objectives would boost student motivation.

General National Vocational Qualifications (GNVQs) have the power to transform learning for a majority of 16–19 year-olds. ... [In respect of A-level courses] young people are entitled to know the objectives of their course, and the definition of excellence. It should raise aspirations.

(CBI, 1993, pp. 15–17)

Of course, their guesswork will doubtless prove correct up to a point. It would indeed be strange if an initiative mounted on the scale of GNVQs did not have some visible effect upon learning. But the CBI's claim is without evidence; it offers no account of the nature of change other than in the most general of terms; it provides no insight into how changes will take place; and, through its omission of any reference to how students may internalize or 'act upon' externally imposed prescriptions, effectively denies the significance of human experience, and of studentship, in the process. It merely presumes a simple causal relationship between prescription and learning, the effect of which is to cast teachers and learners into roles of technician and customer, respectively.

It is apparent that this mode of thought is endorsed at the 'leading edge' of educational thinking and reform as John Major's personal contribution to the White Paper, *Education and Training for the 21st Century,* clearly illustrates:

> The Government are ... launching a new wave of reforms which will give Britain's young people an even better start in life. With the introduction of a new Advanced Diploma, we will end the artificial divide between academic and vocational qualifications.

(DES/DE, 1991, p. i)

This problem, securely rooted in British social, cultural and economic history, is to be solved at a stroke simply by imposing an umbrella qualification upon the divided system. Inequalities will be made equal without any consideration of the qualitative differences between 'academic' and 'vocational' education and with no regard to the cultures which sustain them. Call it 'top-down', 'centre-periphery' or 'inside-out', this is naked determinism. It gives no regard to the lessons from our own recent history when, in the years following the 1944 Act, parity of esteem was bestowed upon grammar, technical and modern schools. A wonderful dream it might have been fifty years ago, but there is no escaping the fact that disparities, even gross disparities, ensued. The declaration of parity amounted to nothing, simply because values and attitudes so firmly embedded in British cultures ensured that a divisive system, whether assessed in terms of pupils' and teachers' experiences or in terms of national economic benefits, was maintained and enhanced.

The problem with determinism in post-16 educational planning and management is simply that it assumes that what is planned is what is taught and that what is taught is what is learned (Bloomer and Morgan, 1993; Clark, 1994), ignoring at each step the significance of human agency. Unanticipated outcomes are, therefore, readily attributable to the failings of either the teacher or the learner, although those unexpected outcomes which can be deemed as successes might be claimed to be not quite so unexpected in the event and, therefore, attributable to successful curriculum design. Such determinism shares its roots with prevailing technical rational models of career decision-making identified in the last chapter. These, too, discount the significance of human agency and assume that once 'correctly matched' to a course or career on the basis of GCSE achievements, aptitude tests, career aspirations, subject interest or other demonstrable criteria at the age of 16, any subsequent 'drop out' or 'failure' is attributable to the teacher, the learner or the efficiency of the matching process. This is a technical determinism, also visible in the 'new managerialism', in accountability mechanisms and in virtually every corner of the 'newly reforming' post-16 sector. But it makes little allowance for human agency excepting where it is countered by strategic, remedial or corrective action. To gain some insight into the inadequacies of determinist models in the provision of post-16 education and to illuminate some of the conditions within which studentship is framed, we shall focus next upon the context and processes of students' post-16 choices.

THE POST-16 CURRICULUM: A MATTER OF CHOICE?

Claims made by central curriculum planners in respect of post-16 provision frequently justify the variety of types of course available in that sector as being a rational response to the varied aptitudes, needs and interests of students, inviting a concentration of attention upon 'matching'.

> This White Paper contains the Government's plans to improve and develop the education and training system for 16 to 19 year olds. It explains how we intend to meet the needs and aspirations of young people. ... Young people should be free at 16 to choose the education or training options which suit them best.
>
> (DES/DE, 1991, pp. 2 and 24)

However, evidence from the Leverhulme study indicates quite clearly that centralist curriculum prescriptions, rational though they may be, do not amount to an effective response in practice. In fact, they are very wide of the mark. Students' choices of post-16 courses are governed more by the social and cultural conditions in which they are made than by careful appraisal by young people of their own strengths, weaknesses and interests or of the intrinsic qualities of the courses available. Choices between A-level and vocational courses are often made on the basis of ill-defined perceptions of those courses as 'more demanding' and 'less demanding' respectively, upon the perceived status of courses, and with reference to some ill-informed notion of progression or career beyond the chosen course. Students' concepts of 'demanding' and, more importantly, how they come to decide whether they are equipped or willing to meet perceived demands, vary significantly by school of origin and catchment area. In one comprehensive school in the study, A-levels were evidently viewed by pupils as the 'natural' progression from GCSEs while vocational courses or employment were seen to be a departure from the norm. This school enjoyed a 'favoured' catchment area and over 60 per cent of its pupils proceeded to post-16 A-level courses. A neighbouring school, which drew pupils from a far less 'favoured' area, appeared to foster the view that the A-level route was confined to an élite and that 'normal' pathways from GCSE led to vocational education or training or work. Only 25 per cent of pupils from this school had entertained the prospect of doing an A-level course. Both of the following examples of reasons given for opting for BTEC National courses were volunteered by students from the second school who were eligible to proceed to A-level courses should they have chosen to do so.

> Because I'm not intelligent enough for A-levels.
>
> (intending BTEC National student)

> I have not enough knowledge to do a A-level. A BTEC would be a little easier.
>
> (intending BTEC National student)

The perceived status of courses appeared to have far more importance for students from the first school.

> A-levels are more highly regarded.
>
> (intending A-level student)

> I feel that (even though we are told the contrary by careers interviewers) we would be looked at more favourably if I do take A-levels.
>
> (intending A-level student)

The influence of family/cultural background upon choice is illustrated by the variation among students in their willingness to defer gratification and by the extent to which their choices are governed by a desire to obtain early employment in order to satisfy personal economic needs. In the first school described above, for instance, 52 per cent of aspiring A-level students stated an intention to leave full-time education to begin work at the age of 21 or over, while in the second school only 22 per cent did so. In the first school, only 19 per cent of all students indicated their desire to leave full-time education at or before the age of 18, while in the second school 39 per cent did so. As one student from the second school put it:

> Because I would only want to do one year at college so's I can get out in the world and get a job.
>
> (intending BTEC First student)

It was certainly the case that many students appeared ill-informed about the progression possibilities offered by their courses:

> So I can be able to learn more about what jobs are available for the future.
>
> (Tessa, intending A-level student)

The evident failure on the part of Tessa to recognize that job searching was not an explicit feature of her chosen A-level courses (she had opted for psychology but had not decided her other two subjects) can be explained by the influence of school culture, family expectations and peer norms in the process of choice-making. All took A-level to be the natural pathway from GCSE and Tessa had not seen fit to question that she should take that path. Her progression to A-level had been culturally framed, 'based on partial information which (was) localised, being based on the familiar and the known' (Hodkinson and Sparkes, 1993a, p. 250). In this context, Tessa's habitus precluded making any critical appraisal of her own needs and/or of the qualities of the courses available to her. Tessa's case, and those of many other students, offer insight into how cultural traditions of one form or another are reproduced from one generation to the next. They cast serious doubts upon the rational action theory of policy-makers and their assumptions of free and informed choice.

Quite a large proportion of students in the study (40 per cent) volunteered intrinsic reasons for their choices. 'Interest' and 'enjoyment' figured frequently. However, closer inspection revealed that while students formed their opinions on the basis of past experiences, they were rarely discriminating between subject knowledge, teaching methods, learning environment and other factors which made up those experiences. They assumed an interdependency between them while rarely considering the problematic nature of each. Thus they were disempowered as prospective learners through having little critical awareness of the very conditions under which their own learning might take place. Consequently, some who in Year 11 had declared a strong attraction to a particular subject were ill-prepared for the profound changes in the nature of subject knowledge or learning environment which they encountered in their transition from GCSE to post-16 courses. To have enjoyed or to have developed an interest in, say, French on the basis of a GCSE course was not, in itself, a very strong indication that A-level French would be an equally rewarding experience.

Only a very small number of students claimed to have made their choices on the basis of some insight into the intrinsic qualities of their post-16 courses and most of these insights concerned arrangements for assessment.

> I would like to do a BTEC National because I think it would be better than A-levels. I prefer course work than just 1 exam after 2 years.
>
> > (intending BTEC National student)
>
> As BTEC are all coursework and some people don't regard them with such a high standard as A-level.
>
> > (intending A-level student)

However, it was again apparent that students' choices were not made as the result of the most critical appraisal. Decisions were more often made on the basis of personal anxieties about one-off terminal examinations or the perceived 'market value' of different forms of assessment than they were upon personal experiences of success and failure in different types of assessment or upon the qualities of the knowledge that was the subject of assessment. Any view of the epistemological foundations of courses ranked fairly low among the criteria that guided students' choices.

Of course, many students cited career prospects among their reasons for choice of course, but there were only small differences between aspiring A-level and vocational course students in the frequency with which they offered career pathways as justifications for their choices. However, A-level and vocational course students' concepts of career and progression did vary considerably. Many intending A-level students, it appeared, were more prepared to suspend commitment to a particular career route, viewing their post-16 studies as a 'general' education that would enhance their eligibility in the 'choice market' at some later stage. For some, it was apparent that this stage might not arrive until the end of their higher education. In contrast, intending vocational course students were less prepared or able to invest faith in a 'general education'; it seemed that they wanted to see a clearer and closer connection between their post-16 studies and their future livelihood. For them, the earlier commitment to some career pathway was a significant personal need; it offered some assurance to them (and their families) that they were routed to a particular career. Despite the rhetoric of policy-makers and its emphasis on providing for students' needs, the reality was that habitus, in the form of culturally sustained values, attitudes and beliefs concerning deferred and spontaneous gratification, future–present time orientation and locus of control (Bernstein, 1961; Coleman *et al.*, 1966; Lewis, 1966; Strodtbeck, 1961; Sugarman, 1967), had a profound effect upon decision-making. Again, rational action theory and its technicist foundations prove inadequate in the face of the powerful effects of habitus and agency in explaining the choice-making process.

From this brief summary of the social conditions of post-16 choice-making it is not only the shortcomings of technicism which are apparent but the very pervasive influence of class, as has been noted elsewhere in this book. School catchment areas, family and cultural values, post-16 course identities (ascribed), students' conceptions of career and, indeed, the scope within which students exercise real choice, are all visibly circumscribed by class. The same is almost certainly true of gender and ethnicity. The choice-making process itself, rather than providing opportunities for them to break from the restraints of class, serves for many students simply to reproduce class differences in their learning, career and social trajectories. While the capacity of education to reproduce or, at least, not counteract inequalities such as this is well documented in European and American literature (Althusser, 1972; Bowles and Gintis, 1976; Bourdieu and Passeron, 1977; Apple, 1979) and also in literature expressly focused on British post-16 education and work (Willis, 1977; Avis, 1991c), the current situation is that of class reproduction being facilitated by the very prescriptions ostensibly geared to the achievement of a classless society.

We have acknowledged the effects of determinism and rational action theory upon curriculum planning and provision and, in earlier chapters, the impact of instrumentalist views of knowledge and learning. But what is most disconcerting is that, by the end of their compulsory education, so many young people have acquired little critical awareness of the very conditions which provide for their own learning. In such circumstances, the prospects of students ever becoming 'knowledge workers' or empowered citizens within a democratic society would seem quite remote unless the post-16 curriculum is expressly geared to promoting among students a critical awareness of self and others. However, as we have noted throughout this volume, the post-16 curriculum is driven by other imperatives and it is against those backdrops that the significance and potential of studentship must be considered.

THE EMERGENCE OF STUDENTSHIP

> **Matt**: I didn't really start considering my A-levels until I was told I'd have to do it and start applying for college and fill out forms and all of that sort of thing. I was just concerned with my GCSEs really and, erm ... My problem I had was that there wasn't any subjects which I was particularly better at at that level than other ones and my GCSE results were sort of ... well I got six As and two Bs or something like that 'cos we only did eight out at school, erm ... I didn't know which direction I wanted to go in and I, sort of, had all my science teachers saying, 'Go on and do science' and, sort of, art teachers saying, 'Go on and do art' and, sort of, like, humanities saying, 'Go on and do history or this and that or whatever' and I just didn't know what to do so I ended up with a really bizarre choice of A-levels. After my GCSEs, first of all I chose philosophy, maths and something ... and then, during the summer, I just thought that was a really silly combination and tried to change to art and English combined with history or communications and I couldn't get on to that and so I ended up doing communications, history and English ... I found it difficult to find out what direction I wanted to go in. I mean I used to go and talk to careers people and stuff like that and they'd say, 'Well, what are your strengths?' and whatever. And I said, 'Well, I feel I could go in any direction' and they didn't really have anything to point me towards. They'd try to say, 'Well, what do you enjoy?' and I'd say, 'Well, I enjoy a bit of this and I enjoy that sometimes', or whatever ...
>
> *So the first 'bizarre' choice which was philosophy, maths and something else ...*
> **Matt**: Yeah, I think it was either, history or communications.
> *What drove you to that? Why maths, say?*
> **Matt**: Maths because that was pressure from my family.

Really?

Matt: Yeah, because I'd done well in sciences – because I got As in the science subjects and an A in maths – and they said, 'Well, this is what'll get you so and so.' Especially my sister because she's an engineer so she's very much into that side of things and she was saying, 'You've got to have maths! If you haven't got maths, you're not going to get into university' and all this sort of rubbish. I was confused, I didn't know what to do so I just put that down as one of my choices. But I had two friends who were both doing maths and couldn't stand it and I realized I really didn't enjoy maths at all.

And why philosophy?

Matt: Philosophy, well I was just getting into thinking about things in a wider sense and philosophical thoughts running round my head and I thought it would be a good excuse to, actually, get more into all that, sort of, side of things.

OK. Then you went to the new choice – the history, English and communication studies ...

Matt: Yeah. Well I tried to get on to do English A-level and art combined course along with history or communications but that was full up ... So I just decided then that maths was a complete ... really not what I wanted to do at all and I wanted to go and do art instead, basically, and English because I enjoyed reading and, sort of, history because it was something I actually found quite interesting and found just came to me quite naturally and I didn't have any problems with it so I thought, well that. And communications I was always interested in as well 'cos that was ... 'cos I had a friend who was doing that and that just struck me as really interesting, the sort of topics that were covered within that. I decided I wanted to go off more into the creative side of things or looking at creative stuff.

So at that time, which would have been just before the September, would it, during the early September?

Matt: Yeah.

At that time you made those new choices, did you have any conception of life beyond 18?

Matt: Oh yeah. Yeah. I was thinking of going on to university, yeah, but going more in an arts direction than a science one. I just thought, 'I'll have to go that way instead of ...' 'cos I think it was more the sort of person I was. But I still had this big conflict between, sort of, visual arts and more, sort of, subjects like communications, English, history and those sort of subjects 'cos I couldn't get on to the English and art combined one. That was just something that I felt just said to me, 'Well, I'll just do that,' 'cos it was something which was decided for me, in a way, I didn't just go for it. I could've gone for a separate art A-level or something else but I just didn't do it in the end.

You said about, 'the sort of person I was'. Are you still that person you were two years ago or ...?

Matt: No. No. I'm a different person now.

The interview with Matt reveals a number of factors which had a bearing upon his choice of A-level courses: his friends, his family, his prior learning experiences and the availability of courses. But these factors alone did not prescribe the choices which Matt made and remade. Rather, as he put it, it was 'more the sort of person I was' or, when viewed in the context of his whole two-year course, the person he was becoming. At 16, Matt did not know the person he was to become. He admitted to some confusion when making his original choices and gave little indication at that stage that the 'person he was' had much of an impact upon his decisions. When revising those choices, however, he did so on the basis of an emerging awareness of his personal relationship to knowledge and the social world. It is quite apparent that the routine experience upon which his personal appraisal had been based was not simply that of the secondary school curriculum. Political, moral and philosophical dilemmas had come to impinge upon Matt's consciousness and he offers a clear indication that the 'person he was becoming' was not merely the product of formally prescribed experiences but a unique expression of human agency.

Matt was not unique among young people proceeding into post-16 education in having made his choices amid some uncertainty about his own needs. However, he was among a minority in reviewing his position during the summer vacation prior to commencing his courses and then seeking to make major changes to his programme of study. His case was considered by his tutors to be 'exceptional' rather than 'normal' in these circumstances. Most of his peers, it seemed, elected to stick with the choices they had made up to a year earlier. A technical rational account of Matt's choice-making process would probably stress that he had lacked sufficient information when making his initial choices and that it was, therefore, quite understandable that he should have discovered himself to be 'ill matched' with the courses he had selected. His peers, under such accounts, would be regarded as being 'well matched' since they had stuck with their initial decisions. However, to adopt such explanations would be to ignore completely the profound influence of Matt's emerging 'person I was' in the process, a person whose identity rested so heavily upon its relationship with knowledge and the social world that it proved in the end to exert the most profound influence over Matt's final settlement with the prescribed post-16 curriculum. It would also be to ignore the emergent persons among Matt's peers.

But that was not the end of the matter, of course. Matt's habitus (what he calls his 'person') did not cease to evolve simply because he had crossed the threshold into post-16 education and made a commitment to certain courses of study. His growth and development continued in the light of newer and newer experiences that the social world in general and his teachers and courses in particular had to offer. So, what 'person' did emerge through this process, and how?

> **Matt**: It's just very bizarre and my mind, I think, was developing in other directions at the time. You know, science was something I was always interested in, like on watching *Tomorrow's World* level really. And maths was ... I was finding I was increasingly more interested in people as opposed to like figures and formulae and that sort of thing – and how people interacted as opposed to how chemicals did, or whatever ...
>
> I think that a lot to do with it was, erm, one of the subjects I was doing, 'cos I was interested in it, especially communications. I got introduced to all sorts of ideas about objective reality and all sort of, like, sociological concepts and the idea that everything is just a construct of things and the media and all that. And I just got really really interested in that and that's influenced the whole way I view the world and the way I feel about myself and whatever and it's helped me work things out. And I just find, sort of, human society incredibly fascinating. I don't know, it just helped clarify some loose ideas that were running around my head of ... And history as well: looking into politics a lot. I became quite interested in politics for a while and worked out my political opinions, really ...
>
> There were quite large elements of what I was learning in college which I wouldn't have divorced from my self-development at all. I mean, it very much assisted it – especially the whole history, reading about fascism and communism, like I was saying ...
>
> *Can we have a look at the A-level courses?*

Matt: Yeah ... He'd [Matt's history teacher] come in with his file. He'd sit down with his file and he'd just sit there and read, lecture to you... There're a lot of people who – he would be talking – you could see it going into their ear and it was like they had a wire connected from their ear to their hand and they were just writing it all down and none of it was really going into their head at all. They were just writing down what he was saying, practically word for word and just filling up sheets and sheets of writing. There was no, sort of, constructive notes going on or whatever. So he was just putting out this knowledge but he wasn't telling people how to process it so I don't think it was that good a way of doing it... It does get a bit tedious after lecture after lecture. It's just like a talking textbook, basically ...

The Tudors component of the course was only made up of four essays which you had to write about a really specific subject within the Tudor period – they give you a really specific question and you have to answer it – and I just came to the conclusion, well, what is the point of learning the entire expanse of Tudor history, going to two hours of lectures a week to only write four essays about a specific thing? So I hardly ever went to them and then when we were given a question, I'd go down to the library, get say five books out about that topic, read up about that and then write the essay and managed ... And I thought I can use my time more constructively than learning about these things.

I mean, I was genuinely interested in the things that I was doing and I do a lot of reading. I mean, I used to do things like, erm, say I needed a course work project in or something in a couple of weeks, I just wouldn't go to my lectures for that week and worked really hard on that course work project at home and get that done and then go to the lectures when I felt I needed to go. I mean, I tried to go regularly but there'd be times when I'd work really hard for a while and then just not really do a lot for a couple of weeks and relax and sort of go out with friends and then get back into it and do a lot of work at home and then go back to the lectures and catch up. Basically, I used college as a resource, really, for my own ends which you could say was unfair in a way on the other students who were in ... I mean, that's what my history lecturer was trying to say to me: 'It's not fair that you're only coming these certain times and they're having to come all the time and you're still, like, getting the grades' and I said, 'Well, that's what the system's all about, really, isn't it?' And he had a paradox running round his head. He couldn't quite decide what was going on... but he was saying, 'You should conform and come to lectures every week' and whatever, even if you don't really need to. And I just thought that was stupid and just carried on the way I was and then he just tried to throw me out again. He tried to get me to pay for my exams as well 'cos he said I hadn't turned up to enough lectures... he invented some bizarre statistic ...

Like I said, he tried to throw me off the course, saying I wasn't turning up to lectures. He actually made this incredible case, saying that I was completely incapable of doing course work and, therefore, I should repeat my first year and do another second year and do an exam-only course, which would have meant I would have had to have stayed for an extra year, just finishing off history A-level. He would say things to me like, 'Look, I tried all my life to work against the system and you just can't do it; it's like hitting your head against a brick wall, you've just got to resign yourself and go with it and go to all this and do this and that and you can't change it from the inside, you can't do anything about it' and all that and I was just thinking, 'Well, maybe not for you but it's working pretty well for me at the moment and I'm getting my work done.'

I mean, I created my own curriculum ... I mean, college was the impetus for that, very much, in that it showed me directions to go in and lecturers were giving me ideas and things like that and talking to me about things but it's like I said, I think, I said the best way to put it was I just used it as a resource. When I felt I needed information to help me in my A-level studies I'd go to lectures and go to college and whatever. But if I didn't, I wouldn't.

His English teacher's prediction was that Matt's A-level grade would fall somewhere between an 'A' and a 'U', while his history and communications tutors were only marginally more decisive. In the event, Matt obtained 'A' grades in all three A-level subjects, a fact that was greeted by one of his tutors with, 'Well, on reflection, I'm not *that* surprised.'

We have used Matt in this chapter to illuminate the conditions of studentship and something of the rich variety of forms that it can take. From Matt's story, it is evident that his post-16 career to 'becoming the person' he became was susceptible to both structure and agency. The structural turning-point of progression from pre- to post-16 education precipitated his decision-making about post-16 courses and doubtless contributed in some way to the self-searching which followed. However, its effect was to release an emerging awareness of self which, in turn, proved so significant in the subsequent development of Matt's learning career. The prescribed curriculum, coupled with what Matt experienced to be the essentially technical rational expectations of his history tutor, gave overt direction and impetus to his learning career. However, although constructed for the purpose of assisting its development, they served more to frustrate than to promote it. In the event, agency counted for far more; Matt had proved a 'successful outcome' not because he had exercised 'consumer choice' over the opportunities made available to him but because he had asserted his agency in order to change those opportunities. While the fact of his success distinguishes him from many of those young people who have been the subject of studies of student resistance, disaffection and rebellion (Corrigan and Frith, 1975; Willis, 1977; Aggleton, 1987), the processes of Matt's retreatism and innovation are closely akin to those of careers of disaffection reported elsewhere. The important point to stress here is that nonconformist adaptations to the requirements of post-16 education are not to be dismissed merely as 'dysfunctional' or 'deviant' but demand proper consideration for their own educative value. While Corrigan and Frith (1975) claim on the basis of their work with working-class youth that young people (and, for that matter, their teachers) have 'no notion of resisting education as *education*' (p. 235) and that class interests and 'educational interests' are fundamentally opposed, the experience of Matt and many of his peers was that what was perceived by others to be resistance was, in fact, profoundly educative.

It must be said that of all the cases witnessed in the Leverhulme study, Matt's studentship proved to be the most starkly innovative. There were, indeed, many others who sought alternative means to the broadly shared ends of A-level success but few who proved so strong as Matt in asserting agency in the face of structure and none who did so to such powerful effect. However, the fact that Matt's learning career was, by any estimation, remarkable should not be allowed to obscure the fact that many other students also made innovative and successful adaptations to the prescribed curriculum. Examples of innovative responses ranged from student-initiated study groups meeting in the 'twilight hours' for the purpose of confirming their understanding of what they believed they were supposed to be studying, to cases of students who, by their own admission, did very little 'out of class' work of any description but who were demonstrably skilled in ensuring that their personal learning needs received tutorial attention within planned lesson time, even where this was at the expense of student peers receiving such attention in equal measure. Some, it was clear, had a marked preference for learning activities which required them to adopt a purely 'receptive' role and retreated from, or even rebelled against, activities demanding their more active engagement with knowledge sources. For others, a majority, the reverse was true. While many students made some innovative response that was to be explained, at least in part, by their dispositions to learning activities, most were strategically compliant in the event. Unlike Matt, they rarely absented themselves or challenged their tutors' expectations. Rather, they would take pains to ensure the outward appearance of their engagement while visible to their tutor, confining their mental or practical innovations to themselves or their friends.

A further case of innovative studentship which contrasts on a number of counts with Matt's was that of Sarah, who had joined the A-level chemistry course with the intention of continuing into higher education and a career 'in the scientific field'. Her choices were rational in the sense that her post-16 and higher education decisions were made in the light of her career ambitions. Her career choice, though not firmly decided, was based upon her assessment of her own strengths and personal preferences, an assessment of employment prospects and, most certainly, confirmation by her family, peers and teachers that a scientific career following a university education was a realistic ambition. She was well-qualified at GCSE level, with ten grade As and one grade E. Although she was not alone among the chemistry students in being very well-qualified at GCSE level, Sarah's attitude to learning was markedly different from that of many of her peers. She stated a clear preference for learning activities which afforded the opportunity to adopt a critical perspective on knowledge and attached far less value to those activities which entailed a more passive and receptive student role (Bloomer, forthcoming). In many respects, Sarah seemed to be the 'ideal student' and this was cautiously acknowledged by her tutor, Richard.

> *Richard*: Ah, it's funny you should mention Sarah. She's quite an able girl, I think, but so... er, airy-fairy. I mean she doesn't seem to be with us at times. She asks some strange questions ... Sometimes she's quite perceptive but quite a lot of the time it's as though she's in another world ... day-dreaming, almost.
>
> *Airy-fairy?*
>
> *Richard*: Yes. What I mean is that there's a lot of foundation work to do in the first year, chemical equations and calculations and new techniques, and at times Sarah appears disinterested almost. She is sometimes late and has missed the odd lecture or two. But when she asks questions during a practical, for example, they often seem to be off at a tangent or related to something we've done earlier in the year or not at all, whereas most students – those who do ask the questions, that is – are much more concerned with the thing we're doing at the time.

Sarah's tutor appeared to have a clear view as to what counted as admissible knowledge at any given point in time in the course. His views on planning stressed that the 'factual content' and 'new techniques' were to be mastered in the first year of the course while 'answering A-level questions', 'applying chemical knowledge' and 'working things out for themselves' provided the main diet for year two. On the matter of student learning, it was apparent that he expected his students to follow his own lines of reasoning quite closely, so deepening their understanding of specific selections of chemical knowledge even, it appeared, at the expense of understanding the place of that knowledge in a wider scheme of chemical or non-chemical knowledge.

But Sarah was 'airy-fairy'. She lived in a world where views of knowledge and expectations of learners were quite different from those held by her chemistry teacher. Sarah's world lay outside the boundaries of her teacher's visions of chemistry, of chemistry education and of studentship. Sarah was a puzzle.

> *Richard*: She could do very well, I think. She's quite able. But I doubt she'll actually be able to rise to the challenges ahead without some change in outlook. There's a lot of hard work to do in A-level chemistry, you know.

Sarah's view of her chemistry education, on the other hand, did not mirror her teacher's concerns about her. Sarah, like Matt, knew exactly where she stood in relation to her A-level course. Her vision of learning and studentship was of enjoyment, not hard work, and of finding knowledge from a variety of sources, not merely receiving it in an uncontestable form.

> *Sarah*: Learning about chemistry is fun ... I like [to listen to] others' opinions. Any problems, you can ask questions and get answers, not just from the tutor but from other people as well.

Sarah's studentship was *innovative* in so far as she sought novel and eclectic sources to assist the development of her personal chemical knowledge, *retreatist* inasmuch as she was 'airy-fairy' and distanced herself from her tutor's concepts of knowledge and learning, *rebellious* only in so far as her 'strange questions' could be perceived as disruptive, and *strategically compliant* inasmuch as she attended and did the work she was expected to. But she was by no means unique, as we have already demonstrated in Matt's case. There were many students who, in some way or other, sought to detach themselves from dependency upon their tutors' views of legitimate knowledge sources and forms. Moreover, there was ample evidence that, although some students' responses were an expression of individual agency, as in the cases of Sarah and Matt, others were more readily recognizable as bound up in group agency. But only a minority, it appeared, had the confidence or ability to assume control over their learning affairs to the degree that Sarah and Matt did. Both cases illustrate the potential and the will, at least, of some students to claim responsibility for the selection of knowledge sources and for the creation of a unique, personal knowledge through a critical engagement with knowledge in a variety of forms. Any curriculum claiming to provide for the 'knowledge worker' will be seriously lacking if it does not *require* students to exert themselves over knowledge and learning in ways that Sarah and Matt have shown. Only through such individualistic or group studentship will the concepts of empowerment, autonomy and independence have value beyond that of a rhetoric colonized in the interests of capitalism.

These few illustrations from the Leverhulme study help locate some of the major flaws in centralist planning. Current policy-making carries with it assumptions that students are well-informed about the qualities of their proposed courses, that they make choices on the basis of a careful examination of their needs as learners and persons, that they are 'ready' to make choices, and that they have unrestrained opportunities to exercise choice. The reality is that, for many students, post-16 progression is not a matter of open choice. For others, choices are ill-informed or made for a variety of pragmatic reasons rarely acknowledged as legitimate in local or national advice on the subject. In practice, progression into post-16 education is rarely achieved solely through a careful 'matching' of students with courses, ambitions with routes, needs with opportunities or learning with teaching, as the technical rationalism of centralist policy presupposes. Students make sense of post-16 progression in quite different ways to those which planners have in mind and make their decisions in accordance with their own interpretations of the situation – interpretations which are governed by evolving habitus.

But the culturally-derived agency of young people does not cease when they take up their places on post-16 courses. While contemporary curriculum prescriptions frequently reinforce an illusion that courses are designed in response to a variety of human interests and needs (e.g., DES/DE, 1991), the reality is that students do not perceive them in the same way. While the rhetoric of centralist planning may claim that curriculum prescriptions are sufficiently flexible to provide for a diversity of human interests and needs, students' experiences frequently stress that, at least to some degree, prescriptions are limiting and stifling rather than embracing and liberating of personal interests and human agency. In those cases, such as Matt's, where key teachers acted so as to confirm and reinforce the restrictive nature of prescriptions, the tension between personal interests and prescriptive practices was most visible of all; in other cases, tension was diffused through teachers acting upon prescriptions in such ways as to create opportunities for the expression, even harnessing, of personal interests. Reality for most students witnessed in the Leverhulme study was not of matching or meeting course prescriptions but of 'acting upon' prescriptions through various forms of studentship in the creation of their learning careers. That reality was visibly contained within the ever-moving boundaries of their habitus, propelled by a newly emerging consciousness of self, of 'becoming a person'. While technical rational curriculum planning is based upon assumptions that curriculum prescriptions determine personal careers, the students in the Leverhulme study offered numerous indications of the contrary: of the power of human agency in determining curriculum through studentship.

Given these observations, we shall now turn to specific features of post-16 curriculum which relate most strongly to the central themes of this book. We have already alluded to technicism as treating people as objects and how this obscures an active view of both citizenship and learning. While the present chapter, thus far, has focused on learning and on how the presence of an active studentship helps to illuminate major flaws in an essentially technicist culture of planning, we shall now turn to the problem of citizenship and to the potential among young people for the development of that critical thinking which is an essential condition of their full and responsible participation in a democratic society.

A CURRICULUM FOR CITIZENSHIP?

Earlier chapters have noted the widespread use of such concepts as empowerment, autonomy, democracy and citizenship in contemporary literature originating from a variety of sources. The terms are freely used by both Right and Left and have never been satisfactorily articulated in curriculum planning (Gore, 1993; Troyna, 1994). They are hugely problematic concepts whose value rests more in their rhetorical power than in any clarity or direction they give to curriculum planning or implementation. Empowerment, for instance, for the Right means the opportunity for young people to exercise choice or take greater control of their working and learning careers within narrowly prescribed limits on matters such as training credits or learning vouchers (CBI, 1993; White Paper, 1994), while for the liberal educator it can mean encouraging young people to exercise their studentship – qualitatively different rights – within the far broader limitations of a moral democracy. To students, empowerment might well entail exercising power across both of these spheres and far beyond. The promotion of student autonomy and independence is similarly problematic, with no agreement and little evidence of clear thought about the criteria to be used in judging whether or not autonomy or independence has been achieved. Whether such concepts concern independence from adult control, from established versions of knowledge and of knowing or from given ways of learning is seldom made explicit. However, while they may amount to little more than empty rhetorical devices, they command considerable authority when used to provide assurances to disparate interest groups on matters ranging from the needs of the 'knowledge worker' to the social construction of knowledge in post-16 education to the deinfantilization of learning. Citizenship and democratic participation are also widely used to describe key values and purposes of new curriculum developments. Students' rights to voice their views, to be listened to, and to participate in determining their own destinies within some democratic framework are now widely acclaimed principles. However, such acclaim obscures fundamental conflicts inherent in the concepts of citizenship and democracy while giving little regard to the opportunities to achieve them in practice.

The 'buzz' words have much in common. They are contested concepts, given the context in which they are used, but they have all been summoned in one formulation or another to legitimize by their rhetorical power current post-16 curriculum innovations. They are related concepts in so far as they each seek to describe the relationship of the learner to the wider social (or educational) structures in which learning takes place. There is agreement among them inasmuch as they each attach importance to self-fulfilment, self-determination and self-actualization (Giddens, 1991). But unless their essentially contested nature is rendered explicit they have little meaning when applied to post-16 education.

An analysis of citizenship is provided by Carr (1991), who notes that the National Curriculum Council's (1990) treatment of the subject is a clear example of a failure to provide anything in the way of clarification.

> [It] defines 'Education for Citizenship' as developing 'the knowledge, skills and attitudes necessary ... for exercising responsibilities and rights in a democratic society' without making any effort to clarify the complex relationship between 'citizenship', 'democracy' and 'education'.
>
> (Carr, 1991, p. 374)

Carr reveals opportunities for different interpretations of necessary knowledge, skills and attitudes as he pursues the distinction between rights and responsibilities and the dual roles of 'ruling' and 'being ruled' that citizenship embraces. He claims, on the authority of Aristotle, that education for citizenship is a general education which includes a political education. It has to be, since citizenship and democracy, which are inextricably linked, are political concepts. Participation, empowerment, autonomy and independence have political dimensions, too.

Carr also makes it plain that the concept of democracy, as it is used in contemporary Britain, does not rest upon any single, unified theoretical position. He sees fit to distinguish between a 'moral model of democracy' and a 'market model'. The former needs a 'knowledgeable and informed citizenry' and is an 'intrinsically justified form of social life' which enables individuals to achieve 'self-development, self-fulfilment and self-determination' through political participation. The market model, on the other hand, requires an individualistic society with 'a politically passive citizenry and a strong active political leadership ... circumscribed by the rule of law'. It is justified extrinsically by its instrumental effectiveness 'in securing the core principle of individual liberty ... to pursue private interests with minimal state interference' (*ibid.*, pp. 378–9). It does not require participation.

There are three essential conditions for an education for citizenship (based on the moral model of democracy). Firstly, there must be a *general education* to ensure that citizens have the wide knowledge-base necessary to enable them to participate effectively in all aspects of the political life of the community and that they are not disadvantaged through having abandoned study in (and, hence, familiarity with) key areas of knowledge. Secondly, there must be a *political education* to enable all citizens to develop skills in participation and, in particular, critical appraisal, reasoning and argument. Such an education would entail an understanding of the dual role of citizenship ('ruling' and 'being ruled') and would be as much concerned with the analysis of the moral basis of rights as it would with those of responsibilities. Thirdly, there have to be *opportunities to exercise independence, autonomy and empowerment* in the achievement of citizenship.

While there have been many attempts to 'broaden' or 'enhance' post-16 education, none could ever be described as constituting a general education and few could be regarded as achieving anything more than a modest level of success. In fact, they have been half-hearted attempts, largely failing in their recognition of the critical importance of a broad-based education for both economic growth (Green, 1995) and personal development. With the possible exception of the International Baccalauréat, no current British post-16 course provides for either a general education or a political education. Those proposals, such as Higginson's five A-levels (HMSO, 1988) and the British Baccalaureate (Finegold *et al.*, 1990), which might have provided a more general education have been firmly rejected, while NVQs, the very antithesis of a general education, are being imposed upon increasing proportions of the student population. It is indeed significant that the small number of institutions to break the mould have found it necessary to reach beyond the offerings of nation-state policy-makers and planners to the International Baccalauréat in order to provide a general education, albeit only for an élite group of students. For the rest, the vast majority, there is no systematic provision of a general education, while the growth of subject content-laden syllabuses, product-orientated assessment procedures and the commodification of knowledge for accountability in a market-place serves to ensure that the prospect of a political education remains extremely remote.

CREATING OPPORTUNITIES

To say that the conditions for an education for citizenship and studentship are not provided simply because there is no curriculum prescription for them would be to assume that what is taught and learned is simply a function of what is prescribed. Drawing upon evidence from the Leverhulme study, we shall illustrate the nature of teachers' interventions in curriculum and highlight ways in which teachers manage to create some of the conditions for an education for citizenship and studentship despite working under the restrictions of prescribed curricula.

A number of teachers in the study claimed that syllabus versions of knowledge were inadequate for their purposes. Knowledge, for these teachers, did not lie in discrete compartments suggested by themes, topics or even subject disciplines (see Bruner, 1973). To them, all knowledge is interrelated somehow and its partitioning into subjects and syllabus headings restricted opportunities to engage with knowledge in its full richness and complexity. The 'ideal student' for these teachers was one who possessed the will and the capacity to search beyond the immediate requirements of a given task, to locate problems in a wider conceptual framework than that intrinsic to the subject and to draw upon knowledge from 'other' sources in seeking a solution.

> [An outstanding student is] bright, clever, intelligent ... incredibly self-motivated, disciplined; good at self-management ... They have flair. You don't want someone who is blinkered. You want someone who is interested in lots of things, not just history, history, history.
>
> (A-level history teacher)

> One who is happy to talk; ... is prepared to think and read around the subject ... one who is in touch with the world.
>
> (A-level French teacher)

> The ability to make connections between ideas discussed at the time and things covered in the past and, say, things in the media.
>
> (A-level sociology teacher)

> You're restricted by the syllabus. Anyone would be. Learning goes on inside and outside of the classroom. You need to spend more time out of the classroom to gain the learning experience.
>
> (A-level chemistry teacher)

> They need a broader knowledge outside of the syllabus – for example, knowledge of current affairs. They are very narrow-minded and their general knowledge is not open to other issues – general literature, politics, etc. They don't know what is going on in their own country.
>
> (A-level French teacher)

Indeed, a common source of discontent among teachers was that only a few students conformed to their 'ideal type' and that the effort consumed in encouraging others to this extra-syllabus view went largely unrewarded.

> If something is not on the syllabus, there is no point in being at college. It's a waste; I've better things to do with my time. At the end of the day, it's not going to help.
>
> (A-level French student)

The view held by teachers, that students who were prepared to reach outside subject or syllabus knowledge in order to further their own understanding proved the most successful learners, is not itself a novel claim. Psychologists have made comparable claims in respect of elaborated conceptual knowledge, as Coles (1990) has illustrated.

Many teachers experience syllabuses and other formal prescriptions of their work as inadequate and even limiting. They attach importance to enabling students to transcend knowledge boundaries in order to achieve the essential conditions for what they deem to be the most effective learning. These conditions which provide for and promote the 'free exchange' of knowledge across syllabus boundaries are among the conditions required for a general education and, in so far as they release opportunities for the formulation of critical perspectives, are essential conditions for a political education. There is an evident will among many, but by no means all, teachers to move in this direction. However, opportunities to do so are hindered by subject and topic-specific syllabuses and traditions in practical teaching (see Keddie, 1971), on the one hand, and resisted by those students whose orientation to knowledge and learning is shaped by utilitarian values on the other. Student resistance of this type bears witness to the impact of agency – agency which, in this case, is rooted in a culturally derived utilitarianism.

The third of the conditions for an education for citizenship which we referred to earlier relates specifically to studentship and concerns opportunities for students to exercise independence, autonomy and empowerment. However, it is this terminology, we have claimed, which has never been satisfactorily articulated in curriculum planning; while it appears to have found favour with many audiences, it has given clear direction to none. Evidence from the Leverhulme study, in supporting this claim, illustrates the variations in practice between tutors who claim to subscribe to similar educational values and whose courses are guided by common aims and principles. The examples that we shall draw upon here are two BTEC National courses whose tutors each stressed the importance of 'students taking responsibility for their learning' and of 'developing understanding through problem-solving activities'. For each tutor, course assignments were the principal means by which their aims in respect of student independence, autonomy and empowerment would be realized. However, in practice they proved very different indeed.

In the first case, the tutor presented students with a novel problem and required them to devise a solution. Students were provided with necessary basic information but were left entirely to their own devices to conceptualize the problem and to decide how to tackle it. The tutor was available to provide such information as students requested but not to assist directly in the discovery of a strategy or a solution. Tutorial intervention occurred only when students were likely to put themselves or their work at serious risk. It was perhaps significant that the tutor's responses to student enquiries very often themselves took the form of questions, ensuring that it was the student who made the important decisions. In this first case of assignment-based learning, students were to take responsibility for *seeking* information and *devising* a solution; they were to solve a problem and through this process *develop their own understanding*.

In the second case, the assignment required that students applied a strategy that they were familiar with to a novel problem. The problem was partly conceptualized and the method given. Students were required to interpret the problem within a given scheme, to make minor adaptations to a solution that they knew in principle, and to apply it. The tutor provided a mass of information which students had to sift in order to extract the details that were required for the task, and periodically intervened to correct students and to provide specific answers to their questions. The purpose of the task, it was apparent, was for students to gain experience of applying the given strategy and to increase their competence in its application through practice. In this second case of assignment-based learning, students were to take responsibility for *selecting* information from a readily available stock; they were to solve a problem by *applying* a known solution and, through this, *consolidate their understanding* of both the problem and the strategy concerned.

Of course, these two examples should not be taken to suggest that there was some unambiguous correspondence between the tutors' aims and their students' learning. Student agency did exert a powerful effect and, within each class, there were numerous examples of students 'acting upon' the opportunities made available to them as they created their own curricula through studentship. However, in so far as tutors' expectations and creation of learning opportunities did impact upon the students – and they certainly did – these two examples of student assignment-based learning gave rise to different forms of knowledge and required quite different learning skills. This was despite being described by their tutors in very similar terms. The rhetoric, although commonly used in formal statements of course philosophy and frequently by tutors in their justifications of their practices, had provided no clear, or at least no common, direction. The nature of the independence, autonomy and empowerment that students acquired through these activities varied greatly, the experiences of students in the second group being more tightly circumscribed than those of the first group. But neither the teachers nor the students knew this.

The evidence offered by cases such as this serves to confirm the problematic nature of the concepts of independence, autonomy and empowerment. But it also points to the potential that teachers have, and which some teachers utilize, to enable young people to increase their control over the selection, creation and evaluation of knowledge. In the second example, above, opportunities for students to obtain a critical perspective on course knowledge were severely limited, while in the first they were considerably enhanced. Opportunities such as those offered in the first example confront students with the need to make choices which draw from a potentially wide range of subject knowledge, further knowledge and personal experience; they require that students experience the full effects of their decisions; they demand that participation with others is collaborative and negotiated for the purpose of achieving the task in hand rather than simply contrived in response to a requirement that students should somehow engage in work with others. It is opportunities such as these which provide for a critical engagement with knowledge and which are the essential conditions of an education for studentship and, in turn, for an active citizenship in a moral democracy. They provide for the liberation of what Habermas (1972) calls the emancipatory interest.

> At the level of practice, the emancipatory curriculum will involve the participants in the educational encounter, both teacher and pupil, in action which attempts to change structures within which learning occurs and which constrain freedom in often unrecognised ways. An emancipatory curriculum entails a reciprocal relationship between self-reflection and action.
>
> (Grundy, 1987, p. 19)

> Hence, 'practical wisdom' is manifest in a knowledge of what is required in a particular moral situation, and a willingness to act so that this knowledge can take a concrete form.
>
> (Carr, 1987, p. 172)

> The teacher is no longer merely the-one-who-teaches, but one who is himself taught in dialogue with the students, who in their turn while being taught also teach.
>
> (Freire, 1972, p. 53)

It is such opportunities which must provide the cornerstones for a new curriculum, not merely be added to it as appendages, if the demise of citizenship through globalization and the consequent unleashing of an aggressive nationalism are to be averted. But the assertion of such values in public education will not always be received sympathetically. It will be met with a most fierce resistance, given the extent to which the predominant market ideologies and technical interests of recent and present governments have impregnated British cultural institutions. It demands, as we have already claimed, that a critical and self-critical population is not, in itself, taken to be a dangerous thing (Beck, 1992).

OPPORTUNITIES FOR STUDENTSHIP

While some teachers may be inclined to create opportunities for a critical engagement with knowledge, we cannot simply presume that students will respond to those opportunities with equal enthusiasm or success. Just as teachers act upon centrally imposed prescriptions of their work to create opportunities for learning, so, as we have shown in our discussion of studentship, students act upon the opportunities created by their teachers by taking, adapting, selecting from, filtering, missing or rejecting them as they strive to create their personal learning careers. Largely through the expression of group or individual agency, as illustrated in Matt's and Sarah's cases, some succeeded in becoming autonomous, critical, independent and individual learner citizens in the face of counter-pressures from centrally inspired curriculum plans.

This chapter has illustrated a number of ways in which culturally located values and beliefs impact upon choice-making and also upon young people's opportunities, through studentship, to create their own careers as learners. A number of arguments have been put forward here. These have concerned the relative impact of structure and agency upon student learning. Determinist and technicist assumptions which underpin many examples of nation-state planning are deeply flawed inasmuch as they ignore the significant influence of teachers and learners in curriculum-making. Changes at a structural level, although often couched in terms of responses to student needs, are an inadequate response to those needs. They are dominated by a concern to equip young people for rationally defined roles, ignoring powerful claims that roles are created in response to complex, culturally bound networks of expectations. Change-makers presume 'role-taking' and have little vision of 'role-making'. Thus the significance of agency comes to be disregarded. Such technical rational planning also excludes any recognition of habitus and its part in the creation of learning careers.

This chapter has also addressed the problematic nature of empowerment, autonomy, independence, participation and democracy. There is much to suggest that these notions are exploited for their rhetorical value, but little to support the view that they contribute usefully to the aims of either an education for citizenship or for economic well-being. They attract widespread support on the basis of their surface features but, in so far as they remain uncontested, they serve to deflect attention from, rather than focus it upon, both the essential qualities of citizenship and the specifics of economic need. Effective, participant citizenship is not simply a matter of digging old people's gardens, talking to drug addicts or playing collaborative games; it rests upon a political education, achieved through the critical examination of all that impinges upon moral, social, political, intellectual or economic life. Moreover, economic needs will not be met by simplistic formulaic solutions such as 'upskilling the workforce' in its technical competence; rather, they demand that the full complexity of the employment–education nexus is examined and that policy is formulated with full regard to the economic, social, moral and epistemological conditions which sustain it. Both broad aims will be achieved only when policy-makers are able to transcend illusory nation-state interests and engage properly with the demands of globalization.

The existing state of educational provision will not do. It does not serve even one of the varied interests which bear upon post-16 education effectively or efficiently. Most importantly, it disenfranchises young people as citizens and as workers through the 'dependency culture' which it engenders by its institutional discourse, contributing to the perpetuation of hegemonic relations and the maintenance of a low-skill, low-trust society in the process. Radical change, guided by principles of moral democracy, social unity and community and recognizing the need to combine knowledge with democracy, is the only way forward if we are to liberate for both personal and public benefit the wealth of human interest and ability which is our natural resource. Only then will there be any realistic prospect of shifting to a high-skill, high-trust equilibrium. Moreover, only through such radical change can there be any real prospect of reconstructing social relations in a manner suited to the demands of globalization. But change must free educational provision from dominance by blinkered technical rational thought, managerialism and the confines of market 'competences' and 'outcomes' which define students as 'customers' or 'skills carriers', and must make a proper response to the potentialities and limitations afforded by habitus and to the broader conception of student as *learner*. Change will be slow, indeed, since structural alterations in the form of syllabus and course reform alone will be insufficient. There needs to be systematic support for cultural accommodation of the values embedded in a radical alternative. A programme for change must

> suggest to individuals alternative ways of interpreting their actions and defining their 'reality'. But to provide individuals with new concepts is not simply to offer them a new way of thinking. It is also to offer them the possibility of becoming more self-conscious about the basic pattern of thought in terms of which they usually make their own actions intelligible ... Practices are changed by changing the ways in which they are understood.
>
> (Carr and Kemmis, 1986, p. 91)

In the first instance, change will require careful attention to aims and principles of post-16 education rather than to content, or even learning processes. It will require comprehensive recognition of the value of a general and political education as the means of promoting global awareness and the critical appreciation of knowledge required of an informed and participating citizenry and labour force. This will entail a successful challenge to current orthodoxies and the regimes of truth which sustain them. It will also require a careful reappraisal of studentship and the development of opportunities for learner independence and empowerment which extend beyond those of current practice. Not only will the rhetoric of empowerment, autonomy and independence require translating into meaningful and achievable curriculum aims, but the translation itself must take account of the social conditions in which aims become transformed into teaching practice. This, in turn, demands that the apparent failure of the State Syllabus for Schools (Golby, 1994) to provide for proper stimulus to the enquiring mind be researched and remedied and that those parts of learning which pencil-and-paper tests cannot reach be accorded value. It also demands that the cultural conditions which foster utilitarianism, dependency, fatalism and other anti-educational values be changed and that educational planners make a positive, rather than negative, response to the potential which agency might offer to the achievement of a truly educative post-16 curriculum for the knowledge worker and participant citizen. Above all, it requires recognition that economic development and social well-being are inextricably linked and must be addressed by a common strategy. That strategy must, first of all, be secured in principles and values of democracy, professionalism and participation as opposed to those of marketism, managerialism and exclusion.

> But in a secular society those beliefs are under siege – and ... belief cannot be reinvented because it might serve a helpful social and moral purpose. The task is more complicated. It

is to reinvent a value system in which obligations are stressed along with rights – and so underpin democracy and the wider society.

The way forward must be to transform the institutions of market capitalism so that, instead of embodying networks of unravellable spot-market relations, there are new legal obligations to acknowledge a reciprocity of obligation.

(Hutton, 1995b)

In our final chapter, we draw upon the various themes developed in this book in order to indicate the shape and direction of reforms so urgently needed for tackling the many problems we have illustrated here.

Chapter 8

Where Next? Education and Democratic Politics

As teachers and researchers, together with our colleagues and students, we have spent most of our professional lives working within the contradictions set by Conservative education policies. It is clearly now time for a change, but not for the reasons so often associated with this cliché. One of the key issues we have sought to address in this book is the association between the shaping of public knowledge and the cultivation of nationhood – which has been such a fundamental feature of the New Right agenda for education. In the Introduction we argued that so central has this process been that it has become the legitimating base for most of the reform of the past two decades. Despite its populist power, our view is that the New Right's concept of nationhood can no longer sustain credibility. Yet, as the tentative proposals so far put forward by opposition parties indicate, there is as yet no clear intellectual focus for an alternative future policy.

So far, this book has been structured around a number of critiques of British, mainly English, education and training policy. It is our claim that, although much of this policy has been ostensibly formulated to promote economic well-being, social cohesion and personal growth, it is grossly ill-informed and simplistic. The reasons why this should be so are essentially twofold. Firstly, the deleterious influence of New Right ideology and dogma upon policy-making in the 1980s and 1990s is inescapable and has been illustrated in various ways in all of the chapters of this book. The uncritical commitment of government to principles of 'free marketism' (neo-liberalism) in all spheres of social and fiscal activity and to a mythical 'golden ageism' (neo-conservatism) in prescriptions of societal and educational values has been the principal driving force behind recent changes. Such ideological commitments have denied opportunities for critical examination of education and public policy through their tight circumscription of the scope of analysis and enquiry and, hence, of informed and open decision-making. Through delineating and controlling the admissible questions, ideology and dogma have exerted a profound effect upon policy formation.

Secondly, the political will to address academic–vocational divisions in English education has been lacking in most post-war British governments. The underlying tension between academic and vocational education within the secondary and post-school curriculum has been a recurring theme of the English education system (Reeder, 1979) and arguably reflects more fundamental features of English culture, sometimes seen to be associated with Britain's overall lack of economic competitiveness (Wiener, 1981). If Sir Ron Dearing's (1995) proposals turn out to side-step a lasting resolution of that tension, contradictions in government policy remain. Ironically, on the day (19 July 1995) that Dearing unveiled plans for the future integration of academic and vocational education across the 14–19 age range, the Secretary of State for Education and Employment, Gillian Shephard, announced a quite separate initiative to allow disaffected 14-year-olds to spend significant amounts of time training in the workplace. Again, this not only spells confusion in government ranks over the aims of vocational education, as part of a skills revolution or as a form of social control, but it also contradicts two central tenets of Conservative education policy: the first, to establish parity of esteem of vocational education across the curriculum, and the second, to enhance both pupil motivation and school effectiveness by improving the quality of teaching and learning for pupils already in school. Allowing the least advantaged and motivated to opt for work-based training, as a means of influencing their attitude and behaviour, bypasses historic contradictions which have led to early specialization and low achievement, including declining national skill levels. Paradoxically, at a time when significant improvements are taking place in post-16 student participation in further education and training, this recent initiative is more reminiscent of the old vocationalism than the new enterprise culture. The *real* irony here is that after a century of state policy designed to take children out of the workplace and into school, the Conservative government should decide to reverse the process at a time when work for many is a thing of the past. Yet, behind the long line of compromises, of which TVEI and GNVQ have been the most recent, the conflict between old humanists, industrial trainers and public educators that has dogged the history of state education in England (Williams, 1961) has continued through the influence of the New Right and, more recently, with New Labour's apparent accommodation of Conservative education policies.

Secure in office for four- or five-year periods, successive governments have been conspicuous in their failure to undertake projects which will not guarantee them short-term political kudos. The reform of A-levels is a case in point. While there is widespread support for reform, governments have failed to take on the challenge for fear that they will have no demonstrable success to claim by the end of their terms of office and, possibly, little more than the fruits of upheaval to offer the electorate. But electorates will not sit idly by as governments fail to take decisive action. Thus it is that the action which governments have taken has been hastily planned, often without wide consultation and frequently without the necessary penetrating and critical examination of the problems in question. The answers that governments have provided in these circumstances – and they have provided many 'answers' – have been singularly lacking and often contradictory, driven as they have been by the short-termism of market and political expediency, including the nationalist one.

The pursuit of these particular political interests is enhanced by the 'discourse of derision' whose political function of policy prescription is to direct attention from the important critical scrutiny of ideas (S. J. Ball, 1994). One consequence has been to blame teachers, parents and young people for wider failures within education, the economy and the criminal justice system. This is exactly what has happened with the school and post-compulsory education agendas: the proliferation of centrally imposed policies and initiatives has been powerful and coercive in its impact upon the minds of practitioners and students at all levels as the scope for thought, action and employment has been progressively narrowed. At the same time, the rhetoric, employed in what can best be described as the 'vocationalization of everyday life', has functioned to disguise the complex and hugely problematic nature of the economizing of education. Put simply, the proliferation of policies and initiatives has smothered the *educational* questions which needed to be asked. The upshot has been to remove from practitioners many of the opportunities necessary to exercise professional judgement as, increasingly, they have become redefined as recipients, implementors or 'deliverers' of curriculum content, either as technicians or as 'part of the problem' to be overcome. While policy may prescribe technicianship, it is the full engagement with the problematic nature of practice which defines professionalism. Professional educators need to formulate their own strategies in the full knowledge of the particular situations within which they carry out their work, and it is for this reason that universalized, imposed policies serve more often to frustrate than to assist educational practice, parents and young people. What is the relevance of this to our analysis so far?

A recurring theme from the preceding discussion is that too much current thinking about post-compulsory education and training is locked in idealistic and ideological views about an over-economized society. This can be seen in the contrast between the idealism of post-Fordism and the more common practice of neo-Fordism; in the assumptions about the top-down impact of curriculum design and innovation on teacher activity and student learning; in the attempts to build careers guidance policies on assumptions about technical rational choice; and in the assumptions about the workings of an education and training market lubricated by contracts, credits and vouchers. It is typified by an erroneous assumption that improving educational achievement can and should necessarily result in economic improvement, greater prosperity and more jobs.

The danger for New Labour and various policy advisors on its fringes is one of retaining a vision of classlessness while, at the same time, ignoring the constraints of class, race and gender. Currently, the tendency to wrap up such constraints in the nomenclature of communitarianism, stakeholding, diversity and choice suggests an accommodation with, rather than a challenge to, New Right thinking. Above all it is typified by bland assumptions concerning the possibility of some prevailing consensus about educational objectives, where the interests of workers and employers, privileged and under-privileged, members of both genders, different social classes and different ethnic groups are somehow seen to be all the same. Thus, far from embracing pluralism and heterogeneity, such an assumed consensus fudges important issues to do with equality and cultural difference. The issue here is not just one of policy but the discourse of concepts and meanings which inform it. In his chapter 'The Service of Democratic Politics', Rorty argues that,

> We should stay on the lookout for marginalised people – people whom we still instinctively think of as 'they' rather than 'us'. We should try to notice our similarities with them. The right way to construe the slogan is as urging us to create a more expansive sense of solidarity than we presently have. The wrong way is to think of it as urging us to recognise such a solidarity, as something that exists antecedently to our recognition of it. For then we leave ourselves open to the pointlessly skeptical question 'is this solidarity real?'
>
> (Rorty, 1989, p. 196)

Here, Rorty points to ways in which our vocabulary betrays principles of inclusion and exclusion. Currently, in Britain, principles of exclusion rather than inclusion are high on the personal and policy agenda with new market rhetoric – opting out, deregulation and choice – legitimating new forms of inequality and privatization at home and in the labour market. But, in reality, fashionable policy concepts associated with public institutions opting out of state control have compounded the displacement of the unemployed, the sick and elderly, excluded from society by New Right social policy. The concealed social contradictions are many. Perhaps the most trivial are those resource-based struggles within the training field, hidden under the mythical assumption that young people choose an employer and training provider, rather than being chosen by them as we have shown in Chapter 6. Of greater concern is the invisibility of long-term, high unemployment for young people and others (Roberts, 1991). The inconsistency of current government training policy is that it is Janus-faced on this issue. On the one hand, policy-makers and analysts alike accept publicly the inevitability of high, structural unemployment for the foreseeable future. On the other hand, they espouse policy stances that exhort the individual to 'take responsibility' for their own careers, as if by so doing the problem of structural unemployment would evaporate. Even more serious is the invisibility of structurally linked disadvantage within the paradigm. Rampant individualism flies in the face of the evidence: class, gender, ethnicity and disability all have a powerful and persisting influence on patterns of educational achievement, job choice and broader life chances. Any policy actively concealing these, rather than trying to address them, must be challenged as a matter of principle, no matter how effective it might be in achieving other ends.

The gains such an ideology brings to the dominant groups in society are obvious. A tax-cutting government can ignore those deeper, potentially expensive, structural problems of unemployment and inequality, and blame individuals – young people, parents, training providers, employers, TECs and teachers – when things apparently go wrong. It cannot be the policy, because individuals determine their own futures. Similarly, the policy serves the purposes of industry – especially large employers. Once more, it is highly convenient to parrot the new mantra that each individual employee or unemployed person is responsible for their own education and training, so that if 'resting' – as actors would say – they should build their own portfolio of skills in order to make themselves employable once more (Ainley, 1994). Employers, on the other hand, have no statutory or other responsibility for employees who suddenly become surplus to requirements, which is not the case in many of Britain's major economic partners and competitors. At an individual level, the current policy ideology also serves the interests of those people, including us, who have reasonably secure and well-paid jobs as part of the core British workforce. The ideology legitimates personal, privileged status, excuses responsibility by blaming the victim for his/her own disadvantage, and legitimates cuts in direct taxation that raise disposable incomes. To paraphrase Hutton (1995a), this is the state we are in. So then, what are the alternatives?

NEW AGENDAS, OLD ISSUES

A concern throughout this book has been the emerging set of ideas and assumptions which frame post-compulsory education. These ideas have been counterposed to those of the New Right. We have examined ways in which a rhetorical reading of the progressive possibilities of post-Fordism is seen as *the* way forward. However, the promise of emancipatory work-relations built around post-Fordism is seriously compromised by the failure of the British economy. Such failure, overlaid by obsessive nation-state protectionism, has taken precedence over the construction of imaginative economic, employment and education policies appropriate to European and global markets. In fact, closure rather than openness has been the order of the day. Consistent with a determination to suppress resistance to its value system, the New Right has recognized that the most effective way to subordinate education and training to its interests is through the construction of a regime of truth that celebrates market and management effectiveness. Yet, by suppressing debate of the wider implications of globalization for education and citizenship, and by installing divided, minimalist, managerialist systems of learning and training for the majority of learners, there has arisen a policy shortfall which will take major political effort and will-power to reverse.

Optimistically, despite its pervading influence, New Right ideology is now more vulnerable than it has been in the past. Its contradictions have become increasingly apparent, if not embarrassing, to its supporters. It is, therefore, important that all who have a legitimate interest in education and training are not trapped by pessimism or by a political purism that rejects their engagement with policy. Rather, their participation in the debate over post-compulsory education is crucial. Even if that debate is set within an economistic discourse, it can still provide room for new thinking and strategic intervention. As Connell notes:

> The strategic problem is to generate pressures that will cumulate towards a transformation of the whole structure; the structural mutation is the end of the process, not the beginning. In earlier stages any initiative that sets up pressure towards that historical change is worth having.
>
> (Connell, 1995, p. 238)

Following on these comments, the limitations of an economistic view of education and training are becoming increasingly apparent (National Commission on Education, 1995). Such recognition is linked to the return of an interest in communitarianism and social justice, including concern on the part of both Left and Right about social solidarity and ethical issues. The result of such a shift in the intellectual and political climate is the realization that we can now start to think about school, post-compulsory and higher education in a much broader context than that of simply serving the interests of the economy. Questions around the curriculum, its usefulness, its ability to inspire as well as illuminate wider social relations, are raised together with the development of citizenship and the skills needed to participate in the polity. One of the dangers we have sought to avoid is the construction of an homogeneous notion of citizenship and value. We therefore want to retain notions of difference and yet move beyond the relativism of pluralism. What is needed is a view of citizenship that rejects absolutes and celebrates dialogue. Such a dialogue would also recognize points of antagonism across and within areas of difference within society. The democratic concern with social justice would recognize the potential for antagonism and should comprehend the real difficulty of moving beyond it. In fact, the commitment to democracy and social justice is an aspiration, for as one set of antagonisms are resolved others come to the fore. There are, as we have argued, a number of issues here that revolve around broadly post-modern concerns.

Post-modernism, or rather the post-modern age, is said to be marked by fragmentation. Capital becomes split into a variety of forms, some of which are benign and others less so. Here, we meet discussions of the Rhine model of capitalism set against the neo-American model (Albert, 1993). The former places importance upon collective success, co-operation and long-term objectives, whereas the latter stresses individual success, competition and short-term financial gain. In other words, capital *per se* is no longer simply the enemy – only those particular forms which are highly exploitative. Those which centre upon Fordist work-relations, seeking to maximize control over labour and minimize wages, would be a case in point. The time is set to transcend these. If we wish to live and work in a society that values and develops human potential, we should align ourselves with forms of education, work and capital that offer this promise. There is no real alternative to such a strategy in current conditions. Capital, therefore, is no longer *the* problem as such: some types are harmful but not all. Those forms that dwell on value-addedness should be at the forefront of current debate and policy, encouraging social and economic innovation and change. A number of writers have engaged with these issues (Ainley, 1994; Lipietz, 1993). Similar to our call for an innovative form of capitalism, Lipietz argues for one that uses and values the creativity of labour, rewarding it accordingly. His argument is set within a framework of global economic relations that embody an awareness of ecological and world development issues. Moves towards new economic relations are, therefore, to be encouraged, even though there are some losses to be incurred. A consequence of the easy assumption of consensus and goodwill is the masking of patterns of antagonism and oppression that criss-cross capitalist societies. This is particularly the case within British debates centred around New Labour. A notion of real struggle, the stakes and investments that people have in existing relations, is often overlooked. The result is innovation without change: newer economic relations are grafted on to old patterns of exploitation, serving to mask the latter in 'new' concepts such as the *stakeholder society*.

A sense of what is possible, a new form of political realism, requires us to recognize the constraints within which we operate. Undoubtedly, to encourage the more human forms of capital is appropriate. However, there is a real danger that by ignoring the logic of capital accumulation we overlook the antagonism that sets capital against human and ecological interests. The duality between the Rhine and neo-American models can be overstated, and if Saunders (1995) is correct in suggesting that the latter is gaining ascendancy, a simple alignment with the more human forms of capital is seriously compromised. Firms in this position will, if they are to survive, have to modify their practices to compete in the global market-place. The language of partnership between labour and capital, stakeholder capitalism and the like is thus seriously flawed. If we really are committed to the principles of democracy and social justice we have to go beyond such constraints. The material conditions within which we are located provide the potential for such moves: global impoverishment, ecological devastation and socially damaging rates of unemployment are the basis from which new developments must arise.

The move towards communitarianism, and more recently *stakeholding*, is an interesting, though perhaps flawed, example of the desire to develop new forms of solidarity. It can, for instance, easily camouflage underlying patterns of economic and social inequality and itself become inward-looking. Values, community and solidarity can readily be linked with pathology and nationalism by the Right. On the Left, without a radical politics, such notions can similarly lead to amelioration, fracture and a failure to challenge the conditions that generate social and economic inequality. If, for example, New Labour is to avoid the parochial nation-state response of the New Right to changes in international capital, it must first recognize the nature of what it is up against and tackle its policy consequences head on. Loose talk about values will not do. Embracing recognition that private monopoly capital is now dominant over state capital does not necessarily mean an uncritical acceptance of its worst-case implications. Currently, such change finds its expression in the dominance of a minority of transnational companies which control a majority of world trade. One consequence of this, in addition to financial deregulation and the freeing up of global information, is that one-third of the world's population is without work, with 20 per cent unemployed in Europe. At national level it is reflected in the demise of the old education and welfare state, premised upon demand management and full employment. According to Ainley and Green (1995), the British education and welfare state is being deconstructed into a contracting state which corresponds to a new mixed economy. As they see it, private and public sectors are no longer separate, as they were when government brought them together as 'social partners'. Instead, a semi-privatized contract state sector is becoming indistinguishable from a state-subsidized private sector. Not only is such a mixed economy reflected in the state-subsidized privatization of education and training, but it also finds expression in the marketization of education policy itself. Education, like jobs, like any other currency or commodity, is now being floated on the international exchange.

As we have argued, instead of facing up to the geopolitical implications of such change in Britain, the New Right has sought to utilize market forces to its own parochial advantage, by exerting its political and ideological will on the education reform process. In so doing, the New Right nation-state has accepted rather than challenged the basis of social and economic inequalities generated by geopolitical crisis in capital. Overwhelmed by such crisis in the late 1980s and early 1990s the Conservative government retreated into a nationalistic bunker while, at the same time, proclaiming the virtues of the enterprise state, vocationalism and the 'skills revolution' as keys to reviving the British economy. Such rhetoric, as we have argued, has little to do with reskilling the economy or with school improvement. Rather it concerns the political objectives of the New Right and, in particular, its determination to control the content and organization of education, welfare and public provision. By downsizing industry, education, welfare, housing and health in the face of fierce international economic competition, the Conservative government did little more than its traditional duty to protect the interests of the British political and economic élite which had no desire to invest in or pay for economic recession or the fall-out from market experimentation.

In so doing, the New Right has sought to achieve such objectives not just for the sake of it, but to control conflict and social divisions generated by its own economic policies. Thus, despite brave policy statements proclaiming the importance of a highly skilled workforce to the future of the British economy (DES/DE, 1991; White Paper, 1994), Conservative education and training reforms have been marginal in creating real employment opportunities and highly skilled jobs. More accurately, the introduction of a series of youth training initiatives and low-level NVQs has had a negative impact on the job market by reinforcing the low-skills equilibrium arising from Britain's narrowing industrial base. Moreover, the limited ambitions of the National Curriculum, coupled with a failure to get to grips with post-compulsory education reforms, has further locked British education into a declining economy. Yet, with so much emphasis placed on an over-idealized *laissez-faire* conception of the role of the state, it could hardly be otherwise.

If, in theory, education has been left to the vagaries of the market, the strong hand of the state has sought to control education in the service of declining capital rather than in the service of democratic politics. In so doing, the state has camouflaged its direct interest and influence, as pupils, institutions, parents, employers and others have competed for their survival in the market. Inevitably there are more losers than winners in this game. As the 1980s progressed, increasing regulation of school, further and higher education took place, accompanied by more detailed specifications of teachers' work and of the duties expected of senior management. By the early 1990s, a framework of greater regulation and accountability had been achieved, based largely on business and market values, within which a largely behaviouristic model of curriculum, learning and assessment was installed. Such reluctance to address recurring failures within British education reminds us of Katz's (1965) observation that British politicians and their policy advisers, by seeking

> to preserve the traditional and respond to the modern by avoiding the resolutions of uncomfortable dilemmas – and their evasions of the essential confrontations – have left Britain with unresolved and debilitating tensions.
>
> (Katz, 1965, p. 287)

The historic reminder here is clear. The real crisis in Britain represents a recurring *political* failure to address changes in the capital relationship between education, nation-state and wider geopolitical trends. The New Right's retreat into a narrow form of nationhood to secure for its own purposes, rather than share, a declining capital market, is now apparent. Increasingly, this finds its expression in huge disparities of wealth, income and poverty which surpass those of the 1930s (Rowntree Trust, 1995), and which have opened up further divisions between 'winners and losers' in school, college and job market.

A major problem for educationists, policy-makers and New Labour is how to respond effectively without adopting the New Right agenda. This is important, as current principles of marketism, managerialism and exclusion, as well as conventional values of democracy and professionalism, are under siege. Some policy rapprochement between the two looks likely, but will it be enough? In many ways the question is more complicated than it appears here. Put another way, what values should inform new policy-thinking, whose values should these be and how should they be represented? An additional complication is that what is meant by policy remains obscure: is it fashioned from the top, or from the bottom, and what should be the relationship between community, professionals, researchers and policy-makers? Addressing such questions suggests that any new settlement has to be underpinned by democracy and wider concerns of society.

The time has come to acknowledge changing economic realities and to consider how they should be dealt with at local, national and international level. It may be, for example, that full employment for all is a thing of the past: but that does not necessarily mean full-time employment is at an end (Ainley, 1994). Rather, it requires new thinking about the nature of work, including its construction, distribution and relationship with education and society. Planning rather than market arbitration is the key here. In education, as we have argued, a new critique is called for which unmasks the pretence of vocational education as the generator of secure employment. Such a critique should, maintain Ainley and Green (1995), start with the social situation of the learner – or studentship as we refer to it in Chapter 7 – placing learning at the heart of democratic rather than market arrangements. The current discourse presents a grossly misleading and over-simplified view of the link between these two. In essence, social interests are currently to be served by each individual maximizing his/her advantage within the constraints of what is centrally acceptable.

Yet, as Chapters 6 and 7 demonstrate, the choices and actions which young people make have a significant impact on both their own lives and the effectiveness of national policies. Furthermore, for active citizenship in a robust and participatory democracy, *some* notion of empowerment of young people to take up active roles is essential. Earlier, we attempted to describe such empowerment as having three dimensions – critical autonomy, personal effectiveness and community. Is this model a useful starting-point for a reconsideration of this issue? Given the recent fashionable interest in stake-holding, how can a balance be found between individual interests and wider social needs? Perhaps most intractably of all, how can we develop and encourage individual and group empowerment, while simultaneously doing something real to address the gross inequalities of late twentieth-century society?

In addressing these questions there is an obvious need to scrutinize the relationship between empowerment and choice, and where guidance and learning fit into the equation. Current systems in further and higher education, for example, emphasize credit accumulation and transfer which, with modular structures, are supposed to free up young people to control their own education and career development (Robertson, 1994). Central to such systems are the notions of guidance and learner autonomy. In further education, guidance is now a mandatory requirement under programme funding, while in higher education it is being promoted by the Department for Education and Employment initiative, *Guidance and Learner Autonomy in Higher Education,* and is included in current Higher Education Quality Council criteria. But there is no reason to believe that choosing modules or transferring credit is any different in kind from students' pragmatically rational choices of subjects, courses and training described in Chapters 6 and 7. Far more sophisticated and informed notions of autonomy, empowerment and 'choice-making' are called for if young people are truly to gain greater control over their education and career development and if current initiatives are to amount to anything more than persuasive rhetoric.

Two key problems relate to choice-making within current market-driven funding regimes. Firstly, choices within educational markets are often mythical rather than real. As we have argued, the hope of the New Right was that markets would shift the focus of educational institutions away from the supposed obsession with their own self-interests towards the interests of their customers. However, there is evidence that the opposite is now happening (Hyland, 1994). If the funding for an organization depends on the triple targets of recruitment, retention and successful course completion, tutors and managers within the organization cannot allow young people to make choices, (i) to attempt a course they might fail, (ii) to leave before completion, or (iii) to go somewhere else to study. There is a paradox within current policies. The new funding regimes were introduced on the assumption that institutions and staff would respond rationally to the new funding mechanisms in order to maximize their income. Yet, when they do that, for example through the hard sell or through course structures designed to retain students and restrict choice, they undermine the expressed intentions of the funding mechanisms, prompting the proponents of market-force policy to retaliate by accusing their critics of a 'lack of professionalism' or naïvety.

Secondly, to suggest that 'neutral guidance' can counteract such pressures, or that issuing vouchers will somehow change the power balance to prevent such activity occurring, is either naïve or dishonest. The scope of choice and progression in education depends crucially upon interactions between young people, teachers and others, all fed by vastly unequal resources. We need to know a great deal more about what kinds of choice young people are able to exercise, and do exercise, within the context of modular systems and credit transfer arrangements; we need careful consideration of balances between mandatory requirements, entitlement and freedom of choice within post-compulsory education and training; and we need a full, open and critical investigation of the functions of guidance within the post-compulsory curriculum framework. A related problem centres on different views of learner autonomy and the relationships between models of choice and models of learning. Current British approaches to modules, credit accumulation and learner autonomy are muddled about the relationship between three related elements: choice, subject expertise and personal growth. In Chapter 7, we argued that learning is inevitably influenced by students, as they make sense of the opportunities mediated by the beliefs and actions of their teachers. From such a perspective, it is possible to see one ideal of learner autonomy deriving from an ongoing relationship between the expert teacher and the student, especially if the teacher sees his/her primary task as to encourage the development of autonomy and criticality in the student. However, in the context of large student numbers and increasing work pressure found in most universities and further education colleges, modularization risks fragmenting learning and, as students move from teacher to teacher, any chance to realize learner autonomy along such a model evaporates. Other key questions which need to be asked, therefore, concern the extent to which such a model of autonomy can or should be part of a future educational vision, what relationship can be developed between such a view and models of autonomy based on choice, and the role of the learner in helping determine the nature of the learning programme he/she is to follow. As Ainley and Green (1995) have observed,

> In place of the rhetoric of empowerment through consumer choice of modules in the market, learning contracts negotiated on terms of equality with individuals and groups could lead to higher levels of learning, discovery and creation.
>
> (Ainley and Green, 1995, p. 52)

This returns us to the central theme of the book, to the nature of *knowledge* and how it finds its expression and meaning in the new post-16 curriculum. Current fascination with market packaging of the post-16 curriculum has discredited some potentially interesting and novel approaches to teaching and learning. Accentuating the vehicle of delivery (in terms of modules, credits, contracts and vouchers) without due attention to professional considerations, knowledge and studentship, has resulted in an atomization and fragmentation of the curriculum in both further and higher education. The supermarket window of student choice has obscured the same deep divisions between the academic and vocational aspects of education which post-16 reforms were ostensibly designed to ameliorate. It is to this neglected aspect of the policy debate that we now wish to turn.

THE PLACE OF VOCATIONALISM IN POST-COMPULSORY EDUCATION

Though vocationalism has been a recurrent theme throughout this book, we have, until now, not addressed it directly. It is important to do so, for the debate around vocational provision too often fails to engage with the issues of citizenship and democracy (Dewey, 1916). For many of its ardent advocates, vocationalism is an uncontroversial, essential component of post-compulsory provision, so that the only debate concerns what form it takes.

Advocates of vocationalism come from a widely divergent political spectrum. The CBI (1989, 1993) and the government, for example, view vocationalism as an essential part of the drive to economic competitiveness. Academics such as Smithers (1993) advocate their own brand of vocationalism for those young people unable to succeed on an academic route. Influential groups such as the National Commission on Education (1993, 1995) and the Institute of Public Policy Research (Finegold *et al.*, 1990), on the other hand, see vocationalism as an essential part of a unified post-compulsory curriculum. Elsewhere are a group of beleaguered academics who argue that vocationalism is best left until after full-time education is completed (Holt, 1987). The result is that there has been far too little discussion about what the nature and purpose of vocational education should be. This is partly because current policy debates have been dominated by the NCVQ and its slogan of competences, linking the content of vocational education unproblematically to what employers want and to a functional analysis of a wide range of jobs as they were performed in the recent past. This, linked with the current fascination with NVQs and competence-based approaches to education and training, is, as we and others have argued, wholly inappropriate given our education and training needs (Hyland, 1994). In order to move beyond this sterile and reductionist context, we need to ask some rather difficult questions about the place of vocationalism. This is important if vocational education is to be shifted away from its present primary concern with social control and its strong dependency upon assumptions of economic rationalism. It is crucial in order to free up vocationalism's ghetto association with the lowest achievers.

Where such discussion has already taken place, it has almost always been predicated on the uncritical assumption that vocational education has two main purposes – to serve the needs of employers and the national economy, and to provide appropriate education or training to those young people who have failed on the academic route, or for whom academic education is unsuitable. Earlier in this book, we disputed both parts of this argument and suggested instead that we need a rationale for post-compulsory education and training which is based on wider notions of democracy and citizenship. What is needed is a radically different analysis of the role and place of so-called 'vocational' education. Central to this analysis is the question: what is the place of vocational education as an integral part of a general education for all? Here, we attempt to further refine that question, always in the context of a general education for citizenship within a robust democracy – issues explored towards the end of the previous chapter.

Breaking out from the current discourse of neo-Fordism and economic rationalism is not easy. Various curriculum modernizers, of both the Right and the Left, have attempted this. Some have called for the development of a new educationally orientated vocationalism that offers students a critical purchase on the social world, and which combines a general education with vocational interests. For example, Jamieson argues as follows:

Fundamental changes in the economic infrastructure and the structure of occupations have forced increasing parallels to be drawn between vocational education and liberal education or, to use more conventional terms, education and training. In essence the argument is straightforward. It is claimed that we have seen the passing, at least in the advanced industrial world, of the sort of semi-permanent occupations which require an easily identifiable set of skills for which training could be designed and given. In the 'post-industrial' world, citizens and workers are required to master an ever widening range of complex information. What is needed, it is claimed, is the ability independently to acquire new knowledge and skill, so that learning how to learn becomes increasingly important. People also need to understand the procedural nature of work, to improve their problem solving skills and to be able to move flexibly from one task to another as the situation demands.

(Jamieson, 1993, pp. 200–1)

In this passage Jamieson suggests that changing post-industrial conditions require the abandonment of outmoded distinctions between the vocational and the academic. Such a duality is seen to belong to earlier economic conditions such as those found in Fordism. The argument is also tied to observations concerning the rapidity of change in a post-modern age in which specialist skills are highly perishable, and to claims that new economic conditions undermine the old vocationalism. Such a view suggests that changing technology and work organization provide the potential for students and workers to become multi-skilled, celebrating skills that enable individuals to participate in team work and contribute to economic wealth in which they have a stake. The danger here, as we have argued in Chapters 3 and 4, is one of causally linking progressive changes in education with those in the economy and workplace. That linkage is founded upon a form of economic rationalism which accepts, rather than critically challenges, the assumption that a new progressive post-Fordist correspondence between education and work is now under way. If only that were the case. Our concern is that evidence supporting the assertion that corporate institutions and everyday workplaces are becoming less bureaucratic, more flexible, participative and knowledge-based, is mixed and contradictory. If, for different reasons, curriculum modernizers of various persuasions have found it convenient to exploit the post-Fordist ideal, that ideal has not translated into the reality of practical policy. Given our line of argument, how could it be otherwise? Essentially, our criticism is that alternative agendas are subordinated to an economic logic which denies the very real conflicts present within our society. There is an assumption that meeting the needs of the economy for value-added labour will lead to the satisfaction of wider societal needs and that this will, somehow, ameliorate deep-seated obstacles to economic and educational progress.

In our view, these conflicts and obstacles must be addressed, but not in a context in which economic needs are hegemonic. It is now apparent that the neo-Fordist policies of the New Right have failed to secure the long-term interests of the economy, nation and workplace. However, the development of an alternative policy strategy by New Labour cannot be seen as self-evidently progressive, as such strategy remains locked into the same dominance of economic interests. Most recently, this has become a problem for New Labour as New Right appropriation of the post-industrial vision collapses. New Right appeals, for example, for a 'skills revolution' for the twenty-first century have been exposed as little more than attempts to revive 'old' models of imperialism and global dominance, supported by domestic forms of selection, hierarchy and exclusion. The problem facing New Labour is one of how to avoid economizing education and training in the same way as the New Right. The sort of economic rationalism which binds current Right and Left thinking is not only deterministic but is also detrimental to the long-term interests of education, learning and economic prosperity. Another way of looking at this must include recognition of the collective and transformative power of education as a means of transforming educational organizations and corporations, rather than simply servicing their here and now skill requirements. As Pring (1995) has observed, the likely 'returns' accruing from investing in a more vibrant, educated community are more liable to bring about improvements in cultural and economic growth than those parochial forms of market individualism which currently prevail.

However, in attempting to do this, it is important to build on existing thinking and writing. Much has now been done to win the argument that the latest transmogrification of tripartism, with parallel A-level, GNVQ and NVQ tracks, is a recipe for innovation without change. The division between academic and vocational pathways remains at the root of many of Britain's educational problems. The origins of tripartism lie in British social and educational history: academic studies have always been associated with a general education for the middle classes, while occupational training has been seen as meeting economic needs and, in the nineteenth century, was explicitly associated with obedience. Repeated attempts to establish some viable 'middle' route have failed, as the very people at whom they have been aimed have frequently aspired to the higher status of academic provision. For this reason, GNVQs face an uphill struggle without a radical restructuring of all post-16 education.

There has been much talk in the 1990s of 'bridging' the academic–vocational divide simply by the creation of new 'pathways' through modular-style course programmes. But these are technically rational solutions which fail to take account of the powerful effects of culturally embedded traditions and expectations and, inasmuch as they have been implemented at all, have proved far less than effective. Post-compulsory educational opportunities are still viewed by users through the bifocal lens of the academic–vocational divide, as 'either/or'. At the time of writing (July 1995), it seems as if the battle for a more unified post-16 curriculum in Britain may have been partly won. In his interim report, Dearing (1995) acknowledged the need for an over-arching National Certificate of the type advocated earlier by the National Commission on Education (1993, 1995). However, simply overlaying a certificate across unchanged A-level, GNVQ and NVQ provision will not go far enough.

An important feature of both the academic and vocational traditions of post-compulsory education is the extent to which courses are, or have been, narrowly subject or occupationally specific. This feature, most noticeable in A-level and NVQs, sets Britain, and particularly England and Wales, apart from most other nations, and provides further indication of the tension between nation-state planning and the requirements issuing from progressive globalization. It also ignores Hutton's (1995a) analysis of a '30–30–40 workforce', where many are unemployed while others have to survive on insecure short-term contracts. Traditional specialisms have been based on assumptions of full employment and careers for life. In a twenty-first century that promises a further acceleration in the explosion of knowledge and, at the very least, a continuation of endemic and rapid change, young people will not be well served by a post-compulsory education focused *within* specialisms defined largely on the basis of past experience and employers' current needs.

New concepts of specialism must be found in which a broader integration of theoreti-

cal and practical knowledge is provided for and in which traditional knowledge categories and boundaries are transcended. This will not be provided for by 'bridges' or
by bolted-on core skills or general studies. Rather, the platform for the curriculum must
be a general education which amounts to more than simply an increase in the number of
'subjects' or 'options' to be studied. Young's (1992, 1993) work on organic specialization could be very important here, for we would argue that his arguments do not depend
upon a correspondence between education and post-Fordism. What is needed, as we
have claimed repeatedly throughout this book, is a general education which allows
young people to utilize critically a wide range of knowledge and experience in the
development of their expertise in the creation of new knowledge. Moreover, that
general education must not exclude what has, in the past, been labelled vocational. It is
necessary, then, to explore the role of the vocational in a curriculum for personal development, democratic social cohesion and lifelong learning, and which allows proper
meaning to be given to concepts of empowerment, autonomy, citizenship and social
justice. Building on points raised in earlier chapters, notably Chapters 4, 6 and 7, the
following are just some of the questions that such an exploration must confront.

1. Does vocational education have to be non-academic?

We know that many forms of education directly linked to employment are not seen as
'vocational' education. These include the high-status courses such as degrees in medicine and law. Their place in higher education is never challenged. But what of those
which do not command such status? Can we not devise courses in catering, engineering,
hairdressing or business and administration that also contain an unproblematic mix of
critical theory and practical application? Within 16–19 education in Britain, there is a
strange polarization in current vocational provision. For those in work, NVQs emphasize practice to the extent that theory can be entirely missing. On the other hand,
GNVQs, designed for full-time education, have no requirement for practical experience
in the workplace – real or simulated; and both are fundamentally uncritical.

2. Why does vocational education have to be closely tied to assumptions about employers' interests?

There are two related issues here. The first relates to the desires of some young people
for an education that prepares them for work and training. If this is acceptable for those
studying science in order to go on and read medicine to become doctors, why should it
not also apply to those who wish to have an education that can lead them to a career in
catering or motor vehicle maintenance? Perhaps we need to consider the links between
education and employment from the young person's perspective, rather than assuming
this is always the same as that of employers. We also need to examine more carefully
the balance between specialisms which are seen by some as career specific, and the
benefits of a broader based general education.

The second issue relates to one of our central themes. We have argued that education
should be freed from an economic imperative. Therefore, if what are now called vocational studies are to be included across the post-compulsory curriculum, and we argue

that they must be, should they also be subjected to scrutiny for the intrinsic interest they can command and for their contribution to citizenship, democracy and a sound general education? This is the kind of question that we believe Dearing, among others, must bring much more to the fore in his deliberations.

3. What is the place of the practical in general education?

Once the vocational curriculum is separated from the 'causal' link with employer needs, we require other reasons for its inclusion. One of these must relate to the need for practical education to balance more restrictedly academic approaches. This raises the currently neglected question about what practical education is and what and who it is for. Here, we suggest four different types of answer, and hence four different reasons for the inclusion of the practical, although we are sure our list is not definitive.

- The first concerns the benefits of learning from practical experience. If our key aims of learner autonomy and citizenship are to have more than rhetorical value, all learners must acquire the means of generating their own theoretical understanding. The uncritical rehearsal of others' theorizing is not sufficient. Knowledge and understanding must square with learners' personal practical experiences if they are to have proper meaning and value and, for this, learners will need at their disposal the skills necessary for their continual critical examination of practical experience.
- The second stresses the practical application of theory or knowledge. This can take place in almost any subject, and might include putting on a play, conducting a scientific experiment or running a simulated business. The important point is that knowing and understanding are not enough – that education must go further.
- The third type of practical concerns physical dexterity and the notion that education should not neglect physical skills. Once more, these skills could be developed in a wide variety of contexts, not all currently included in 'vocational' education. Hairdressing, cooking, mechanical engineering, laboratory experiments and making electronic circuits are just a few examples.
- The fourth type is of a different order. Practical, in this sense, implies the ability to be proactive in a practical way, rather than expecting someone else either to give a lead or do things for you. Often, though not always, this type of 'practicality' is a team effort. Examples would be when students organize their own events, intervene in local community politics, run a college newsletter or produce their own concert. Matt's innovative approach to his A-level studies (see Chapter 7) is an extreme and individual case of this. The central question then becomes, can we ever justify a general education that does not celebrate and develop all these forms of the experimental and practical, for all young people?

4. What should be the role of learning in the workplace?

We have already drawn attention to the current paradox whereby vocational courses in full-time education may have no requirement for work-based experience, while work-based training programmes have no requirement for off-the-job experience. Yet we know that most young people identify with work experience of various types, not least because they are treated as adults in adult surroundings, in sharp contrast to what they see as the infantilization of full-time schooling. As school-leaving ages continue to rise, with a growing number staying in full-time further education until they are 20 or older, this issue is of growing importance. Furthermore, is it not at least plausible that work environments could release novel learning opportunities which, for many young people, could be profitably blended with other experiences in their post-16 education? This relates to the previous question. Where relevant, the understanding of applied practical skills is likely to be greatly enhanced in a working environment linked with post-compulsory education and training. It is time to be less squeamish about such matters if policy-makers are to take the education–industry relationship seriously.

CONCLUSION

Addressing such questions brings us full circle to the central concern of this book: how to enhance a curriculum for earning, learning, active citizenship and economic growth for *all*. Meeting the terms of any such curriculum requires, as we have argued, parallel initiatives linked with two preconditions: one, a rejection of New Right ideology and, two, placing *studentship* rather than markets at the centre of learning. At the same time any economic vision requires new thinking about the nature of, and relationships between, work organization, capital, technology, popular culture and leisure. As Hutton (1995a) has reminded us, this will require concerted efforts which combine City reform, fiscal policy, planning and energizing private finance to raise investment levels in both private and public sectors of the economy, health, education, housing and welfare. Fat chance, you might say, but what realistically are the alternatives, given the crumbling state of British education, economy and society? As Reich (1991) points out, the choice is ours to make.

> We are no more slaves to present trends than vestiges of the past. We can, if we choose, assert that our mutual obligations as citizens extend beyond our economic usefulness to one another, and act accordingly.
>
> (Reich, 1991, p. 315)

Whether this can be achieved by individuals acting alone, through government legislation or policy initiatives, or through new principles of stakeholding remains to be seen. We suspect that all three areas, including the 'rediscovery' of the relationship between family and education, will be significant in the process of national reconstruction in the years to come. The challenge will be not to lose sight of the collective bonds which bind relations between education, economy and society, already the subject of extensive research (Halsey *et al.*, 1961). As we have sought to argue, in spite of the apparent importance attached by the New Right to education and training in revitalizing the British economy, the reality has been an economizing of education (Kenway, 1994), dominated by financial and fiscal objectives, the pursuit of which has led to a serious fracturing of Britain's social, industrial and education base. Instead of becoming the socially progressive *post-Fordist* society advocated by some commentators, Britain has adopted the *neo-Fordist* route, in which the rights and opportunities of citizens and workers have been increasingly diminished. If this book has contributed anything to this debate, it is to demonstrate that the future of cultural and economic wealth is contingent upon investment in human potential, public services and an *educated community* (Pring,

1995). If this sounds like a familiar variation of the 1960s human capital theme, the difference this time around emphasizes *the social purposes of public investment in the service of democratic politics*. It also recognizes that individual and collective responses to the sort of social, economic and educational issues raised so far in this book will have more productive and lasting outcomes in people's lives than those founded on market individualism. To date, markets have demonstrated that they are too fragile and unreliable to deliver on this, and are susceptible to short-termism, downsizing and low achievement as divisions between 'winners' and 'losers' become ever more apparent. As the demands of globalization become more pressing, Britain's adherence to an inward looking nation-state view of its role, based on a divided and authoritarian system of education and training, appears increasingly inadequate and inflexible. Serious attention now needs to be given to *educating* as opposed to training a majority of the population hitherto denied access to further and higher education. If a more enlightened education reform process is to achieve a distinctive ethos and practice for *all*, it must also stress values for the future rather than simply reproduce those of the past. The search is now on for a new political economy of education and training which recognizes the strategic importance of investing in an educated community and which will address the profound changes now taking place in the relationship between the economy, the nation and global citizenship and, with it, all our futures.

References

Abegglen, J. C. (1994) *Sea Change: Pacific Asia as the New World Industrial Center.* New York: Free Press.

Adamski, W. and Grootings, P. (eds) (1990) *Youth, Education and Work in Europe.* London: Routledge.

Aggleton, P. (1987) *Rebels Without a Cause?* London: Falmer.

Ahier, J. (1995) Hidden controversies in two cross-curricular themes. In J. Ahier and A. Ross (eds), *The Social Subjects within the Curriculum: Children's Social Learning within the National Curriculum.* London: Falmer.

Ainley, P. (1993) *Class and Skill.* London: Cassell.

Ainley, P. (1994) *Degrees of Difference.* London: Lawrence and Wishart.

Ainley, P. (1995) Unpublished letter to Hayes, Fonda and Hillman, 11 March.

Ainley, P. and Green, A. (1995) *Progression and Targets in Post 16 Education and Training.* Post 16 Centre Education Report No. 11. London: Institute of Education.

Albert, M. (1993) *Capitalism against Capitalism.* London: Whurr.

Althusser, L. (1972) Ideology and ideological state apparatus. In B. Cosin (ed.), *Education: Structure and Society.* Harmondsworth: Penguin.

Alvesson, M. (1987) *Organisation Theory and Technocratic Consciousness: Rationality, Ideology and Quality of Work.* New York: de Gruyter.

Apple, M. W. (1979) *Ideology and Curriculum.* London: Routledge and Kegan Paul.

Apple, M. W. (1990) *Ideology and Curriculum.* 2nd edition. London: Routledge.

Archer, M. (1984) *Social Origins of Educational Systems.* London: Sage.

Arnot, M. and Weiner, G. (1987) *Gender and the Politics of Schooling.* London: Hutchinson.

Audit Commission (1993) *Unfinished Business: Full-time Educational Courses for 16–19 Year Olds.* London: HMSO.

Austin, M. (1992) Health checks for FE bodies. *Times Educational Supplement,* 11 September.

Avis, J. (1991a) Teaching practice, professionalism and social relations. In Education Group II, *Education Limited.* London: Unwin Hyman.

Avis, J. (1991b) Social difference and antagonism within the 16–19 core curriculum. *British Journal of Sociology of Education,* 13 (3), 361–74.

Avis, J. (1991c) Curriculum categories and student identities in FE. In Education Group II, *Education Limited.* London: Unwin Hyman.

Avis, J. (1991d) The strange fate of progressive education. In Education Group II, *Education Limited.* London: Unwin Hyman.

Avis, J. (1993a) A new orthodoxy, old problems: post-16 reforms. *British Journal of Sociology of Education,* 14 (3), 245–60.

Avis, J. (1993b) Post-Fordism, curriculum modernisers and radical practice: the case of vocational education and training in England. *The Vocational Aspects of Education*, **45** (1), 3–14.

Avis, J. (1994) Teacher professionalism: one more time. *Educational Review*, **46** (1), 63–72.

Ball, C. (1990) *More Means Different: Widening Access to Higher Education*. London: Royal Society of Arts.

Ball, C. (1991) *Learning Pays*. London: Royal Society of Arts.

Ball, S. J. (1981) *Beachside Comprehensive: A Case Study of Secondary Schooling*. Cambridge: Cambridge University Press.

Ball, S. J. (1990a) *Politics and Policy Making in Education: Explorations in Policy Sociology*. London: Routledge.

Ball, S. J. (1990b) Management as moral technology: a Luddite analysis. In S. J. Ball (ed.), *Foucault and Education: Disciplines and Knowledge*. London: Routledge.

Ball, S. J. (1994) *Education Reform: A Critical and Post-structural Approach*. Buckingham: Open University Press.

Ball, S. J. and Shilling, C. (1994) At the cross-roads: education policy studies. *British Journal of Educational Studies*, **42** (1), 1–5.

Banks, M., Bates, I., Breakwell, G., Bynner, J., Elmer, N., Jamieson, L. and Roberts, K. (1992) *Careers and Identities: Adolescent Attitudes to Employment, Training and Education, Their Home Life, Leisure and Politics*. Milton Keynes: Open University Press.

Baran, P. and Sweezy, P. (1966) *Monopoly Capital*. New York: Monthly Review Press.

Barnett, C. (1986) *The Audit of War*. London: Macmillan.

Bates, I. (1990) No bleeding, whining Minnies. *British Journal of Education and Work*, **3** (2), 91–110.

Bates, I. and Riseborough, G. (eds) (1993a) *Youth and Inequality*. Buckingham: Open University Press.

Bates, I. and Riseborough, G. (1993b) Introduction: deepening divisions, fading solutions. In I. Bates and G. Riseborough (eds), *Youth and Inequality*. Buckingham: Open University Press.

Batteson, C. and Ball, S. J. (1995) Autobiographies and interviews as means of 'access' to elite policy making in education. *British Journal of Educational Studies*, **43** (2).

Beck, U. (1992) *Risk Society: Toward a New Modernity*. London: Sage.

Bell, D. (1974) *The Coming of the Post-industrial Society*. London: Heinemann.

Benington, J. and Taylor, M. (1993) Changes and challenges facing the UK welfare state in the Europe of the 1990s. *Policy and Politics*, **21** (2), 121–34.

Bennett, R. J., Glennester, H. and Nevison, D. (1992) *Learning Should Pay*. Poole: BP Educational Service.

Bennett, R. J. and McCoshan, A. (1993) *Enterprise and Human Resource Development: Local Capacity Building*. London: Paul Chapman.

Bennett, R. J., Wicks, P. and McCoshan, A. (1994) *Local Empowerment and Business Services: Britain's Experiment with Training and Enterprise Councils*. London: UCL Press.

Bernstein, B. (1961) Social class and linguistic development: a theory of social learning. In A. H. Halsey, J. Floud and C. A. Anderson (eds), *Education, Economy and Society*. New York: Free Press.

Bernstein, B. (1971) On the classification and framing of educational knowledge. In M.F.D. Young (ed.), *Knowledge and Control*. London: Collier-Macmillan.

Bernstein, B. (1972) Sociology and the sociology of education: some aspects. In Open University Course Unit E282, 15/17.

Blair, T. (1994) Change and national renewal: leadership election statement. London: Labour Party.

Blair, T. (1995) The rights we enjoy reflect the duties we owe. The Spectator Lecture, the Queen Elizabeth Conference Centre, London, 22 March.

Bloomer, M. (forthcoming) *Studentship in Post-16 Education* (working title). London: Routledge.

Bloomer, M. and Morgan, D. (1993) It is planned, therefore it happens – or does it? *Journal of Further and Higher Education*, **17** (1), 22–37.

Board of Trade (1994) *Competitiveness: Helping Business to Win*. Cmnd 2563. London: HMSO.

Bolton, E. (1994) One last push. *Education Guardian*, 17 May.

Bourdieu, P. (1971) Systems of education and systems of thought. In M. F. D. Young (ed.),

Knowledge and Control. London: Collier-Macmillan.

Bourdieu, P. (1977) Cultural reproduction and social reproduction. In J. Karabel and A. H. Halsey (eds), *Power and Ideology in Education*. Oxford: Oxford University Press.

Bourdieu, P. and Passeron, J. (1977) *Reproduction in Education, Society and Culture*. London: Sage.

Bourdieu, P. and Wacquant, L. J. D. (1992) *An Invitation to Reflexive Sociology*. Cambridge: Polity.

Bowles, S. and Gintis, H. (1976) *Schooling in Capitalist America*. London: Routledge and Kegan Paul.

Brause, R. S. (1992) *Enduring Schools: Problems and Possibilities*. London: Falmer.

Braverman, H. (1974) *Labor and Monopoly Capital: The Degradation of Work in the Twentieth Century*. New York: Monthly Review Press.

Brosio, R. A. (1988) The present economic sea changes and the corresponding consequences for education. *Teacher Education Quarterly,* **15** (1), 4–37.

Brown, A. and Evans, K. (1994) Changing the training culture: lessons from Anglo-German comparisons of vocational education and training. *British Journal of Education and Work,* **7** (2), 5–16.

Brown, J. S., Collins, A. and Duguid, P. (1989) Situated cognition and the culture of learning. *Educational Researcher,* **18** (1), 32–42.

Brown, P. and Lauder, H. (eds) (1992a) *Education for Economic Survival: From Fordism to Post-Fordism?* London: Routledge.

Brown, P. and Lauder, H. (1992b) Education, economy, and society: an introduction to a new agenda. In P. Brown and H. Lauder (eds), *Education for Economic Survival: From Fordism to Post-Fordism?* London: Routledge.

Brown, P. and Scase, R. (1994) *Higher Education and Corporate Realities: Class, Culture and the Decline of Graduate Careers*. London: UCL Press.

Bruner, J. S. (1973) *Beyond the Information Given*. New York: Boston.

Burke, J. (ed.) (1995) *Outcome Based Learning*. London: Falmer.

Burns, T. and Stalker, G. M. (1961) *The Management of Innovation*. London: Tavistock.

Buxton, T., Chapman, P. and Temple, P. (eds) (1994) *Britain's Economic Performance*. London: Routledge.

Cain, P. J. and Hopkins, A. G. (1993) *British Imperialism: Crisis and Deconstruction 1914–1990*. London: Longman.

Callaghan, J. (1987) *Time and Chance*. Glasgow: Collins.

Callan, P. (1994) Future scenarios: education and work. Paper presented at the International Conference on *Directions: Education and Training for 15–24 Year Olds*, Sydney, NSW, Government Department of Education, Australia, September.

Cantor, L. and Roberts, I. (1983) *Further Education Today*. London: Routledge and Kegan Paul.

Carlen, P., Gleeson, D. and Wardhaugh, J. (1992) *Truancy: The Politics of Compulsory Schooling*. Milton Keynes: Open University Press.

Carr, W. (1987) What is an educational practice? *Journal of Philosophy of Education,* **21** (2), 163–75.

Carr, W. (1991) Education for citizenship. *British Journal of Educational Studies,* **39** (4), 373–85.

Carr, W. and Kemmis, S. (1986) *Becoming Critical*. London: The Falmer Press.

Cassels, J. (1990) *Britain's Real Skill Shortages: And What to Do about It*. London: Policy Studies Institute.

CBI (1989) *Toward a Skills Revolution*. London: CBI.

CBI (1993) *Routes to Success*. London: CBI.

CBI (1994) *Thinking Ahead*. London: CBI.

Cecchini, P. (1988) *The European Challenge, 1992: The Benefits of a Single Market* (The Cecchini Report). Aldershot: Gower.

Centre for Contemporary Cultural Studies Education Group (1981) *Unpopular Education: Schooling and Social Democracy in England since 1944*. London: Hutchinson.

Chubb, J. and Moe, T. (1990) *Politics, Markets and America's Schools*. Washington: The Brookings Institute.

Clark, G. (1994) The changing context of post-16 education and training. Paper presented at Keele University (CSRE) Postgraduate Seminar Programme, December.

Clarke, J., Hall, S., Jefferson, T. and Roberts, B. (1981) Subcultures, cultures and class. In T. Bennet, G. Martin, C. Mercer and J. Wallacott (eds), *Culture, Ideology and Social Process*. London: Batsford.

Clarke, J., Cochrane, A. and McLaughlin, E. (1994) (eds) *Managing Social Policy*. London: Sage.

Coates, D. (1994) *The Question of UK Decline: State, Society and Economy*. Hemel Hempstead: Harvester Wheatsheaf.

Coffey, D. (1992) *Schools and Work: Developments in Vocational Education*. London: Cassell.

Coffield, F. (1990) From the decade of the enterprise culture to the decade of the TECs. *British Journal of Education and Work,* **4** (1), 59–78.

Cohen, N. (1994) One-party Britain. *Independent on Sunday,* 3 April.

Coleman, J. S., Campbell, C. J., McPartland, J., Mood, A. M., Weinfield, F. D. and York, R. L. (1966) *Equality of Educational Opportunity*. Washington, DC: US Government Printing Office, OE3–8001.

Coles, C.R. (1990) Elaborated learning in undergraduate medical education. *Medical Education,* **24**, 14–22.

Commission on Social Justice (1994) *Social Justice Strategies for National Renewal*. London: Vintage.

Commission on Wealth Creation and Social Cohesion (1995) *Report on Wealth Creation and Social Cohesion in a Free Society* (Dahrendorf Report). London: Commission on Wealth Creation and Social Cohesion.

Committee of Vice Chancellors and Principals (1985) *Report of the Steering Committee for Efficiency Studies in Universities* (Jarratt Report). London: Committee of Vice Chancellors and Principals.

Connell, R.W. (1995) *Masculinities*. Cambridge: Polity.

Coopers and Lybrand Deloitte (1992) *Training Credits Evaluation: National Coordinator's Report of the 11 Case Studies*. Employment Department Mimeo.

Corrigan, P. and Frith, S. (1975) The politics of youth culture. In S. Hall and T. Jefferson (eds), *Resistance through Rituals*. London: Hutchinson.

Crowther Report (1959) *15–18*. Report of the Minister of Education's Central Advisory Committee. London: HMSO.

Dale, I. R. (1989) *The State and Education Policy*. Milton Keynes: Open University Press.

Davies, H. (1992) *Fighting Leviathan: Building Social Markets That Work*. London: The Social Market Foundation.

Dearing, R. (1994) *The National Curriculum and Its Assessment: Final Report*. London: School Curriculum Assessment Authority.

Dearing, R. (1995) *Review of 16–19 Qualifications: Summary of the Interim Report*. London: HMSO.

Department of Employment (DE) (1988) *Employment in the 1990s*. London: HMSO.

DE (1993) *Assessing the Effects of First Phase Training Credits*. Quality Assurance Study No. 15. Sheffield: Employment Department.

DE (1994) *Labour Market and Skill Trends, 1995/6*. Nottingham: Skills Enterprise Network, Employment Department.

Department of Industry (DI) (1974) *The Regeneration of British Industry*. Cmnd 5710. London: HMSO.

Department of Industry (1977) *Industry, Education and Management: A Discussion Paper*. London: HMSO.

DES (1977) *Education in Schools: A Consultative Document*. Cmnd 6860. London: HMSO.

DES (1991) *Higher Education: A New Framework*. London: HMSO.

DES/DE (1991) *Education and Training for the 21st Century*. Cmnd 1536. London: HMSO.

Dewey, J. (1916) *Democracy and Education*. New York: Macmillan.

Donald, J. (1992a) *Sentimental Education*. London: Verso.

Donald, J. (1992b) Dewey-eyed optimism: the possibility of democratic education. *New Left Review,* No. 192, 133–44.

Donoughue, B. (1987) *Prime Minister: The Conduct of Policy under Harold Wilson and James Callaghan*. London: Cape.

Elliott, L. (1995) Shephard's watch. *Guardian*, 20 September.

Evans, B. (1992) *The Politics of the Training Market: From Manpower Services Commission to Training and Enterprise Councils*. London: Routledge.

Fagan, E. (1984) Competence in educational practice: a rhetorical perspective. In E. Short (ed.), *Competence: Inquiries into Its Meaning and Acquisition in Educational Settings*. New York: University of America Press.

Featherstone, M. (ed.) (1990) *Global Culture: Nationalism, Globalisation and Modernity*. London: Sage.

Fergusson, R. (1994) Managerialism in education. In J. Clarke, A. Cochrane and E. McLaughlin (eds), *Managing Social Policy*. London: Sage.

FEU (1982) *Profiles*. London: FEU.

FEU (1984) *Profiles in Action*. London: FEU.

FEU (1991a) *Flexible Colleges: Access to Learning and Qualification in Further Education*. London: FEU.

FEU (1991b) *Quality Matters*. London: FEU.

FEU (1992) *Supporting Learning: Promoting Equity and Participation*. Parts 1 and 2. London: FEU.

FEU (1994) *Initiating Change: Educational Guidance for Adults 1988–93*. The final report of the National Educational Guidance Initiative. London: FEU.

Field, J. (1995) Reality testing in the work place. Are NVQs employment led? In P. Hodkinson and M. Issitt (eds), *The Challenge of Competence: Professionalism through Vocational Education and Training*. London: Cassell.

Fielding, M. (1988) Democracy and fraternity: towards a new paradigm for the comprehensive school. In H. Lauder and P. Brown (eds), *Education in Search of a Future*. London: Falmer.

Finegold, D. (1991) *Beyond the White Paper*. London: Post 16 Education Centre, Institute of Education, London University.

Finegold, D. (1992) The changing international economy and its impact on education and training. In D. Finegold, L. McFarland and W. Richardson (eds), Something borrowed, something blue? A study of the Thatcher government's appropriation of American education and training policy. *Oxford Studies in Comparative Education*, part 1, vol. 2, no. 2.

Finegold, D. (1993) The emerging post-16 system: analysis and critique. In W. Richardson, J. Woolhouse and D. Finegold (eds), *The Reform of Post-16 Education and Training in England and Wales*. London: Longman.

Finegold, D., Keep, E., Miliband, D., Raffe, D., Spours, K. and Young, M. (1990) *A British Baccalaureat: Ending the Divisions Between Education and Training*. London: Institute for Public Policy Research.

Finegold, D. and Soskice, D. (1988) The failure of training in Britain: analysis and prescription. *Oxford Review of Economic Policy*, **4** (3), 21–53.

Foucault, M. (1980) Truth and power. In C. Gordon (ed.), *Power/Knowledge: Selected Interviews and Other Writings 1972–1977*. New York: Pantheon.

Foucault, M. (1983) On the genealogy of ethics: an overview of work in progress. In H. L. Dreyfus and P. Rabinow (eds), *Michel Foucault: Beyond Structuralism and Hermeneutics*. 2nd edition. Chicago: University of Chicago Press.

Freire, P. (1972) *Pedagogy of the Oppressed*. Harmondsworth: Penguin.

Friedman, A.L. (1977) *Industry and Labour*. London: Macmillan.

Frykholm, C. and Nitzler, R. (1993) Working life as pedagogical discourse: empirical studies of vocational and career education based on theories of Bourdieu and Bernstein. *Journal of Curriculum Studies*, **25** (5), 433–44.

Fullan, M. and Hargreaves, A. (1993) *What Is Worth Fighting for in the Curriculum*. London: Falmer.

Funnell, P. and Muller, D. (eds) (1991) *Delivering Quality in Vocational Education*. London: Kogan Page.

Furlong, A. (1992) *Growing up in a Classless Society? School to Work Transitions*. Edinburgh: Edinburgh University Press.

Gamble, A. and Walton, P. (1976) *Capitalism in Crisis*. London: Macmillan.

Garrahan, P. and Stewart, P. (1992) *The Nissan Enigma*. London: Mansell.

Gibson, R. (1986) *Critical Theory and Education*. London: Hodder and Stoughton.

Giddens, A. (1984) *The Constitution of Society: Outline of the Theory of Structuration*. Cambridge: Polity.

Giddens, A. (1991) *Modernity and Self-Identity: Self and Society in the Late Modern Age*. Cambridge: Polity.

Gilmour, I. (1992) *Dancing with Dogma*. London: Simon and Schuster.

Gleeson, D. (1989) *The Paradox of Training*. Milton Keynes: Open University Press.

Gleeson, D. (1993) Legislating for change: missed opportunities in the Further and Higher Education Act. *British Journal of Education and Work,* **6** (2), 29–40.

Gleeson, D. and Hodkinson, P. (1995) Ideology and curriculum policy: GNVQ and mass post-compulsory education in England and Wales. *British Journal of Education and Work*, **8**(3), 5–19.

Gleeson, D. and McLean, M. (1993) Whatever happened to TVEI? *Journal of Education Policy,* **9** (3), 233–44.

Golby, M. (1994) Personal communication distinguishing the qualities of a curriculum from those of a syllabus.

Gore, J. (1993) *The Struggle for Pedagogies: Critical and Feminist Discourses as Regimes of Truth*. London: Routledge.

Grace, G. (1987) Teachers and the State in Britain: a changing relation. In M. Lawn and G. Grace (eds), *Teachers: The Culture and Politics of Work*. London: Falmer.

Gray, J. (1994a) Against the world. *Guardian,* 4 January.

Gray, J. (1994b) Looting Leviathan. *Guardian,* 2 February.

Gray, J. (1995) Casualties of the carousel. *Guardian,* 27 April.

Green, A. (1990) *Education and State Formation*. London: Macmillan.

Green, A. (1993) Post 16 qualification reform. *Forum,* **35** (1), 13–15.

Green, A. (1994) Post-modernism and state education. *Journal of Education Policy,* **9** (1), 67–83.

Green, A (1995) The European challenge to British vocational education and training. In P. Hodkinson and M. Issitt (eds), *The Challenge of Competence: Professionalism through Vocational Education and Training*. London: Cassell.

Grundy, S. (1987) *Curriculum: Product or Praxis?* London: Falmer Press.

Habermas, J. (1971) *Towards a Rational Society*. London: Heinemann.

Habermas, J. (1972) *Knowledge and Human Interests*. 2nd edition. London: Heinemann.

Hall, S. (1983) The Great Moving Right Show. In S. Hall and M. Jacques (eds), *The Politics of Thatcherism*. London: Lawrence and Wishart.

Hall, S. (1988) *The Hard Road to Renewal: Thatcherism and the Crisis of the Left*. London: Verso.

Hall, S. (1991) The local and the global: globalisation and ethnicity. In A. D. King (ed.), *Culture, Globalisation and the World System*. Basingstoke: Macmillan.

Hall, S. and Jacques, M. (1983) *The Politics of Thatcherism*. London: Lawrence and Wishart.

Halpin, D. (1994) Editorial. *British Journal of Education Studies,* **42** (3), 225–9.

Halpin, D., Power, S. and Fitz, J. (1993) Opting into state control? Headteachers and some paradoxes of grant-maintained status. *International Studies in Sociology of Education,* **3** (1), 3–23.

Halsey, A. H., Floud, J. and Anderson, C. A. (eds) (1961) *Education, Economy, and Society: A Reader in the Sociology of Education*. London: Collier-Macmillan.

Hampden-Turner, C. and Trompenaars, F. (1994) *The Seven Cultures of Capitalism*. London: Piatkus.

Handy, C. (1989) *The Age of Unreason*. Boston: Harvard Business School.

Hargreaves, A. (1994) *Changing Teachers, Changing Times: Teachers' Work and Culture in a Post-Modern Age*. London: Cassell.

Hargreaves, D. H. (1967) *Social Relations in a Secondary School*. London: Routledge and Kegan Paul.

Hargreaves, D. H. (1982) *The Challenge for the Comprehensive School*. London: Routledge and Kegan Paul.

Hartley, D. (1994) Mixed messages in education policy: sign of the times. *British Journal of Educational Studies,* **42** (3), 230–44.

Harvey, D. (1993) Class relations, social justice and the politics of difference. In M. Keth and

S. Pile (eds), *Space and the Politics of Identity*. London: Routledge.

Hatcher, R. (1994) Market relationships and the management of teachers. *British Journal of Sociology of Education*, **15** (1), 41–62.

Hatcher, R. and Troyna, B. (1994) The policy cycle: a ball by ball account. *Journal of Education Policy*, **9** (2), 155–70.

Hayes, C., Fonda, N. and Hillman, J. (1995) *Learning in the New Millennium*. NCE Briefing new series No. 5. London: National Commission for Education.

Healey, N. M. (ed.) (1993) *Britain's Economic Miracle: Myth or Reality?* London: Routledge.

Herzberg, F. (1966) *Work and the Nature of Man*. New York: World Publishing Co.

Hickox, M. and Moore, R. (1992) Education and post-Fordism: a new correspondence. In P. Brown and H. Lauder (eds), *Education for Economic Survival: From Fordism to Post-Fordism*. London: Routledge.

Higher Education Quality Council (HEQC) (1994) *Choosing to Change: Extending Access, Choice and Mobility in Higher Education* (Robertson Report). London: Higher Education Quality Council.

HMSO (1988) *Advancing A-Levels* (Higginson Report). London: HMSO.

Hodkinson, P. (1994) Empowerment as an entitlement in the post-16 curriculum. *Journal of Curriculum Studies*, **26** (5), 491–508.

Hodkinson, P. and Hodkinson, H. (1995) Markets, outcomes and VET quality: some lessons from a Youth Credits pilot scheme. *Vocational Aspects of Education*, **47** (3), 209–55.

Hodkinson, P. and Issitt, M. (1995) The challenge of competence for the caring professions. In P. Hodkinson and M. Issitt (eds), *The Challenge of Competence: Professionalism through Vocational Education and Training*. London: Cassell.

Hodkinson, P. and Sparkes, A. C. (1993a) Young people's choices and careers guidance action planning: a case study of Training Credits in action. *British Journal of Guidance and Counselling*, **21** (3), 246–61.

Hodkinson, P. and Sparkes, A. C. (1993b) To tell or not to tell? Reflecting on ethical dilemmas in stakeholder research. *Evaluation and Research in Education*, **7** (3), 117–32.

Hodkinson, P. and Sparkes, A. C. (1994) The myth of the market: the negotiation of training in a Youth Credits pilot scheme. *British Journal of Education and Work*, **7** (5), 2–20.

Hodkinson, P. and Sparkes, A. C. (1995a) Taking credits: a case study of the guidance process into a Training Credits scheme. *Research Papers in Education*, **10** (1), 75–99.

Hodkinson, P. and Sparkes, A. C. (1995b) Markets and vouchers: the inadequacy of individualist policies for vocational education and training in England and Wales. *Journal of Educational Policy*, **10** (2), 189–207.

Hodkinson, P., Sparkes, A. C. and Hodkinson, H. (in press) *Triumphs and Tears: Young People, Markets and the Transition from School to Work*. London: David Fulton.

Hoggett, P. (1994) The politics of the modernisation of the UK welfare state. In R. Burrows and B. Loader (eds), *Towards a Post-Fordist Welfare State?* London: Routledge.

Holmes, G. (1993) *Essential School Leadership*. London: Kogan Page.

Holt, M. (ed.) (1987) *Skills and Vocationalism: The Easy Answer*. Milton Keynes: Open University Press.

House of Commons (1995) *Standards in Public Life: First Report of the Committee on Standards in Public Life* (The Nolan Committee). London: HMSO.

House of Lords (1985) *Report of the Select Committee on Overseas Trade*. London: HMSO.

House of Lords (1991) *Innovation in Manufacturing Industry: First Report of the Select Committee on Science and Technology*. London: HMSO.

Howard, R. W. (1987) *Concepts and Schemata: An Introduction*. London: Cassell.

Hutton, W. (1995a) *The State We're In*. London: Jonathan Cape.

Hutton, W. (1995b) Healing community requires reform rather than rhetoric. *Guardian*, 27 March, p. 11.

Hutton, W. (1995c) Trade with a tangible return on well-being. *Guardian*, 25 September.

Hyland, T. (1994) *Competence, Education and NVQs: Dissenting Perspectives*. London: Cassell.

Hyland, T. (1995) Behaviourism and the meaning of competence. In P. Hodkinson and M. Issitt (eds), *The Challenge of Competence: Professionalism through Vocational Education and Training*. London: Cassell.

Illich, I. (1973) *Deschooling Society*. Harmondsworth: Penguin.

Jallade, J. P. (1989) Recent trends in vocational education and training. *European Journal of Education,* **24** (2), 103–25.

Jallade, J. P. (1992) Some neighbourly advice: assessment of British further education from a continental perspective. *Times Educational Supplement,* 24 January.

Jamieson, I. (1993) The rise and fall of the work-related curriculum. In J. Wellington (ed.), *The Work-Related Curriculum*. London: Kogan Page.

Jenkins, R. (1992) *Pierre Bourdieu*. London: Routledge.

Johnson, R. (1991a) A new road to serfdom? A critical history of the 1988 Act. In Education Group II, *Education Limited*. London: Unwin Hyman.

Johnson, R. (1991b) My new right education. In Education Group II, *Education Limited*. London: Unwin Hyman.

Johnson, R. W. (1995) Fatal legacy of Tory greed. The Observer Essay. *Observer,* 28 May.

Joseph Rowntree Foundation (1995) *Inquiry into Income and Wealth*. York: Joseph Rowntree Foundation.

Kanter, R. M. (1989) *When Giants Learn to Dance: Mastering the Challenges of Strategy, Management and Careers in the 1990's*. London: Simon and Schuster.

Katz, M. (1965) From Boyce to Newsom: assumptions of British educational reports. *International Review of Education,* **11**, 287–302.

Keat, R. (1991) Introduction: Starship Britain or universal enterprise. In R. Keat and N. Abercrombie, *Enterprise Culture*. London: Routledge.

Keddie, N. (1971) Classroom knowledge. In M. F. D. Young (ed.), *Knowledge and Control*. London: Collier-Macmillan.

Keegan, W. (1992) *The Spectre of Capitalism*. London: Radius.

Keep, E. and Mayhew, K. (1991) The assessment: education, training and economic performance. In G. Esland (ed.), *Education, Training and Employment. Volume 1: Educated Labour – the Changing Basis of Industrial Demand*. Wokingham: Addison-Wesley.

Kenway, J. (ed.) (1994) *Economising Education: The Post-Fordist Directions*. Deakin: Deakin University Press.

Kerckhoff, A. C. (1993) *Diverging Pathways: Social Structure and Career Deflections*. Cambridge: Cambridge University Press.

Kerr, C., Dunlop, J., Harbinson, F. and Myers, C. A. (1973) *Industrialism and Industrial Man*. Harmondsworth: Penguin.

Kickert, W. (1991) Steering at a distance: a new paradigm of public governance in Dutch higher education. Paper presented to the *European Consortium for Political Research*. University of Essex, March.

King, A. D. (ed.) (1991) *Culture, Globalisation and the World System*. Basingstoke: Macmillan.

Knights, D. and Willmott, H. (1989) Power and subjectivity at work: from degradation to subjugation in social relations. *Sociology,* **23** (4), 535–58.

Kuhn, T. S. (1970) *The Structure of Scientific Revolutions*. 2nd edition. London: University of Chicago Press.

Labour Party (1990) *Investing in Britain's Future*. London: Labour Party.

Labour Party (1991) *Today's Education and Training: Tomorrow's Skills*. London: Labour Party

Lacey, C. (1970) *Hightown Grammar*. Manchester: Manchester University Press.

Lacey, C. (1988) The idea of socialist education. In H. Lauder and P. Brown (eds), *Education in Search of a Future*. London: Falmer.

Lawlor, S. (1990) *Teachers Mistaught: Training in Theories or Education in Subjects*. Policy Study No. 116. London: Centre for Policy Studies.

Le Grand, J. and Bartlett, W. (1993) *Quasi-Markets and Social Policy*. London: Macmillan.

Lee, D., Marsden, D., Rickman, P. and Duncombe, J. (1990) *Scheming for Youth: A Study of YTS in the Enterprise Culture*. Milton Keynes: Open University Press.

Letwin, S. R. (1992) *The Anatomy of Thatcherism*. London: Fontana.

Lewis, O. (1966) *La Vida*. New York: Random House.

Lipietz, A. (1993) *Towards a New Economic Order: Post-Fordism, Ecology and Democracy*. Cambridge: Polity.

Lyotard, J. F. (1984) *The Post-Modern Condition: A Report of Knowledge*. Minneapolis: University of Minnesota Press.

Mac an Ghaill, M. (1992) Teachers work: curriculum restructuring, culture power and comprehensive schooling. *British Journal of Sociology of Education*, **13** (2), 177–99.

McCulloch, G. (1989) *The Secondary Technical School: A Usable Past?* Lewes: Falmer.

MacDonald, R. and Coffield, F. (1993) Young people and Training Credits: an early exploration. *British Journal of Education and Work*, **6** (1), 5–22.

Macleod, D. and Beckett, F. (1995) Body and soul. *Guardian*, 6 June.

Maclure, S. (1991) *Missing Links: The Challenge to Further Education*. London: PSI.

Marginson, S. (1993) *Education and Public Policy in Australia*. Cambridge: Cambridge University Press.

Marquand, D. (1995) Flagging fortunes. *Guardian*, 3 July.

Maslow, A. H. (1954) *Motivation and Personality*. New York: Harper.

Mayo, E. (1945) *The Social Problems of an Industrial Civilisation*. Boston: Harvard University Press.

Merton, R. K. (1968) Social structure and anomie. In R. K. Merton, *Social Theory and Social Structure*. New York: Free Press, pp. 185–214.

Metcalfe, L. and Richards, S. (1990) *Improving Public Management*. London: Sage.

Miller, M. (1983) The role of happenstance in career choice. *Vocational Guidance Quarterly*, **32** (1), 16–20.

Mills, C. W. (1971) *The Sociological Imagination*. Harmondsworth: Penguin.

Moore, R. (1988) Education, employment and recruitment. In R. Dale, R. Ferguson and A. Robinson (eds), *Frameworks for Teaching*. London: Hodder and Stoughton.

Mouffe, C. (1992) Democratic citizenship and the political community. In C. Mouffe (ed.), *Dimensions of Radical Democracy*. London: Verso.

Mulgan, G. (1994) *Politics in an Anti-political Age*. Cambridge: Polity.

Murphy, M. (1993) A degree of waste: the economic benefits of educational expansion. *Oxford Review of Education*, **19** (1), 9–31.

Murray, F. (1987) Flexible specialisation in the 'third Italy'. *Capital and Class*, **33**, Winter, 84–95.

National Commission on Education (1993) *Learning to Succeed*. London: Heinemann.

National Commission on Education (1995) *Learning to Succeed after Sixteen*. London: National Commission on Education.

National Curriculum Council (1990) *Curriculum Guidance 8: Education for Citizenship*. London: NCC.

Norris, C. (1993) Old themes for new times, postmodernism, theory and cultural politics. In C. Squires (ed.), *Principled Positions: Postmodernism and the Rediscovery of Values*. London: Verso.

O'Connor, J. (1973) *The Fiscal Crisis of the State*. New York: St Martin's Press.

OECD (1995) *OECD Economic Surveys: United Kingdom, 1995*. Paris: OECD.

Okano, K. (1993) *School to Work Transition in Japan*. Clevedon: Multi-Lingual Matters.

Ormerod, P. (1994) *The Death of Economics*. London: Faber and Faber.

Ozga, J. (1995) New Age traveller, a review essay. *Curriculum Studies*, **3** (1), 90–5.

Ozga, J. (forthcoming) *De-skilling a Profession: Professionalism, De-professionalism and the New Right*.

Payne, J. (1995) *Routes beyond Compulsory Schooling*. Youth Cohort Studies, No. 31/32. London: PSI.

Peters, T. (1987) *Thriving in Chaos*. New York: Knopf.

Peters, T. and Waterson, R. (1982) *In Search of Excellence*. London: Harper and Row.

Piore, M. and Sabel, C. (1984) *The Second Industrial Divide: Possibilities for Prosperity*. New York: Basic Books.

Pollert, A. (1988) Dismantling flexibility. *Capital and Class*, **34**, Spring, 42–75.

Pollitt, C. (1993) *Managerialism and the Public Services*. 2nd edition. Oxford: Blackwell.

Porter, M. E. (1990) *The Competitive Advantage of Nations*. London: Macmillan.

Pring, R. (1995) The community of educated people: the 1994 Lawrence Stenhouse Memorial Lecture. *British Journal of Educational Studies*, **43** (2), 125–45.

Quinlan, K. (1991) *CEMP, an Organisational and Management Development System*. London: FEU.

Raab, C. (1991) Education policy and management: contemporary changes in Britain. Paper presented to The International Institute of Administrative Sciences, Copenhagen, July.

Raffe, D. (1990) The context of the Youth Training Scheme: an analysis of its strategy and development. In D. Gleeson (ed.), *Training and Its Alternatives*. Milton Keynes: Open University Press.

Rajan, A. (1990) *1992: A Zero Sum Game: Business, Know-how and Training Challenges an Integrated Europe*. London: The Industrial Society.

Ranson, S. (1984) Towards a tertiary tripartism: new codes of social control and the 17+. In P. Broadfoot (ed.), *Selection, Certification and Control: Social Issues in Educational Assessment*. Lewes: Falmer.

Ranson, S. (1994) *Toward the Learning Society*. London: Cassell.

Redwood, J. (1993) *The Global Marketplace: Capitalism and its Future*. London: HarperCollins.

Reeder, D. (1979) A recurring debate: education and industry. In G. Bernhaum (ed.), *Schooling in Decline*. London: Macmillan.

Reich, R.B. (1991) *The Work of Nations: Preparing Ourselves for 21st Century Capitalism*. London: Simon and Schuster.

Reid, R.P. (1988) Charter flight. *Times Higher Education Supplement*, 25 March.

Rifkin, J. (1995) *The End of Work: The Decline of the Global Labor Force and the Dawn of the Post-market Era*. New York: Putnam.

Robbins Report (1963) *Higher Education*. London: HMSO.

Roberts, K. (1991) Mass unemployment returns. In G. Esland (ed.), *Education, Training and Employment. Volume 1: Educated Labour – the Changing Basis of Industrial Demand*. Wokingham: Addison-Wesley.

Roberts, K. (1993) Career trajectories and the mirage of increased social mobility. In I. Bates and G. Riseborough (eds), *Youth and Inequality*. Buckingham: Open University Press.

Robertson, D. (1994) Flexibility and mobility in further and higher education: policy continuity and progress. *Journal of Further and Higher Education*, **17** (1), 68–79.

Robertson, D. (1995a) Aspiration, achievement and progression in post-secondary and higher education. In J. Burke (ed.), *Outcomes, Learning and the Curriculum*. London: Falmer.

Robertson, D. (1995b) Policy and the reform of post-compulsory and higher education. Paper presented at the FEFC Annual Conference.

Robinson, P. (1995) Evolution not revolution: have UK labour market changes been vastly overstated? *New Economy*, **2** (3), 167–72.

Roderick, G. and Stephens, M. (eds) (1982) *The British Malaise*. Lewes: Falmer.

Rorty, R. (1989) *Contingency, Irony and Solidarity*. Cambridge: Cambridge University Press.

Ross, A. (ed.) (1988) *Universals Abandoned*. Edinburgh: Edinburgh University Press.

Rowntree Trust (1995) *Income and Wealth*. Report of the Joseph Rowntree Enquiry Group, Vols 1 and 2. Poole: BEBC Distribution.

Royal Society of Arts (1995) *Tomorrow's Company*. London: Royal Society of Arts.

Rudduck, J. and Hopkins, D. (1984) *The Sixth Form and Libraries*. Library and Information Research Report, 24. London: British Library.

Rumelhart, D. E. (1980) Schemata: the building blocks of cognition. In R. Spiro, B. Bruce and W. Brewer (eds), *Theoretical Issues in Reading Comprehension*. Hillsdale, NJ: Lawrence Earlbaum.

Sallis, E. and Hingley, P. (eds) (1992) Total quality management. *Coombe Lodge Report*, **23** (1).

Saunders, P. (1995) *Capitalism: A Social Audit*. Buckingham: Open University Press.

Sawicki, J. (1988) Feminism and the power of Foucauldian discourse. In J. Arac (ed.), *After Foucault: Humanistic Knowledge, Post Modern Challenges*. London: Rutgers University Press.

Schmidt, V.A. (1995) The New World Order, Incorporated: the rise of business and the decline of the nation state. *Daedalus*, Spring, 75–106.

Scruton, R., Ellis-Jones, A. and O'Keeffe, D. (1985) *Education and Indoctrination*. Harrow: Education Research Centre.

SEAC (1990) *General Principles for Advanced and Advanced Supplementary Examinations*. London: SEAC.

Shirley, I. (1991) State policy and employment. In D. Corson (ed.), *Education for Work*. Clevedon: Multi-Lingual Matters.

Simon, H.A. (1982) *Models of Bounded Rationality*. Cambridge, MA: MIT Press.

Sims, D. and Stoney, S. (1993) *Evaluation of the Second Year of Training Credits*. Slough: NFER.

Skeggs, B. (1991) Postmodernism: what is all the fuss about? *British Journal of Sociology of Education*, **12** (2), 255–68.

Smail, D. (1993) *The Origins of Unhappiness*. London: HarperCollins.

Smithers, A. (1993) *All Our Futures: Britain's Education Revolution*. London: Channel 4 Television.

Smithers, A. and Robinson, P. (1993) *Changing Colleges: Further Education in the Market Place*. London: The Council for Industry and Higher Education.

Squires, C. (1993) *Principled Positions: Postmodernism and the Rediscovery of Values*. London: Verso.

Standing, G. (1992) The need for a new social consensus. In P. Van Parijs (ed.), *Arguing for Basic Income: Ethical Foundations for a Radical Reform*. London: Verso.

Stanton, G. (1992) The contribution of Further Education colleges to delivering NVQs. In P. Funnell and D. Muller (eds), *Delivering Quality in Vocational Education*. London: Kogan Page.

Steedman, H. and Hawkins, J. (1994) Shifting foundations: the impact of NVQs on youth training for the building trades. *National Institute Economic Review*, August, 93–102.

Strauss, A. (1962) Transformations of identity. In A. M. Rose (ed.), *Human Behaviour and Social Processes: An Interactionist Approach*. London: Routledge and Kegan Paul.

Strodtbeck, F. (1961) Family integration, values, and achievement. In A. H. Halsey, J. Floud and C. A. Anderson (eds), *Education, Economy and Society*. New York: Free Press.

Sugarman, B. (1967) Involvement in youth culture, academic achievement and conformity in school. *British Journal of Sociology*, **18**, 151–64.

Sweetman, J. (1994) Examining new options. *Guardian*, 1 April.

Tebbit, N. (1991) *Unfinished Business*. London: Weidenfeld and Nicolson.

Temple, J. (1991) Coventry Technical College – a perspective for the year 2000. In S. Maclure, *Missing Links: The Challenge to Further Education*. London: PSI.

Temple, P. (1994) The evolution of UK trading performance: evidence from manufacturing industry. In Buxton *et al.* (1994).

Thurow, L. (1992) *Head to Head: The Coming Economic Battle among Japan, Europe and America*. London: Nicholas Brealey.

Tipton, B. (1973) *Conflict and Change in a Technical College*. London: Hutchinson.

Tomaney, J. (1990) The reality of work place flexibility. *Capital and Class*, **40,** Spring, 29–60.

Tomlinson, S. (1993) No future in the class war. *Times Educational Supplement,* 20 August.

Trades Union Congress (1989) *Skills 2000*. London: Trades Union Congress.

Trades Union Congress (1995) *A New Partnership for Company Training: A Consultative Paper*. London: Trades Union Congress.

Trow, M. (1994) *Managerialism and the Academic Profession: Quality and Control*. London: Open University Quality Support Centre.

Troyna, B. (1987) *Racial Inequality in Education*. London: Tavistock.

Troyna, B. (1994) Blind faith? Empowerment and educational research. *International Studies in Sociology of Education*, **4** (1), 3–24.

Unwin, L. (1993) Training Credits: the pilot doomed to succeed. In W. Richardson, J. Woolhouse and D. Finegold (eds), *The Reform of Education and Training in England and Wales*. London: Longman.

Van Parijs, P. (1992) Competing justifications for basic income. In P. Van Parijs (ed.), *Arguing for Basic Income: Ethical Foundations for a Radical Reform*. London: Verso.

Venables, E. (1967) *The Young Worker at College*. London: Faber and Faber.

Venables, E. (1974) *Apprentices out of Their Time*. London: Faber and Faber.

Walton, J. (1995) *After Learning to Succeed*. NCE Briefing new series No. 1. London: National Commission for Education.

Weber, M. (1948) *From Max Weber*. Translated and edited H. Garth and C. Wright Mills. London: Routledge and Kegan Paul.

Webster, F. (1994) Three cheers for Marx. Sociology subject committee seminar, Oxford Brookes University.

Wells, J. (1993) The economy after ten years: stronger or weaker? In N. M. Healey (ed.), *Britain's Economic Miracle: Myth or Reality?* London: Routledge.

West-Burnham, J. (1992) *Managing Quality in Schools*. London: Longman.

Westergaard, J. (1994) Why is it perverse to set class aside? Sociology subject committee seminar, Oxford Brookes University.

Wexler, P. (1992) *Becoming Somebody: Toward a Social Psychology of the School*. London: Falmer.

White Paper (1994) *Competitiveness: Helping Business to Win*. Cmnd 2563. London: HMSO.

White Paper (1995) *Competitiveness: Forging Ahead*. Cmnd 2867. London: HMSO.

Whitty, G., Edwards, T. and Gewirtz, S. (1993) *Specialisation and Choice in Urban Education: The City Technology Experiment*. London: Routledge.

Wiener, M. (1981) *English Culture and the Decline of the Industrial Spirit, 1850-1980*. Cambridge: Cambridge University Press.

Williams, F. (1994) Social relations, welfare and the post-Fordist debate. In R. Burrows and B. Loader (eds), *Towards a Post-Fordist Welfare State*. London: Routledge.

Williams, R. (1961) *The Long Revolution*. Harmondsworth: Penguin.

Willis, P. (1977) *Learning to Labour*. Farnborough: Saxon House.

Wright, T. (1995) *Beyond the Patronage State*. Fabian Pamphlet 569. London: The Fabian Society.

Wymer, K. (1993) *Further Education Colleges: Adult Learning*. Occasional Paper 3. Bilston: Bilston College.

Yeatman, A. (1993) Corporate managerialism and the shift from the welfare to the competition state. *Discourse*, **13**, 3-9.

Young, H. (1989) *One of Us: A Biography of Margaret Thatcher*. London: Macmillan.

Young, H. (1994) We're all losers in the Tory war on political independence. *Guardian*, 1 November.

Young, M. (1961) *The Rise of the Meritocracy*. Harmondsworth: Penguin.

Young, M. (1992) A curriculum for the 21st century. Paper presented at the International Workshop on Mutual Enrichment and Academic and Vocational Education in Upper Secondary Education, Institute for Educational Research, University of Jyuaskyla, Finland, 23-26 September.

Young, M. (1993) A curriculum for the 21st century? Towards a new basis for overcoming academic/vocational divisions. *British Journal of Educational Studies*, **41** (3), 203-22.

Subject Index